# T.L.S.

ESSAYS AND REVIEWS FROM
*The Times Literary Supplement · 1969*

8

# T.L.S.

ESSAYS AND REVIEWS FROM
*The Times Literary Supplement · 1969*

# 8

*London*
OXFORD UNIVERSITY PRESS
NEW YORK   TORONTO
1970

*Oxford University Press, Ely House, London W.1*
GLASGOW  NEW YORK  TORONTO  MELBOURNE  WELLINGTON
CAPE TOWN  SALISBURY  IBADAN  NAIROBI  DAR ES SALAAM  LUSAKA
ADDIS ABABA  BOMBAY  CALCUTTA  MADRAS  KARACHI  LAHORE  DACCA
KUALA LUMPUR  SINGAPORE  HONG KONG  TOKYO

SBN 19 211544 8

Printed in Great Britain by
Alden & Mowbray Ltd
at the Alden Press, Oxford

# CONTENTS

# NOTE

*T.L.S. 8* contains a varied selection of review articles printed in the *Times Literary Supplement* during 1969. Some of these have been included because they deal with crucial public questions—the future of literary censorship, student unrest; others because the books that prompted them were clearly among the most significant productions of the year—V. S. Naipaul on Imperialism in the West Indies, John Gross on the Man of Letters, George Rudé and Eric Hobsbawm on the Swing Riots; others again because they form valuable summaries of the literary careers of major foreign writers—Günter Grass, João Guimarães Rosa. *T.L.S. 8* also reprints reviews of the year's more discussed novels, including new books by Graham Greene, Nabokov, Philip Roth, and Montherlant, and a selection of poetry reviews.

# I

## BURNING QUESTION

### THE FUTURE OF CENSORSHIP

MR. RICHARD HOGGART, giving evidence in the case of *Lady Chatterley's Lover*, was the ninth of the thirty-five defence witnesses, and if memory serves rightly the first to use the word 'fuck' in Court, with the intention as he said of showing that 'one of the things Lawrence found most worrying was that the word for this most important relationship had become a word of vile abuse'. Later Mr. Gerald Gardiner (now Lord Gardiner), in his address to the jury told them reassuringly that 'No one should think that if the use of these words for this special purpose, by this particular author, in this particular book, is legitimate, it will follow that these words can be used by any scribbler writing any kind of novel'.

The trial took place less than a decade ago, yet in relation to the question of language it took place in a different world. In Britain and the United States 'any scribbler' can now use any word and describe any act in a novel with little fear of prosecution. In many large American cities *Justine* and *Juliette* are on sale, not as they are here in Soho shops devoted solely to sex books, but in drug stores and tobacconists where ordinary paperback works are racked not only with de Sade but beside hard-core sex works like *The Spy Who Came —and Came—and Came* and *Lovers—Oral*. In the Danish 'Sex Shops' photographic magazines showing every sort of coupling are openly sold and sex films openly shown, and an almost equal degree of freedom exists in some other European countries. And naturally enough this freedom is not confined to printed words and pictures. Did members of the cast of *Che* commit sodomy on the New York stage or did they merely simulate it? The question remains open

---

RONALD PEARSALL: *The Worm in the Bud*. 560 pp. Weidenfeld and Nicolson. £3 3s.

CHARLES REMBAR: *The End of Obscenity*. 528 pp. André Deutsch. £3 3s.

C. H. ROLPH: *Books in the Dock*. 144 pp. André Deutsch. 25s.

DONALD THOMAS: *A Long Time Burning*. 546 pp. Routledge and Kegan Paul. £4.

although a grand jury's decision has stopped the performance of the play. Recent films at the Cannes Festival indicated, according to *The Times* critic, that

This was a great year for the 'revealing', the 'outspoken', even at times the outright pornographic. . . . This year, it seems, once characters head towards bed there are just as likely to be three in it as two. One of the *ménages à trois* in Patroni-Griffi's *Metti, una Sera a Cena*, for instance, consists of a married woman, her husband's best friend, and a male prostitute they hire to add zest to their bedroom romps . . . Jonas Cornell's *Like Night and Day* has lesbian sisters in bed together with the (male) lover of one of them . . . *Without a Stitch On*, made by Annelise Meineche, who made the charming *Seventeen*, takes its heroine on a sexual odyssey across Europe in which virtually no experience from flagellation to simultaneous penetration, front and rear, is denied her or withheld from our view.

Such permissiveness is not universal. There are many American small towns in which hard-core sex books could not easily be bought, and the words printed in books are not found acceptable by all newspapers. Yet the climate has changed sufficiently for the words 'obscenity' and 'pornography' to be virtually meaningless. One of the books under review reproduces an illustration from *The Ferret* (1870), which helped to earn the printer a year's hard labour, beside a recent advertisement of an attractive girl wearing nothing except some roses and a pair of French skin boots. Is such an advertisement not likely to arouse erotic feelings? In 1967 it 'suffered no worse fate than being reproduced in a *Times* feature', but it would not have been likely to appear in magazines and newspapers even twenty years ago. The present interest in the open discussion, display, practice of sex goes a long way beyond literature, carrying with it implications about the kind of world we live in, a world of sexual freedom. Yet it is not very useful to talk about freedom without definition of the word. 'Freedom of speech is an abstraction', as Mr. Charles Rembar says in his book about the American trials of *Lady Chatterley*, *Fanny Hill* and *Tropic of Cancer*. Freedom to say what, and for what purpose, and to whom? There is a view often expressed at present that there should be no limitation of any kind upon what can be written and said. There is also a contrary view, less publicized, but probably much more widely held, that in relation to the written and spoken word we are misusing the freedom we possess, and that restriction of our present freedom is necessary for the public good.

It is desirable to disentangle as far as possible the legal and historical aspects of literary censorship as it has been practised in the past before examining these questions of principle. One of the most notable aspects of the cases brought in England since 'expert witnesses' were permitted to give evidence under the 1959 Act about the literary, artistic, scientific, sociological or other merit of works that might be judged obscene has been the difficulty experienced by the prosecution in finding writers and critics of any standing to go into the witness box, and there is undoubtedly a general feeling that to give evidence which might help in the suppression of any book is to place oneself on the wrong side. Historically censorship has always been regarded as inimical to literature and to progressive social thinking.

*The Worm in the Bud*, which deals chiefly with the double standards of Victorian middle and upper-class sexual life, and Donald Thomas's *A Long Time Burning*, which follows closely the history of English literary censorship, contain dozens of examples which show the stupidity and folly of what has been done in pursuit of that famous definition by Sir Alexander Cockburn in 1868 that 'the test of obscenity is whether the tendency of the matter charged as obscenity is to deprave and corrupt those whose minds are open to such immoral influences'. On such a basis the bookseller Edward Truelove was imprisoned for his persistence in selling Robert Dale Owen's *Moral Physiology* and J. H. Palmer's *Individual, Family and National Poverty* (1880), Vizetelly was first fined and then imprisoned for publishing translations of Zola (1889), and Balzac's *Contes Drolatiques* were destroyed (1909). There were of course a great many prosecutions before Cockburn, and Mr. Thomas makes a detailed examination of the operations of the Society for the Suppression of Vice in the early nineteenth century, and of the Proclamation Society who undertook the prosecution of Paine's *Age of Reason*. The basic idea behind most nineteenth-century prosecutions was that ideas which might threaten the mores of the ruling class should be suppressed, and little practical distinction was made in this respect between publishers of what was later called hard-core pornography and people advocating advanced social ideas like Charles Bradlaugh and Annie Besant. The important thing about their publication of *The Fruits of Philosophy*, a work in favour of birth control, was 'not merely whether the book was obscene in the coarser sense of the term, but whether its tendency was to vitiate public morality', as the Lord Chief Justice put it.

Such an attitude was unacceptable to many Victorians, and seems all the more revolting to us because recent research has shown the very considerable trade in sex literature of all kinds that was carried on in the second half of the nineteenth century. *The Worm in the Bud* elaborates on this, and while Mr. Pearsall is a ham-handed and erratic guide to literature, classifying Arthur Machen and Ernest Dowson as 'engaged in pornography' because they translated Casanova, the *Heptameron* and Voltaire, he has collected a formidable mass of evidence from newspapers of the double standard as it operated in life. Sexual assault was often regarded as trivial or comic when made on a working-class woman, but as a lasting social disgrace if attempted on a woman then distinguished by the word lady. He gives several pages to the story of Colonel Valentine Baker who kissed a girl in a railway carriage somewhere between Woking and London, was found guilty of indecent assault ('when this appalling story was first published a thrill of horror rang through the country', the Judge said), sentenced to a year's imprisonment and fined £500 plus costs. Baker was dismissed from the Army and although he was later rehabilitated his career ended in a minor post as inspector-general of the Egyptian constabulary. 'Colonel Baker had been spiked on the spears of Victorian hypocrisy as surely as if his head had been placed on Temple Bar', as Mr. Pearsall says with characteristic floridity.

It was essentially against this hypocrisy that the cohorts of defence witnesses were drawn up in the *Lady Chatterley* case, four clergymen including a Bishop and a Dean, the one time editress of a fashion magazine, a headmaster and a classics mistress, a special brigade of dons and literary critics, male and female, and a girl of twenty-one whose qualifications were, as Mr. Rembar ironically says, 'that she was young, bright, female and a Roman Catholic'. Some of these witnesses had remarkably little basis for making an informed comment on the legal points at issue, their presence merely testifying to the inconsistencies inherent in the 1959 Act and the usefulness to the defence of that word 'other' which allowed them to testify about 'other objects of general concern'. The link that bound them all was perhaps a feeling that in 1960 the prosecution of a book by a greatly respected writer on the ground that it described sexual activities and used certain words in doing so, was so far away from the temper of the time as to be absurd.

Earlier in the decade five novels had been prosecuted in a single year, and although in three cases the defendants were acquitted, publishers (the highly respectable A. S. Frere of Heinemann found himself in the dock) and authors were equally alarmed. The 1959 Act was an indirect result of these prosecutions in the sense that if the 'purge' of 1954 had never been attempted the new Act would no doubt have been delayed. The witnesses were determined to make no concessions to judicial illiberalism, to say nothing that would help the other side. Because of this determination they committed themselves to such statements as that *Lady Chatterley's Lover* was a book that Christians ought to read because Lawrence was trying to portray the sex relationship as something essentially sacred, that he was a writer in the Catholic tradition and that the book should be read by every Catholic priest and every Catholic, that it had great educational merit for the young, that it should be read and discussed in universities and in youth clubs. In relation to the book's theme the witnesses said that it treated sex as a basis for a holy life, or alternatively actually as a sacred act of holy communion. It was an antidote to the idea that sex should be regarded as a physical thrill, it advocated marriage and not adultery, was a puritanical book, essentially a moral tract, emphasized part of the Christian tradition. It was even said by one witness that the novel pointed in a prophetic way to the growth of Nazism and the dangers of Bolshevism. The prosecution case was ineptly conducted, and they called no witnesses, but even if they had been in a position to confront the defence witnesses with Mr. John Sparrow's article later published in *Encounter* persuasively arguing that Mellors had committed sodomy with Lady Chatterley, it is unlikely that many of them would substantially have changed their views. (One envisages a reply to an awkward question: 'Obviously when Lawrence referred to the necessity for "burning out the deepest, oldest shames, in the most secret places", he thought of this act as the necessary although rather disagreeable prelude to leading a Christian life.') Some of the opinions expressed must now be a source of embarrassment, but the point really is that English law as embodied in the 1959 Act is not a suitable instrument for dealing with such matters. As Mr. Rembar says:

The statute was a compromise and had the characteristically bad features of a compromise. The trial by jury opened the way to all the antics and irrelevancies that are perhaps tolerable in ordinary private litigation, but seem violently incongruous where what is involved is a fundamental question of freedom.

In America only two expert witnesses were called for the defence,

Malcolm Cowley and Alfred Kazin, and their examination and
cross-examination was in almost every way more relevant to the book
and the issues involved than the questioning in the Old Bailey trial.
Mr. Rembar is not exaggerating when he says that the British case
was a low parody of the American one (which had already been
decided), that 'the British defence was permitted to do precisely the
kind of thing that those on the side of suppression attempted to do
in our case—to influence judges and juries with irrelevant testimony',
and that the case was decided on better grounds in America than in
England. The trials of *Fanny Hill*, however, found witnesses in
America as in this country bending over backwards in a desperate
attempt to establish the book's ethical basis and sociological importance. John Cleland would have been surprised by Eric Bentley's
discovery in the book of 'a very challenging and far-reaching idea . . .
that there are two situations in ethics and Western civilization . . .
one is called pagan and consists of the enjoyment of the animal part
of our nature, and the other is ascetic, having much to do with
Christian tradition generally', and that 'the author's notion was
through the example of sexual activity to arrive at some middle
ground between these two extremes'. Why could *Fanny Hill* not be
called what it is, a lively and often very amusing sex book containing
a minimal amount of non-sexual activity? Because to describe the
book in such terms would have been to invite an adverse verdict.

It is evident that American law is at present much better equipped
than English to deal with the question of sex literature. In America,
according to the Supreme Court decision of March 21, 1966, a book
will not be condemned unless it is 'utterly without redeeming social
value', so that the works of de Sade although possibly 'found to
possess the requisite prurient appeal and to be patently offensive'
would nevertheless be publishable because the ideas in them are
of interest. In England the 1959 Act still includes the 'deprave
and corrupt' definition, and the opportunity of calling expert
witnesses can lead to utter confusion for a jury which may have
to decide that a book is obscene and yet is for the public good.
The various modifications of the existing law suggested by Mr. C. H.
Rolph in his short study of the past and present position, *Books in
the Dock*, seem only to be tinkering with a basically unworkable
Act. The most important of them are suggestions that 'books'
should be carefully defined and then exempted from the operation of
the obscenity laws, that the right of private prosecution should be

abolished, that proceedings should involve forfeiture of the books and not imprisonment of their publisher, that there should be a time limit between seizure and hearing, and that if 'books' are not to be exempted from obscenity prosecutions there should be a two-stage trial, the first on the obscenity question alone, and then if the book had been found obscene a second trial involving literary merit and public good. Some of these ideas are plainly sensible, others like the attempt to define 'books' seem impracticable—who would make the definition? And of the two-stage trial, in which *the same jury* (our italics) would consider the literary merit of a book they had already found to be obscene, it must be said that it seems likely to weigh the scales against acquittal in the second trial as surely as any procedure that could be devised.

The purely legal position is that the well-intentioned 1959 Act causes hopeless confusion in practice. Some ruthless simplification of it along the lines of American law would be immensely helpful both to the Director of Public Prosecutions and to any defending publisher. The 'deprave and corrupt' definition should be abandoned, and the scope of expert evidence made plain. Such an Act by its clarity would do much to silence the present unrealistic cry for specially literate juries or Lord Goodman's idea that manuscripts could be submitted to a Home Office committee of specially selected 'literate persons' for vetting before publication. From a legal point of view adoption of the American system in some modified version would be infinitely preferable to what we have now.

From a legal point of view: but the problem of sex literature extends outside purely legal considerations, and the present legal confusion in Britain is a faithful reflection of confusion in society. The written and spoken word is part of the social fabric, and what is written or said may damage the nature of that fabric. Those who believe that books can corrupt individuals at least give more importance to literature than those who say that nothing of the kind is possible, for if books cannot corrupt neither can they ennoble. If we are to say that nobody can be seriously influenced by reading the *Protocols of the Elders of Zion* or other anti-Semitic literature, or seeing anti-Negro or anti-Oriental sex strip cartoons, then it must logically be said that they are equally uninfluenced by reading Wordsworth's *Prelude* or seeing Shakespeare's or Brecht's plays. (This is not to agree with those who say that the reading of books about torture decisively influenced the Moors murderers, or that if

they did such books should be banned. Haigh, who sucked his victim's blood, had his first vampiric longings when watching an Angli-
can High Church service. No general conclusions should be drawn
from the effects of words, pictures or rituals on psychopaths.) The
influence art exerts on society is subtle, complex and closely bound
up with the influence new social forms and technical discoveries
exert upon art. The case of Dickens shows clearly this interpene-
tration. More than any other English novelist of his time Dickens was
affected by the social and mechanical changes of the Victorian age—
the rise of an educated middle class and the coming of the railways
helped profoundly to shape what he wrote—but his writings themselves then played a part in changing the ethos of the country and
affected the way that people thought not merely about particular
social causes but about the whole class structure. Yet Dickens worked
always within the pattern of his society, making no conscious
attempt to outrage it by his writings or behaviour. Artists today seem
often to use their freedom to abuse their society and place themselves
outside it, rather than with any wish to change it.

The specific question of freedom in political comment lies outside
the scope of this article, but as Mr. Thomas points out in his admirable book, our present freedom in speech and writing is sexual and
not political. As the publishers of *Private Eye* have found, freedom to
comment on public figures is by no means so great now as it was in
the latter part of the eighteenth and the early part of the nineteenth
century. Nobody today would dare to write as Junius did about the
Royal Family, nobody would be allowed to criticize living people in
the terms used in 1810 about the Duke of York: 'A prodigal spend-
thrift, licentious Debauchee, and double Adulterer'. Attempts even
to criticize the editor of the *New Statesman* in personal terms have
been effectively stifled. The Official Secrets Act and D Notices are
used often to stop discussion of an uncomfortable subject, as in the
case of the Casement Black Diaries. The attempts in *Private Eye*,
*Black Dwarf* and other periodicals to publicize what others find
unprintable should be regarded with sympathy, even though they
descend often to childish abuse. It is an indication of the very limited
nature of the sexual revolution in the last decade that its chief
advocates should be so little concerned with political freedom of
speech. Their concern is with sexual freedom. How much should we
have?

This is a question of general principle, yet principles are always linked to practical considerations. The observation of common decency is such a consideration. The phrase is not susceptible of any permanent definition but it exists in any given time and place, and the proponents of sexual freedom often ignore it. It is stupid to disregard obvious facts, such as the fact that sex acts (or acts of extreme violence and brutality) described in a book are one thing, and sex acts performed on screen or in public quite another. When Mr. Kenneth Tynan, an intelligent man capable of saying silly things, tells us that he sees nothing against the sexual act being performed on the stage, possibly between an old man and a young girl, he is simply ignoring the nature of the society in which he lives. When people point to the example of Denmark and suggest explicitly or by implication that sex magazines and films should be freely available here, they are ignoring the social differences between Denmark and Britain and are in any case asking for something that is of little value. The Danish shops exist, like the idea of copulation on stage, as a substitute for sex rather than for its satisfaction. If the surrogates were turned into reality, if it were suggested that theatre audiences should take part in the stage copulation, they would have a serious interest, but this presupposes a social situation that does not exist. Such a revolutionary situation would have to be one in which most of the apparatus of what we call civilization, including property, money, the family, had been destroyed. Until the arrival through atomic war of such a primitive society the ideas of Mr. Tynan, of the Living Theatre and the Underground movements, of those who attempt to practise a do-nothing personal anarchism within the context of the mechanical Western world, are all more or less feeble variations of the Noble Savage myth. Those who wish to destroy the whole pattern of bourgeois society should work practically to that end. It is a classic though continuing illusion that they can have any effect by becoming saintly or other drop-outs, or by outraging bourgeois susceptibilities in the cinema or theatre. Sexual freedom of any real interest must be closely linked with social freedom, and the present campaign for total sexual freedom in literature and in action is in many ways a substitute for social freedom, as Norman Mailer has recognized.

It is probable that very few people wish to see a state of affairs in which total public sexual freedom is permitted and what is now regarded as common decency ignored, in which (for example) copulation, defecation, urination were freely carried on in public. Mr.

B

Rolph, Mr. Rembar and Mr. Mailer, who contributes a most perceptive foreword to Mr. Rembar's book, all voice their doubts about
this. If we accept that the concept of privacy is one of the positive
virtues marking the emergence of man as a civilized animal we shall
agree with Mr. Rolph's postscript:

Are the various forms of mass communication combining now to annihi-
late our personal integrity? Privacy is the part of the human condition
that has taken the longest to grow: the process must have begun, in a very
small way, soon after we came down from the trees. Apes built and build
no lavatories. There could have been little privacy in the forest clearings
where the early Britons slept, loved and scratched. By Victoria's time,
privacy was a civil right as inalienable as a decent funeral; even the very
poor contrived to get as much as they could. . . . It could hardly last, and
perhaps it was right that it shouldn't. But it was the apex of the privacy
graph: if there was to be a change it could only be downwards, less privacy
and less, down towards the long-lost status of the ape.

And with Mr. Mailer in his foreword:

A war has been won. Writers like myself can now in America write about
any subject; if it is sexual, and we are explicit, no matter, the American
writer has his freedom. . . . We can all congratulate ourselves.
    [Rembar] is, however, as I would remind you, a moral man, and so I was
pleased to see as I read through these pages that he is troubled just a hint by
the liberties won, just indeed as I am troubled. For back of the ogres of
censorship and the comedies of community hypocrisy, there still rests the
last defence of the censor, that sophisticated argument which might urge
that sex is a mystery and men explore it and detail it and define it and
examine it and eventually disembowel it of privacy at their peril.

And with Mr. Rembar:

The current uses of the new freedom are not at all to the good. There is an
acne on our culture. Books enter the best-seller lists distinguished only by
the fact that once they would have put their publishers in gaol. Advertising
plays upon concupiscence in ways that range from foolish to fraudulent.
Theatre marquees promise surrogate thrills, and the movies themselves,
even some of the good ones, include 'daring' scenes—'dare' is a child's
word—that have no meaning except at the box office. Second-hand Freud
gives the film director a line on which to hang his heroine's clothes; psycho-
analytic clichés create his reputation as philosopher-poet, while shots of
skin insure his solvency. Television commercials peddle sex with an idiot
slyness.

It is not the intention of Rolph, Mailer, Rembar, to give comfort
to the Citizens for Decent Literature (in America) or to Mrs.
Whitehouse and her legions in this country. Nor is that the object

of this article. 'If writing will remain free for a sufficient time, some balance will be restored' to quote Mr. Rembar again. The hard-core books in the drug stores, the excrescences in the body of freedom, will disappear in time. The gains that have been made, the liberties that have been won, are of enormous value in helping us to understand the nature of the modern world and of human psychology. It is proper that the writer should have freedom to use any words and describe any actions. Without such freedom today the serious artist must be hampered in any attempt to influence and improve, or even to describe, his society. But in words begin responsibilities. Writers, dramatists, film-makers, need to show a bit of sense in using their freedom. The sort of anti-intellectualism exemplified among many students and some of their elders by the present cult of instant sensation, instant art, instant revolution, can play no part in changing society, and if it is pursued far enough will bring the whole force of the state down to crush the freedoms so painfully won. In America novelists, dramatists, visual artists dealing with sex are free, in England novelists and dramatists have now a high degree of freedom. Legally, what we now need in this country is something as near to the present American law as possible. Morally, artists should be their own censors. There is every reason to suppose that they will be if a minority of artists and intellectuals stop trying to use art as a simpleton's substitute for a non-existent social revolution.

# 2
# STUDENT REVOLUTIONARIES

POLITICS is certainly the art of the possible—but what *is* possible? For the ordinary myopic philistine, nothing very different from what is happening already. Someone has to keep the old ship afloat, and the common sense of mankind will insist that, most of the time, the task is entrusted to a reasonably accomplished navigator. Occasionally, some upstart will try his hand and throw everything out of gear, and there may be trouble in getting rid of him; but sooner or later normality of a kind will be restored.

Unfortunately for this comfortable and comforting view of the political process, we are living in the century of upstarts, the most successful of whom think in terms not of the art of the possible but of the translation of dream (or nightmare) into reality. In pursuit of visions, these men accept 'overwhelming' challenges—and win. One thinks of the lonely Lenin in his sealed train, of Mustapha Kemal surveying the bare ruins of Anatolia, of Mao choosing the desperate expedient of the Long March, or of Fidel Castro, with his twelve companions, confronting an army in the Sierra Maestra. One also remembers, with a shudder, the uttering of wild words by a ridiculous fanatic in a Munich beer cellar, and the donning of a black shirt by a discredited Italian socialist.

In the light of such experiences it would be inadvisable to dismiss the predominantly youthful contributors to *Student Power* and *New Revolutionaries* as mere ranting radicals. Some of them do indeed rant atrociously, in a peculiarly repulsive language, and many of them will certainly have disappeared from public view within a year or two. But a few—and guessing their identity is about the only fun to be had from reading either volume—may have increased their stature; and the point of view they represent may have become even more uncomfortably challenging to the middle-aged, the respectable, the intellectually indolent and the politically apathetic.

---

TARIQ ALI (Editor): *New Revolutionaries.* 299 pp. Peter Owen. 38s.
ALEXANDER COCKBURN and ROBIN BLACKBURN (Editors): *Student Power.* 378 pp. Penguin in association with New Left Review. 7s.

It is not the things they say, which are not highly original; nor the way they say them, which bores more often than it stimulates; but the spirit or—one has to use the wretched word—*Weltanschauung* that they represent. Consider what it is like to be young, educated and idealistic at the beginning of the last third of the twentieth century. With most of one's life still to live, one sees mankind, having just failed in two most determined efforts to destroy its civilization, poised on the brink of nuclear annihilation, while doing its damnedest to ensure that, should it by some miracle escape this fate, it will collectively perish as a result of excessive multiplication or the progressive poisoning of the environment or both.

The image of the Gadarene Swine is inadequate, since the wretched animals are not rushing down a steep slope but being carried down it in vehicles they have proudly paid for, while enjoying the solace of an equally expensive programme of canned entertainment designed to make them forget the direction in which they are going. Can one wonder that it is precisely the young, educated and idealistic who have taken to expressing themselves with such 'shocking' violence and even, on occasion, to using actual physical violence? If we are really surprised, then it is obvious that we richly deserve all the opprobrious things they say of us.

'We didn't behave like this in the 1930s', grumbles the grey-bearded ex-revolutionary. Of course he didn't. Unemployment may have been pushing at the three million mark and Hitler threatening war: but there was no H-Bomb, no population explosion that one would notice, and no threat of a 'silent spring'—and there *was* the new-born Soviet Union, a little disfigured by birth-marks but nevertheless pointing the way forward with a proud and confident Leninist finger. (Let it be whispered, moreover, that young people, at a time when Ph.D.s were conducting buses, were very worried about their jobs and consequently did not want to offend too many of their elders too often.)

Politically, the present generation neither enjoys these advantages nor suffers from these inhibitions. 'The revolution', as formerly conceived, has gone sour on it. Except among a few old cloth-capped party hacks, who have learnt nothing and forgotten nothing since they listened spell-bound to Harry Pollitt, there is no enthusiasm for the Soviet Union. Anyone who still has the temerity to suggest that it is leading anyone anywhere except up the garden path is treated with silent contempt in places where people still think. As for the regimes that claim to have kept their doctrine pure and to have returned to 'sound' revolutionary practice, Yugoslavia is looking a little tarnished, while China has descended into shadows where misshapen monsters wrestle obscurely. The People's Republic, of course, has its shrill advocates among the young, but it is obvious that they know as little of what is going on there as the communists of the 1930s knew of what was going on in the U.S.S.R.; and, on the evidence provided by these two symposia, Maoism divides rather than unites the new radicals.

Whereas some are as prepared to parrot the Thoughts as to repeat any other 'Marxist' formulas that seem to come in handy, others are more critical. In *New Revolutionaries*, Bill Luckin, a journalist who was in China at the beginning of the Cultural Revolution, finds it necessary to warn the reader of his less-than-enthusiastic account against seeing the activities of the Red Guards as *entirely* 'negative', while the two imprisoned Poles, Jacek Kuron and Karel Modzelewski, go so far as to allege that the 'Chinese bureaucracy' has been *driven* into alliance 'with the forces of colonial revolution' only as a result of its conflict with the 'Soviet bureaucracy'. This, no doubt, is Trotskyism —but a lot of the young radicals are Trotskyists of one sort of another.

The only two major revolutionary establishments that now arouse universal enthusiasm among the radicals are the Cuban and the Vietnamese. The latter, of course, offers a David-versus-Goliath image of heroic proportions. Indeed a cynic may well wonder how the radical left could get on without it, so obsessively does it dominate their thoughts. But of necessity it is still an inspiration for struggle rather than a model of achievement—a church militant rather than a church triumphant. As for Cuba, this thorn in America's side provides two figures, Fidel Castro and Che Guevara, of enormous charismatic power. Yet the Cuban regime, which is more open to inspection by sympathizers than any of the others, provokes doubts that find intermittent expression. 'To paint Cuba as a Utopia would be misrepresentation', writes Tariq Ali. 'Admittedly there is total cultural freedom, but there are still considerable political restraints; there is as yet no real inner-Party democracy and the trade unions are too bureaucratised.'

The difficulty of finding a satisfactorily 'libertarian' church triumphant, free from Thermidorian menace, compels these young radicals either to adopt utopian positions or to preach the value of violent struggle almost for its own sake. Hence, while continuing to sympathize with their very real dilemmas, one must take a coldly critical look at their ideas and policies.

The utopianism normally finds expression in a vision of a society, nowhere yet realized, where man will be 'truly free': a vision of the same kind that informed the early works of Marx and sustained the endeavours of all those revolutionary veterans whose hopes—for reasons which few of their present-day successors make much effort to analyse—remain so sadly unfulfilled. The manner of expressing these familiar aspirations for a social order in which there will be no repression, no exploitation, no bureaucracy, no militarism, and universal 'participation' is familiarly vague; for did not Marx himself teach us that the new order will be forged in struggle against the old and that therefore attempts to delineate its contours in advance are futile? Only the two Poles, in *New Revolutionaries*, make any attempt to describe what the new order will be like, and no contributor to either volume seems interested in the political, social and administrative problems which everyone knows are encountered by men who try to engineer drastic changes in established ways of living. But all, in spite of the clearest lessons of experience, appear to assume that however severe the new order's birth-pangs may be, any disfigurement that may result can be readily rectified.

Thus devotion to the new easily merges into formal adherence to a myth whose sole justification is ideological fortification of those who are waging the struggle. In some of the contributions, particularly to Tariq Ali's symposium, revolutionary violence is presented as a 'cleansing' experience valuable almost irrespective of its actual consequences. We are asked to approve of Che's horrifyingly mindless slogan, 'Create Two, Three, Many Vietnams', and to admire his advocacy of a hatred 'that impels us over and beyond the natural limitations of man and transforms us into an effective, violent, selected and cold killing machine'. Eldridge Cleaver, in a 'Black Panther' contribution of stark brutality, boasts of his party's determination to encompass the 'total destruction of America' should 'total liberty for black people' be refused. No one who is not himself a fanatic of comparable single-mindedness can imagine that these are the men who hold the keys to the solution of the agonizingly complicated problems of the modern world. Thinking of themselves as potentially all-powerful witch-doctors, purveying a universal panacea, they are in fact no more than symptoms of the sicknesses of the societies that have reared them.

By contrast with the Guevaras and the Cleavers the students and junior teachers responsible for *Student Power* are a pretty provincially-minded lot, despite the frequent violence of their language. Those who write directly to the subject say little that is not already painfully familiar to dons and administrators involved in the weary, repetitive and time-consuming process of 'confrontation'. However much one may sympathize with the dislike felt by these young people for the society in which they, like the rest of us, are doomed to spend their lives, one does wish that they would direct their shafts of frustrated anger towards some object other than the university itself—an institution which, with all its faults, is one of the best and not one of the worst that the 'bourgeois' social order has created. One wishes this not only for the university's sake but for their own sake. One longs to make them see that they themselves, who are contributing a radical critique of society for which the university, so long as it retains its liberal traditions, provides the best possible forum, are in danger of destroying the base from which they operate.

Radical students, in a society such as ours, are in a peculiarly dangerous and exposed position. Only in very special circumstances (e.g., France in May, 1968) can they form an effective—and even then temporary and highly unstable—alliance with the working class in whose name they affect to speak. More normally, they are looked upon with suspicion and distrust as privileged trouble-makers, and all too often, as a recent writer in *Survey* has demonstrated, the only effect of their activities is to provoke a reaction in which they and the university suffer alike.

That they, as a new generation 'permissively' brought up, feeling scant respect for their elders, and regarding university education as a right rather than as a privilege, should press vigorously for curricular and organizational reforms is natural enough; and reforms there will be—although the smashing of gates and similar behaviour is likely to delay rather than to accelerate them. But that they should regard themselves as a kind of surrogate for a working class at present too besotted by bread and circuses to 'do the job' for itself, and as revolutionary pioneers whose task is to capture the university fort and hold it until the proletariat, having learnt from bitter experience that bread is dry and circuses are tawdry, joins them in an assault on the main citadel of bourgeois power—all this would be comic if it were not so tragic.

As for the equation of 'student power' with 'workers' control', and the belief that, in defying the university authorities, students are waging the class struggle, these illusions scarcely merit serious criticism. Fortunately, there is a little evidence in this symposium itself that some of the radicals are beginning to become aware of the distasteful consequences to which such absurdities lead. Do they really want to 'go Japanese' and spend their time in pitched battles with the police, while the university remains closed? Does this really help the proletarian revolution, or scare the daylights out of the American imperialists? The answers, one would have thought, are obvious; yet experience now suggests that there will always be some who deliberately refuse to listen to them—a hard core of coldly determined destroyers whose fanaticism will be assuaged by nothing less than the wrecking of university education. These, undoubtedly, will have to be dealt with—even, if necessary, at the cost of a temporary alliance with elements whose political illiberality is itself a danger.

Yet what of the critique of bourgeois ideology with which *Student Power* tries to justify its attempt to intensify any distrust that already exists between the students and most of their teachers? In the hands of Robin Blackburn, a university teacher himself, and Perry Anderson, the editor of *New Left Review*, it is not very effective. Neither writer appears to possess the intellectual capacity of the older generation of Marxist scholars, as represented by a Hobsbawm or Kiernan. Mr. Blackburn, in his 'Brief Guide to Bourgeois Ideology', tells us that, although 'the first concern of a revolutionary student movement will be direct confrontation with authority whether in the colleges or on the barricades', the 'preparation and development of such a movement has always entailed a searching critique of the dominant ideas about politics and society', since 'in this way practice and theory reinforce one another'. His method of reinforcement is to wield a great big Marxist stick, heavy with quotations. Naturally, he finds plenty of suitable targets, particularly in his own field of sociology, but is betrayed, as people of his stamp generally are, by dogmatic over-confidence. He *knows* the answers, because Marx has told him, while his motley collection of bourgeois opponents are mere apologists for the indefensible, to be exposed and ridiculed. Mr. Anderson is more serious. His theme is that, in most of its components, British national culture is irredeemably philistine and that it has been rescued from complete sterility only by the importation of a number of 'White' refugee savants (e.g. Wittgenstein, Malinowski, Namier, Popper, Berlin, Gombrich, Eysenck and Klein) who, in performing their rescue operation, have simultaneously reinforced its reactionary characteristics.

The nice thing about Mr. Anderson is his real appreciation of intellectual originality, even when he disagrees most fundamentally with the point of view of its possessor. His thesis, however, rests on the shakiest of foundations. It begins by excluding 'two major disciplines', economics and literary criticism, in which the intellectual domination of two 'natives', Keynes and Leavis, is both admitted and proclaimed. Oddly enough, it also excludes 'the natural sciences at the one extreme and creative art at the other' on the curious ground that these are not 'obviously relevant and amenable to a political and structural analysis' (would Engels have shirked it?)

So out go 'at one extreme', our great 'native' physicists, chemists and biologists, not to mention a very distinguished collection of technologists, and 'at the other', a most splendid array of 'native' painters, sculptors, poets and musicians. Having accepted these exclusions on Mr. Anderson's say-so, one is left wondering why, in political science, Sir Isaiah Berlin should be regarded as so much more important than—say—Harold Laski or R. H. Tawney or even T. D. Weldon, W. G. Runciman and W. J. M. Mackenzie; why, in history, Sir Lewis Namier should be boosted to such an extent at the expense of Hugh Trevor-Roper, Arnold Toynbee, E. H. Carr, Christopher Hill, Lawrence Stone, Rodney Hilton, Edward Thompson, Eric Hobsbawm and George Rudé (don't Marxists count in this particular exercise?); or why, in aesthetics, no notice should be taken of the work of Herbert Read, Donald Tovey, Deryck Cooke, or the two Bells, Clive and Quentin? Even more curiously, this highly selective discourse is suddenly interrupted to take note of a worthy 'native' tradition of anthropology—which, alas, is not considered sufficient compensation for our sociological infantilism and our philosophical senility.

Is it true that 'a White emigration rolled across the flat expanse of English intellectual life, capturing sector after sector, until this traditionally insular culture became dominated by expatriates of heterogeneous calibre'? It is not true; it is merely a piece of special pleading to 'prove' that the 'chloroforming effect' of our 'cultural configuration' (what words!) has deprived the left of 'any source of concepts or categories with which to analyse its own society', and that therefore the only critique possible today is that provided by 'a revolutionary practice within culture' of which 'student struggle' is the 'initial form'. In contrast to Mr. Blackburn, who finds Marxism enough, Mr. Anderson is reduced to advocating a mindless militancy. Why should you disregard your teachers, Oh Students? Because they have no minds of their own, being the slaves of clever 'White' expatriates. What should you then think? We should not think, we should act. Come off it, Mr. Anderson; we have heard this kind of drivel before, and in some pretty sinister contexts.

The other contributions, as one might expect, are of unequal value. Alexander Cockburn makes suitably fierce noises; Gareth Stedman Jones, on 'The Meaning of the Student Revolt', generalizes widely and wildly; David Adelstein displays his knowledge of the British system of higher education; Linda Tinkham produces a very perceptive and (for this book) moderate vignette of conditions in colleges of education; poor Tom Fawthrop, the Hull student who tore up his papers, says his set piece about the iniquity of examinations; Tom Nairn and Jim Singh-Sandu explain the reasons for 'Chaos in the Art Colleges'; David Widgery gives a detailed, boring and biased account of the alleged 'muffling' role of the National Union of Students; David Triesman slams the C.I.A.; Fred Halliday provides a useful comparative account of student movements in other countries; and Carl Davidson, in 'Campaigning on the Campus', like Edwin Luttwak in his recent and much-publicized *Coup d'Etat*, deals with strategy and tactics in a way that should be as useful to the opponents as to the advocates of Student Power. The book ends with a typical piece of 'Marxist' mystification from Herbert Marcuse and a manifesto by the Nanterre students.

Both symposia deserve to be read; for the new revolutionaries, whether on or off the campus, must be taken seriously. In some parts of the world (e.g., Latin America) they may well have history on their side; in others, particularly the more developed parts, they may help to loosen things up a bit, by inducing our more wooden 'establishment' figures to change their ominously set postures, or, alternatively, may push our society just a little farther and faster towards dissolution. All one can say with certainty is that everywhere the results of their activities will be entirely different from any that they may expect. That is the fate of revolutionaries.

# 3

## THE HIGHER JOURNALISM

### (a) HACKS AND HEROES

ALEXANDER MACMILLAN was pregnant with a multiple birth of literary biographies. The midwife was to be John Morley. How to name the progeny? Short Books on English Authors? Masters of Literature? 'I am more and more averse', wrote Morley, 'to "Men of Letters". To call Bunyan or Burns—to say nothing of Shakespeare or Bacon—by that title is not good.' To which Macmillan replied: 'Carlyle applies it in his *Hero-Worship*'—Macmillan hero-worshipped his great compatriots—'to Johnson, Rousseau, AND BURNS.' So Carlyle, for whom the man of letters was 'our most important modern person', stood fairy-godfather, good or bad, to the nineteenth century's most influential series of short books on British masters of literature. Two generations at least were brought up on Macmillan's *English Men of Letters* without stopping to think about the aptness of the baptismal name. It has been left to a later generation, in the person of Mr. John Gross, to set us thinking.

What Englishman today would declare his profession as 'man of letters'? Yet *homme-de-lettres* would not look pretentious in a Frenchman's passport or on his *déclaration de l'impôt sur le revenu*. What English writer would, without whimsicality or affectation, address an older writer by the English equivalent of *Cher maître*?— as indeed, in French and in England, the Polish Joseph Conrad was wont to address the American Henry James. For all we have a Royal Academy of (visual) Arts, and a British Academy devoted to the

---

(a) JOHN GROSS: *The Rise and Fall of the Man of Letters*. Aspects of English Literary Life since 1800. 322 pp. Weidenfeld and Nicolson. £3 3s.

(b) LOVAT DICKSON: *H. G. Wells: His Turbulent Life and Times*. 330 pp. Macmillan. £3 3s.

KENNETH B. NEWELL: *Structure in Four Novels by H. G. Wells*. 120 pp. The Hague: Mouton. 18 guilders.

COLIN WILSON: *Bernard Shaw: A Reassessment*. 306 pp. Hutchinson. £2 5s.

ALLAN CHAPPELOW: *Shaw—'The Chucker-Out'*. 558 pp. Allen and Unwin. £3 15s.

moral and political sciences, we either do not take ourselves seriously enough as a nation of scribblers, or we are too modest, or too self-conscious, to set up anything as pontifical as an equivalent of the Académie Française. A step in this direction was taken half a century ago, largely at the instigation of that *homme-de-lettres par excellence*, Edmund Gosse, with the formation of an 'academic committee' within the Royal Society of Literature. Like Robert Bridges's Society for Pure English a few years later, this was altogether too un-English an activity to last long.

Yet the designation 'man of letters' has, or has had, its uses. Mr. Gross applies it, not to Shakespeare or Burns or to any creative writer as such, but to critics and essayists, belletrists and littérateurs, expositors and dons. Such men existed before 1800, where this book begins, but there is some logic in beginning where the rise on the graph was nearing the top and tracing the descent to our own day. There are two descents, that of the respectability of the designation itself, and that which records the decay of a culture. Mr. Gross's avowed concern in this book is 'with the shaping of nineteenth-century literary culture and with its gradual disintegration'. The graph starts with Francis Jeffrey and the *Edinburgh Review* and ends with Dr. Leavis and *Scrutiny*. It starts with one kind of high-level journalism and ends with another.

'Journalism is a career', writes Mr. Gross; 'literature is, or ought to be, a vocation.' This is a matter of definition. 'The main reason why a satisfactory history of journalism will never be written is that journalism itself is such an elastic term.' What Mr. Gross has attempted is a history of that elastic character, the man of letters, who at his best has a foot in both camps: his vocation is not for imaginative literature—though he may also be a Coleridge, a Thackeray, or a Bernard Shaw—but for a form, or forms, of writing which can only reach the public through periodicals of one level or another.

The history is organized in a series of chapters, generally chronological but overlapping, in each of which the tendencies of the period are exemplified in the persons of one or more outstanding characters. The chapters might have been titled in the manner of Carlyle's *Hero-Worship* lectures. First comes the man of letters as gentleman-reviewer, with Jeffrey as hero. The eighteenth-century idea that to write for money was ungentlemanly died hard. The laird of Abbotsford was reluctantly forced into it: the bard of Newstead became reconciled to it. Jeffrey regarded his twenty-five years of editing the *Edinburgh* as an amateur interlude in the life of a professional politician, advocate and judge.

His influence as editor and critic was none the less forceful for his anonymity—an anonymity that characterized, and was all too often abused by, almost all the great nineteenth-century reviews and magazines. (It has been estimated that 90 per cent of the criticism and fiction in such periodicals in Victoria's reign was anonymous or pseudonymous.) He was the first and, for all his prejudices, the most respected of that lustrous regiment of Scotsmen which not only dominated the quarterlies and monthlies—Macvey Napier, 'Christopher North', Lockhart, John Scott and David Masson among them—but included, as Mr. Gross points out, the first editors of the serious weeklies, the *Spectator*, *Economist* and *Saturday Review*. Among the exceptions it is pleasant to find Mr. Gross lauding that in many respects most unsatisfactory personality, the arch-Cockney Leigh Hunt, founder of the weekly *Examiner*,

a far more enterprising editor than any of his Tory assailants. A timeless setter-up of periodicals, at one time or another he provided a platform for most of the outstanding anti-establishment poets and critics of the age.

There was nothing of the gentleman-reviewer about Leigh Hunt: editing and writing for money was as much a bread-and-butter affair in Surrey gaol as it had been in Grub Street and was to become in Fleet Street.

The second chapter, on the man of letters as prophet, takes Carlyle (another Scot, and *sui generis*) and Matthew Arnold as exemplars. Mr. Gross has a great deal to say *about* Carlyle, but not much *for* him. It is in fact both a strength and a weakness of this history that a great deal is said, and said well, about a small number of famous men of letters, and less is said, in too small a space, about others who, though their names are not household words, should in the context be recognized as equally significant in the rise and decline of the genre. Carlyle was a towering figure, posthumously judged to have feet of clay. He is shown up by Mr. Gross, not without reservations, as a man worth remembering only for his letters and his overtly autobiographical writings, and one whose prophetic books—his lectures, his essays, his histories—with their philistine precepts and ur-fascist philosophy, are little more than camouflage for covert autobiography, for glorification of the hero as Carlyle. Nevertheless it is admitted that 'with all his snarls, no writer of his generation can have done more to raise the whole moral prestige of literature'.

By way of Mill, self-styled logician-in-ordinary, who only latterly and grudgingly accepted the 'aesthetic branch' of education as runner-up to the moral and intellectual branches, we arrive at Arnold, scholar, poet, sage. Mr. Gross accords Arnold the sympathy he withholds from Carlyle, a sympathy grounded in politics and sociology rather than in literature. Arnold looked forward to the welfare, not the servile, state. His efforts in the field of education, says Mr. Gross with justice, are not nearly as well known as they ought to be, adding, more arguably: 'I don't know that, even as literature, one would willingly forgo his reports on elementary schools for the sake of another "Thyrsis".' Arnold, who gave up writing poetry in his forties, was never more than a part-time man of letters.

While Mr. Gross can claim for Carlyle that he raised the moral prestige of literature, he can also approve René Wellek's judgment that 'around 1850', the year of *Latter-Day Pamphlets*, 'English criticism had reached a nadir'. In Chapters III and IV, which treat of the man of letters as higher journalist, we start with the impetus the abolition of the taxes on knowledge gave to a cheap press, the launching of the penny *Daily Telegraph*, the disgust of Arnold that a newspaper should boast the biggest circulation in the world. The 1850s and 1860s witnessed a vastly wider spread of more-or-less serious journals and more-or-less higher journalists. The first group of heroes comprises G. H. Lewes, Bagehot and Leslie Stephen. The portrait, more accurately the anatomizing, of Stephen is one of the best short essays in the book. Mr. Gross sums up this too often forgotten man:

A little more personal resonance, one feels, a higher degree of social involve-ment, and his criticism might have ranked beside Arnold's. As it is, he played safe: he is the Gentleman in the Library, content not to ask too many embarrassing questions. This sets a definite limit on his value to posterity. Unlike Arnold, he never seems an indispensable critic—except, that is, in the sense of there being no finer example of his type available. Without him, we should scarcely have guessed quite how formidable a Gentleman in a Library could be.

'A higher degree of social involvement. . . .' This is one criterion by which men of letters are being judged, and by which many of them, heroes and anti-heroes alike, are found wanting. The second group of higher journalists, classed as 'Liberal Practitioners'—John Morley, Frederic Harrison, Augustine Birrell, Herbert Paul—pass at least that test.

Not so men of letters as 'book-men'—another appellative that time has debased—who held sway over a wide public for half a century from the early 1870s. Saintsbury and Henley were indeed committed, but to the Tory side: the rest began as purveyors of *vers-de-société*, and ended as elegant essayists and arm-chair critics, or were dons turned journalists or journalists turned dons. The principal anti-heroes this time are Andrew Lang and Edmund Gosse, and little use has Mr. Gross for either. For Lang he reserves his sharpest barbs:

one of the most sought-after journalists of the day, famous for his facility at dashing off an article in a railway compartment or a cricket pavilion or wherever he could snatch a few minutes. Dozens of books, hundreds of essays, thousands of reviews: there was no stopping him. By the end of his career, life's tired-out guest must have produced enough fugitive journalism to stock a small library.

Lang was 'the droopy aristocrat of letters . . . much approved of by the tweedier sort of schoolmasters and dons, especially on account of the learned levity with which he celebrated the pleasures of cricket and angling and golf'.

And for serious criticism? For Lang, says Mr. Gross, 'Milton was literature, and so was Stanley J. Weyman'—or Rider Haggard and Anthony Hope. His enthusiasm for, and puffing of, 'the straight-forward tuppence-coloured adventure story', 'the trashiest melodrama . . . provided it had its quota of swashbuckling', is set against the ridicule and disparagement he consistently meted out to 'practically every truly important novel which came his way', to Hardy and James, Tolstoy and Dostoevsky and Zola. Can anything, Mr. Gross asks, be saved from this wreck? The answer is, the *Fairy Books*.

All this may seem a little unfair. The fault, if fault there be, lies not so much with Lang as with the age, with an educated public which liked its escape-literature well written. Lang till he was nearly seventy and Gosse till he was nearly eighty were both assured of a forum for their causeries, which they would not have been if editors and press barons had not known that their clientèle liked it. Mr. Gross should blame the public. Indeed by his jibe against tweedy schoolmasters he seems to say so. Yet may not a schoolmaster who appreciates *Areopagitica* also enjoy *King Solomon's Mines*?

While Lang was dishing out learned levity to the average educated man, two other influences were at work. In a chapter happily titled 'Early English' we are introduced to the beginnings of 'Eng. Lit.' as an academic discipline (in Oxford not until the 1890s though Anglo-Saxon had been taught there since the eighteenth century), and so to the seeds of academic literary criticism as we know it today—to Furnivall and Henry Morley, Churton Collins and Raleigh and Quiller-Couch. Of none of these, except perhaps Morley, a man with a mission, does Mr. Gross fully approve, though he pays tributes to Raleigh and Quiller-Couch as ambassadors of letters no less than heads of, by modern standards, unprofessionalized departments.

The other new influence—and here again Morley, as *vulgarisateur*, plays a part—was the cashing-in by spry publishers and hired men of letters on the hunger for learning of the newly literate, the products of W. E. Forster's Education Act. Forster, incidentally, rates mention by Mr. Gross for the repressive Irish Coercion Act of 1881, but not for the enlightened Education Act of 1870. Incidentally, also, Mr. Gross's side-swipe at the Oxford University Press for the 'agreeable anomaly' of the title The World's Classics—a series including insular non-classics—is misdirected: the title was not of the Press's coining.

The World's Classics was neither the first, nor at first among the more successful, of the cheap series to bring literary works—however 'classical' may be defined—within the purchasing power of the new readers. This area has been well charted, from the viewpoint of reader and publisher, by the American scholar Dr. Richard D. Altick. Mr. Gross's contribution is to view the scene through the eyes of the men of good will who promoted vulgarization, and the men of letters who edited reprint series, or provided brief and often super-ficial introductions to individual volumes, or wrote elementary histories of English or world literature. Some were scholars, some hacks. (Morley could at times be as superficial a hack as any of them.) The benefit of the popularization of literature in the late nineteenth century is well attested by readers of humble origins who rose to eminence in other than literary fields. If Mr. Gross had acknowledged this fact he might have been less harsh towards Sir John Lubbock's 'crash-course' of *The Hundred Best Books*—

Any reader capable of profiting from [such lists] is *ipso facto* perfectly capable of compiling a list of his own, and also of recognizing how pre-posterous the whole idea is, except as a parlour game.

It does not seem to have occurred to Mr. Gross that one must begin

C

by reading some best books before one is capable of whittling world literature down to one hundred titles, or that some humble souls can profit by crash-courses.

A brief chapter on the Edwardians leads to 'Modern Times' and to 'Cross-Currents of the Thirties'. It is only at this point that Mr. Gross shows his true colours. It is now that he begins to distinguish clearly between the academic and the non-academic critic, and between the academic critic who, in his view, is to be trusted and his fellow who, by the same token, is not to be trusted. There are some excellent pen-portraits in these chapters—of Chesterton, Squire, Desmond MacCarthy, Middleton Murry—and sidelights on the periodicals with which they were associated. The most understanding is a long appreciation of T. S. Eliot. That his political views—'the occasional tenderness shown towards Nazism'—are repugnant does not blind Mr. Gross to his virtues as a critic of literature and an influence for the good.

The last of the anti-heroes is the academic critic who is not to be trusted. Mr. Gross's analysis of what he sees as the arbitrary judgments, illogicalities and self-deceptions of Dr. Leavis is strong stuff. A 'Leavisite' might regard it as prejudiced, but he should recognize it as more cogently reasoned than attacks by those who have allowed judgment to be obfuscated by what they see as arrogance, dogmatism and a self-justifying martyrdom. The sixteen pages devoted to Leavis end with a passage that reveals one of Mr. Gross's two fears for the future.

One would no doubt feel very differently about him if he were not a university teacher, and a potent influence on the educational world. After all there have been critics with strong views before. Carlyle was far more bigoted, but at least he didn't have his critical opinions inculcated in teachers' training colleges. Arnold had his prejudices, but I doubt whether many Victorian sixth-formers were encouraged to reproduce them in their essays. And coming down to our own time, and to someone more comparable to Leavis in intellectual stature, supposing, say, Geoffrey Grigson had been able to inflict his views on generations of freshmen. . . . What seems certain is that any future critical *chef d'école* will be more likely than ever to be an academic.

Here, still virtually in the 1930s, the book ends, except for an epilogue voicing Mr. Gross's second foreboding. He shies away from 'the Two Cultures episode', but sees literary appreciation, indeed literature itself, passing through perilous straits. On one side is the Scylla of the Other Culture beckoning potential humanists into the physical, and also the social, sciences. On the other side, the Charybdis of the mass media lures potential readers to the screens of the cinema and the TV set. Against such hazards 'the literary tradition quite simply needs the protection of the universities. But it would be a sad day if it ever came to be positively identified with them.'

Who, finally, is this Mr. Gross? We learn from the book-jacket, if we did not know before, that he was a publisher before he became a Cambridge don, and that he is now a freelance writer. The *homme-de-lettres de nos jours*? While there is an historian so thorough, a critic at once so acute and so provocative, a writer with so sure a command of English prose, we need not despair lest the discipline of Dr. Leavis and the Other Culture of Lord Snow have exterminated the genre, at its best, of English Men of Letters. This is no backhanded compliment.

## (b) EDWARDIAN POLYMATHS

IN BEATRICE WEBB HOUSE, at Leith Hill, Surrey, a stained-glass window commemorates the Edwardian makers of the Fabian Society. Shaw is prominent there; with Sidney Webb he is hammering out a new world on the Fabian anvil, while in a row below, the lesser Fabians kneel before an altar made of the works of Shaw and the Webbs. Only one figure offends the mood of energetic piety that the window playfully expresses; in the lower left-hand corner H. G. Wells cocks a snook at the whole tableau (and one notices then that one of the reverent kneelers is irreverently reading Wells's *New Worlds for Old*).

The Fabian window was commissioned by Shaw in 1910, and it is a properly Shavian version of the Society's situation at that time: Shaw-the-Maker, cheerful and dominating: and Wells-the-Mocker, impudently opposing, but nearly out of the picture. One can imagine another window, commissioned by Wells, in which the roles of hero and imp would have been reversed, and the altar made of *Anticipations*, *A Modern Utopia*, and *The Faults of Fabian*; and if events had taken a different turn this window would have had its validity, too. But the point to be made is that in any representation of the most significant political group of the Edwardian period, the two best-known writers of the time would necessarily have figured. One cannot avoid seeing them as public faces in public places.

It is surely this quality of public and various activity, of enormous energies scattered in many causes, that has left both Shaw and Wells with such unstable reputations. Shaw expected a 'period of staleness and out-of-dateness' after his death, but this is not in fact what has happened; critics have gone on writing about him, his plays are revived, and professors lecture on his works, but his place in English letters is still uncertain, and no settled canon of his writings has emerged (is *Saint Joan* a good play? should *Back to Methuselah* have been revived? is there any life left in *Mrs. Warren's Profession*? has anyone here read *Everybody's Political What's What*?). And the same is true of Wells—so many books, so few established judgments. That Wells's novels are readable and Shaw's plays playable is apparently not enough; Wells has not found a secure place in the histories of modern fiction, and Shaw figures among modern dramatists as an example of nineteenth-century technique. Nor has either had any formal influence on his chosen form (though both thought of themselves as innovators).

Certainly the critical common-places of the Age of Eliot do not work very well in these hard cases: the autonomy of the work of art, the impersonality of the artist, the importance of significant form— in these terms, Shaw and Wells simply don't pass. For one thing, they took the wrong matters seriously: Wells worried about the specialization of function, but not about the form of the novel ('I was disposed to regard a novel as about as much an art form as a market place or a boulevard'); and Shaw, though he worked hard at the structure of governments, let his plays come as they would ('I have never claimed a greater respect for playmaking than for the commoner crafts'). At a time when the idea of the Conscious Artist was becoming current, neither writer was content to play that role with a seemly single-mindedness: Wells wrote more than a hundred books, but only half of them could be called fiction, and some of those are scarcely novels; and Shaw wrote far more non-dramatic prose than plays.

Most of all, Shaw and Wells are as far from the ideal of the impersonal artist as could be. Wells drew so shamelessly on his own life and the lives of his acquaintances for material that his works can be read virtually as a hundred-volume autobiography; and Shaw not only thrust Shavian characters into his plays to speak his piece, but surrounded them with even more Shavian stage directions, and then attached most Shavian prefaces that were often longer than the play.

Paradoxically, though their fictions were like life, their lives had the quality of fiction. Shaw created a public role for himself of such precise definition that he could give it a name, and having created 'G.B.S.' could refer to him thereafter as a tedious but useful fiction. And 'H.G.' was a similar sort of invention—a scientific prophet with lower-class manners and a gift for publicity. One might take it as a measure of the distance of the actual men from their inventions that both could write mocking third-person biographies of their public selves. Shaw's begins, characteristically: 'I declare at once that Shaw was the just man made perfect.' Wells is equally characteristic in his ironic self-denigration: 'First we have to realize that this Mr. H. G. Wells, in spite of the inexplicable prestige he has contrived for himself, is an individual of the lowest extraction and the most haphazard education.'

These are self-caricatures as bold and simplified as the figures in Low's cartoons, and one's first response to them is that though they might have written the lesser works, they could not have created *Man and Superman* or *Kipps*. But perhaps this is the point that neither Shaw nor Wells played the artist's role in public. We must take them, if we take them at all, on other terms—beard and knickerbockers, limp moustache and baggy eyes, and all. Those other terms are complex, because the men were complex, and the twentieth century seems to have no critical machinery adequate to deal with a playwright-philosopher-politician-novelist-phonetician, or a novelist-romancer-scientist-philosopher-historian.

One might propose as a beginning that Shaw and Wells are best regarded not as a playwright and a novelist, but as two Edwardian polymaths. *Edwardian* because, though Shaw was forty-five when Edward ascended the throne, and Wells wrote more than half of his books after Edward died, both men represent that point of intersection between Victorian and Modern, and both express in their lives and works the preoccupation of that time; like the Webbs and Galsworthy and Forster, they carried the advanced ideas of the late-Victorian reformers into the twentieth century, and watched them grow out-of-date and useless there. *Polymaths* because they believed that man could seize knowledge in a wide embrace, and that through much knowing he could affect the future of his species, and earn a place in the story. Both were humanists in the most generous and impressive sense, engaging themselves in human affairs as agents rather than as critics. They suffered, to use Shaw's term, from *Weltverbesserungswahn*—a rage to better the world.

Since their medium was the written word, they were both polemicists in everything they wrote. There is no useful distinction to be
made between Shaw's prefaces and his plays, or between the Wells
of *Tono-Bungay* and the Wells of *The Open Conspiracy*—all are
polemical, for if one aspires to turn words into actions, then all
words are equally instrumental. (This is what Virginia Woolf found
so unsatisfactory in Wells's novels: 'in order to complete them it
seems necessary to do something—to join a society, or, more
desperately, to write a cheque'. Mrs. Woolf did not include Shaw
among her bad Edwardian examples, but she might have—he was as
guilty of what she condemned as Wells was.)

The effect of polemical intentions on judgment is nicely illustrated
in the relations between Shaw and Wells and Henry James. Both men
quarrelled with James, and neither understood what he was getting
at. Shaw, writing to explain why the Incorporated Stage Society was
rejecting a James play, said:

I, as a socialist, have had to preach, as much as anyone, the enormous
power of the environment as a dead destiny. We can change it: we must
change it: there is absolutely no other sense in life than the work of changing
it....

and he urged James to forsake art and join with the forces of change.
And Wells, though admired by James, cruelly attacked him in *Boon*,
and later, mulling over his relations with the Master, concluded that
James 'had no idea of the possible use of the novel as a help to conduct'. To which James would no doubt have replied that Wells had
no idea that the novel might nobly exist *without* uses.

It might be argued—and indeed it has been argued—that in both
men the polemicist eventually dominated the artist. One could find
considerable evidence for this view in their later writings, and especially in those vast works of the 1920s, *Back to Methuselah* and *The
World of William Clissold*—two distended, ill-constructed, un-
dramatic monsters over which Creative Evolution and The Open
Conspiracy have spread like some dreadful Wellsian plague, and
have left imagination quite dead.

But even in such cases, the canons of aesthetics seem inadequate
bases for condemnation. 'You cannot be an artist', Shaw wrote in an
early letter, 'until you have contracted yourself with the limits of
your art.' Neither he nor Wells found that contraction easy, and it is
a necessary condition of just judgment of either writer that the critic
realize that the limits of the art cannot be held. One must see Wells,

not as a spoiled Dickens, but *sui generis*, as a complete Wells; and similarly with Shaw. The coordinates of art are too strict to contain them, and to say simply that *Back to Methuselah* is a bad play, or *William Clissold* a bad novel, is to have missed the point. Perhaps an aesthetics of polemics is what is called for.

On the other hand, one must not let a preoccupation with polemical concerns blind one to essential excellences in both writers. There must be many readers of Shaw who first discovered that discursive prose could be pleasurable by reading his prefaces, and who learnt there the meaning of style. And though no one is likely to miss the fact that Shaw was a gifted comic dramatist, it is worth noting that he was at least as good in comic narrative: 'The Life and Death of Uncle William', for example, in Shaw's preface to *Immaturity* is as good as Sterne. And in Wells, behind and below the myths of science and the satirical grotesques of society, lies a gift for particularizing ordinariness and imagining new actualities that makes the comparison with Dickens legitimate.

The polemical road may lead to fame—artists don't visit Stalin, but polemicists do, and both Shaw and Wells did—but it also leads to disappointment. These two men had set out to change the world, and how far had they succeeded? Shaw had played his part in the Fabian Society, and had lived to see the Labour Party governing England; but how many of the words he wrote had touched that change? And did he admire what socialism had come to? Wells had imposed his views of history on more people than any other historian ever reached, and by writing frankly about sex, and frankly living his convictions, he had contributed to the sexual revolution in this century; but these were not the achievement he had imagined.

No, in spite of their endeavours, mankind remained unreformed. 'Man is so far a failure as a political animal', Shaw observed, and Wells in a novella of the 1930s, has a psychiatrist darkly conclude:

Man is still what he was. Invincibly bestial, envious, malicious, greedy. Man, Sir, unmasked and disillusioned, is the same fearing, snarling, fighting beast he was a hundred thousand years ago. These are no metaphors, Sir. What I tell you is the monstrous reality.

It was as though *The Island of Doctor Moreau* had come true.

One must conclude that both men lived too long. They belonged to the Edwardian era, when optimism was still possible, and they lived to see the failure of their hopes. 'I have produced no permanent impression', Shaw once said, 'because nobody has ever believed me';

and almost nobody ever did. And Wells said sadly, near the end of his life, that he was tired of talking in parables to a world engaged in destroying itself.

But if both had a sense of ultimate failure, they expressed it very differently, and the difference points to a fundamental difference of temperament. Compare, for example, the epitaphs that they imagined for themselves, Shaw's was to be

Hic Jacet
**BERNARD SHAW**
*Who the devil was he?*

while Wells proposed for his own,

'God damn you all, I told you so'.

There was a cosmic indifference in Shaw that made it possible for him to contemplate being forgotten, and even to provide for that eventuality in his will. It was not coldness (though careless men mistook it for that), for Shaw had, if not a warm heart, then a warm intellect; it was, rather, an abnormal tolerance for reality. Wells didn't have it—the actual made him furious (perhaps one does not invent futures unless the present is intolerable), and he spent his life —both his public life and his private one—in trying to exchange new worlds for old. And it was Wells who came in the end to despair; his last book, *Mind at the End of its Tether*, is a cry of anguish and pain, like that last Martian howling alone on Primrose Hill in *The War of the Worlds*. Whereas Shaw, like one of his Ancients, waited for death with at most a slight irritation that it was so long in coming.

If Shaw and Wells, viewed as artists, rank below the very greatest, this is partly because they refused to be *merely* artists, and partly because they nevertheless invite comparison with the best: Shaw is one of the Great Irishmen, and shares the ambience of Joyce and Yeats, and Wells's novels are in the greatest English tradition; if neither is at the top, yet both are in honoured company. Shaw himself said: 'Either I shall be remembered as a playwright as long as Aristophanes and rank with Shakespeare and Molière, or I shall be a forgotten clown before the end of the century.' But there is a third possibility: to be remembered as a man who was great in the multitudinousness of his imagination, and who realized his greatness in the amplitude of his work. Writing of Charles Doughty, Shaw remarked that 'there must have been something majestic or gigantic about the man that made him classic in himself'. Perhaps that is the best way to treat Shaw and Wells, as giants who were classics in themselves. Few men of letters have lived such fully engaged lives in the world, and put that fullness into their work, so that here one can rightly say that the work is the man. The truest and most useful judgment of either will be that which encompasses the life and the work together, as one record of a great imagination.

Of the four books under review, only one fully meets that standard. Lovat Dickson's *H. G. Wells* is a true and sensitive account of Wells's life, written with elegance and generosity. Mr. Dickson has made use of the Wells-Macmillan files, to which his position as a publisher has given him special access, and though this gives the firm of Macmillan a somewhat inflated role in the narrative, it provides valuable social history and one would not wish the account abridged. Admirers of Wells may feel that Mr. Dickson has been too severe in some of his judgments—that Wells was a man 'who did not know what intellectual rigour was', and who was inherently incapable of clear, rational thinking, but that, on the other hand, 'he was all brains and very little heart'—and not everyone will share his quirky admirations (for *The Undying Fire*, for example), but these are the marks of a clear and individual critical intelligence at work, and the book is a fine and permanent addition to Wells criticism and biography.

If the principles sketched above for judging Wells have any validity, then it should follow that a book titled *Structure in Four Novels by H. G. Wells* will not be adequate to its subject. And that is indeed the case. Mr. Newell discusses a 'framework of abstract thinking' in *Love and Mr. Lewisham*, *Kipps*, *Tono-Bungay*, and *The History of Mr. Polly*, but his method demonstrates nothing so clearly as that it is the wrong method; he has sealed off the books from Wells and his world, and has made them seem less various and alive than they are. Still, the novels have never had the attention that Wells's science fiction has, and it is good to see what may be a critical shift of interest.

It is difficult to write objectively about a book that is at once bad and pretentious, but the following points may be made quite objectively of Mr. Colin Wilson's *Bernard Shaw*: that it is careless in its documentation, wrong-headed in its critical judgments, confused in its reasoning, and clumsy and humourless in its style. When one considers that the subject of the book was exact, rational, witty and stylish in everything he did, then the offence committed by Mr. Wilson seems unpardonable. His 'reassessment' does not seem to be based on any new materials, though without a bibliography, and with only very uncertain footnotes for guidance, one cannot be sure. His sources appear to be standard published sources, and though this is a perfectly reasonable way of going about a re-assessment of a major writer, it puts a burden on the author, since whatever is new in his book must come out of his own head. And on these terms Mr. Wilson performs badly. For he takes Shaw to be an *Ur*-philosopher in the School of Wilson, and so turns a witty and unpredictable genius into a lumpish messiah of Creative Evolution. And he caps his performance with a final chapter entitled 'My own part in the matter', in which he explains his kinship with Shaw and offers a sketch of his own philosophical musings. Readers who feel reverence or affection for Shaw are advised to skip this chapter; or better still, skip the whole book.

There is no reason to skip Allan Chappelow's *Shaw—'The Chucker-Out'* except its enormous weight. Like Mr. Chappelow's earlier *Shaw the Villager*, this book is a collection of biographical materials and opinions, often trivial but, because the source is Shaw, usually entertaining—for instance, the texts of Shaw's printed postcards, and the various versions of his will. It is a book *for* the convinced Shavian, *by* a convinced Shavian—copious, scholarly, a bit eccentric in its evident devotion, but accurate and useful. Shaw would have approved.

No doubt he would also approve of the definitive edition of the plays, which The Bodley Head has just announced. The edition, in six or seven volumes, will contain all fifty-two of the plays Shaw included in his official canon, the prefaces, an index of characters and of subjects discussed. Volume One, containing 'Plays Pleasant' and 'Plays Unpleasant', is promised for June 1970.

# 4

## IMPERIAL ISSUES

### (a) VISION AND REALITY

WRITING SEVEN YEARS AGO in *The Middle Passage* V. S. Naipaul gloomily concluded that the history of the West Indian islands could not be satisfactorily told. 'History is built around achievement and creation; and nothing was created in the West Indies.' Nevertheless, in his latest book he has ventured into the history of futility and failure. His theme is the origin of modern Trinidad viewed in terms of the myth of El Dorado, dramatically highlighting the contrast between metropolitan vision and provincial reality.

The twin poles of his inquiry are two forgotten stories. The first is the late sixteenth-century search for El Dorado, the golden city of Indian legend in the South American interior, by an ageing Spaniard, Antonio de Berrio, to whose initial quest Ralegh became heir. The second is the British capture of Trinidad in 1797 and the opening years of British rule there, culminating in the trial, on the charge of torturing a young mulatto girl, of General Picton, the first governor of the new colony. In Picton's failure we are made to see, in microcosm, imperial hopes worked out as colonial despair. He was made the scapegoat for the failure of the Venezuelan revolution which, it was believed, would have broken open the Spanish Empire to the merchants of the Industrial Revolution.

Berrio was for long only a name in Ralegh's *A Voyage for the Discovery of Guiana*; he left no published writings but here he is rescued from oblivion in order to expose metropolitan indifference. With God's aid, he argued, Trinidad would become the richest trade

---

(a) V. S. NAIPAUL: *The Loss of El Dorado*. 334 pp. André Deutsch. 35s.
(b) B. N. PANDEY: *The Break-up of British India*. 246 pp. Macmillan. 40s. (Paperback, 18s.).
H. V. HODSON: *The Great Divide*. 563 pp. Hutchinson. £4 4s.
(c) PHILLIP KNIGHTLEY and COLIN SIMPSON: *The Secret Lives of Lawrence of Arabia*. 293 pp. Nelson. 42s.
RICHARD ALDINGTON: *Lawrence of Arabia*. Introduced by Christopher Sykes. 448 pp. Collins. 42s.

centre in the Indies, but his pleas for help from Spain went un-answered. He dreamt of a Third Marquisate to rival Mexico and Lima but even his paltry settlement of straw huts at St. Joseph was destroyed by Ralegh and he himself left to die half-crazed in the jungle. Philip II, nearing his death, showed interest only when it was too late. Spanish Trinidad remained a forgotten outpost of empire. Another generation of Spaniards were drawn to the New World by the tangible riches of Potosí, not the hypothetical wealth of the upper Orinoco.

For Ralegh it was different. The Renaissance yearning for paradise which had earlier inspired the Spaniards still echoed in the Eliza-bethan court, finding fantastic expression in his writings: the sexual paradise where Devonian sailors would sire a new mestizo race; the religious paradise where 'infinite numbers of souls may be brought from their idolatry, bloody sacrifices, ignorance and incivility to the worshipping of the true God aright to civil conversation'. But in any case he had an ulterior motive. El Dorado was a way back into the queen's favour. Hence the urgency of his tone: 'After the first or second year I doubt not but to see in London a Contratation house of more receipt for Guiana than there is now in Seville for the West Indies.' Ralegh's ideas about El Dorado were taken from Berrio who in turn had taken them from mainland Indians. Thus Indian myths fused with those of the Spanish conquistadors and English courtiers who found in them a reflection of their own deepest yearnings. But apart from one of Othello's most memorable lines Ralegh's work fell on deaf ears in England, although on the Conti-nent, and especially in Holland, many translations roused interest in the Guiana interior.

Mr. Naipaul's account is built up from standard secondary sources but in addition he has used the Venezuelan Boundary Arbitration Papers in the British Museum, collected from the Archives of the Indies at the time of the Venezuelan-British Guiana border dispute of 1897. They may well be still being consulted in what is perhaps the most dangerous frontier flashpoint in South America today, caused ironically by diamond reserves in that part of Guyana claimed by Venezuela, which was also a location of El Dorado.

After the death of Berrio and Ralegh, Trinidad relapsed into somnolence; its Spanish population remaining below two hundred well into the eighteenth century. In the 1770s, however, its tempo changed. The appointment to governor of Chacon, the one person of any consequence in the history of Spanish Trinidad, brought the rationalizing efficiency of the Bourbons, though Spain was not to be the beneficiary of this. In 1797 the island fell to the British with scarcely a shot being fired. The striking feature of its population, now nearly 31,000, was its racial variety. Only 2,500 were white and of these less than half were British, the rest French or Spanish. The French free coloureds, overwhelmingly republican in sympathy, outnumbered the whites by two to one, while slaves made up two-thirds of the total population. Faced with this potentially explosive mixture Picton imposed an impartial terror, although his sympathies soon came to lie with the plantocracy.

Mr. Naipaul's second theme centres on Picton's term of office, his conflict with Fullarton the vindictive commissioner charged to investigate his office, and on the subsequent trial for illegal use of torture—a trial which divided British opinion much as did the great Governor Eyre controversy in Jamaica during the late 1860s. Mr. Naipaul shows the impossibility of Picton's task—policies outrunning the abilities of the men administering them. The Picton affair is used to expose the personal feuds, the legal and administrative complexities of colonial government; but by stopping with Picton's retrial and acquittal it is not possible to appreciate the subsequent problems posed and tensions created by Trinidad at a time when the abolitionists were questioning the whole basis of British rule in the Caribbean. Others have analysed the Saints' mentality; Mr. Naipaul is concerned to bring out the limitations of the officials formed under their influence, thus by implication exposing the flaw in future Crown Colony theory. No policy can succeed in spite of the quality of the men expected to enforce it.

In the eighteenth century the Caribbean had been the fulcrum of the overseas empire. But by 1797 the days of the slave colonies were numbered. Soil exhaustion in the older British islands focused attention on the potentialities of undeveloped and under-populated Trinidad. Merchants and planters, with whom Picton agreed, argued for a slave plantation economy there. These views were challenged by the abolitionists, whose main spokesman for Trinidad was George Stephen. 'You have in this acquisition', he wrote in 1802, 'the means of most favourably trying an experiment of unspeakable importance to mankind.' Trinidad must become a model colony of small proprietors with a free Negro labour force. But to do this the metropolitan government must keep power out of the hands of colonial assemblies (and out of the hands of republican French free coloured immigrants). Thus a Burkean theory of trusteeship replaces that Lockean tradition of colonial assemblies as the guardians of 'popular' rights against an alien executive which prevailed in the older British islands. The new Crown Colony system presupposed an enlightened governor fighting local vested interests on behalf of the people.

The Spaniards had early developed a theory of Empire. The British, commercially inspired, were more pragmatic, but the acquisition of Trinidad, abolitionist critiques and the new utilitarianism were forcing the Imperial issue into the open. The change in colonial government practice has been studied already in some detail, but here the human dimension, absent from those accounts, is built up with a sharp eye for significant detail. Mr. Naipaul has pinned down the moment when the balance of empire was changing. Laisser faire and informal empire were to take care of British interests in the newly emancipated continent: with the decline of sugar and the opening up of South America to British trade there was a shift of imperial interest to India, an interest which was slow to return. Few now cared whether or not Trinidad was a model colony. 'The quality of controversy declined and the stature of men.' There was no longer a carry-over from the metropolis. What was left was a colony as peripheral to the interests of the British as it had been to the Spaniards.

But where, it might be asked, is there any public concern today about India, which for the nineteenth century was the centre-piece of empire? It is the Caribbean which impinges on our consciousness as rarely before; Enoch Powell and Cuba have seen to that. One value of Mr. Naipaul's book is that it sharpens the focus once again on the Caribbean; not on the sun-drenched beaches of the bingo prize but on what James Pope-Hennessy has called the 'sunless and fungoid region' of our past. As Mr. Naipaul shows, race became the reference point of all major and most minor conflicts:

> in the end it was the only colonial battleground. This was what stalled and perverted every stated metropolitan advance, law, social drive, justice and freedom; race, the taint of slavery; it helped to make the colonial society simple.

Race, as we now know to our cost, is not simple. Attitudes are buried deep in the historical as well as the psychological past and an imperative which socially conscious historians ought not to evade is how to uncover and explain these attitudes. It is a matter of changing historical perspectives, of changing sensibility: cliché has blunted perception and atrocity has become domesticated so that we now need a new style, a new tone, to relate the larger issues to a recognizable experience. In this *The Loss of El Dorado* has a valuable contribution to make. To meticulous research is added the novelist's eye for character and situation. The form of the book, although it might irritate the professional historian as well as being complex for the general reader, presupposing a wide knowledge of what was happening in the rest of the Caribbean and in Venezuela, nevertheless enables the author to break the tyranny of the usual historical categories. Thus the central figure in the last half of the book is not Picton so much as Luisa Calderón, the illiterate mulatto girl whom he ordered to be tortured for an unproven civil offence. At the trial (for which she and her torturer were brought to London, where they consoled each other as the long process dragged on) the comedy of determining her precise age heightened the enormity and irrelevance of the crucial legal point in Spanish law of whether or not she was old enough (fourteen was the dividing line) to be tortured.

No historian has attempted to weave together in so subtle a manner the threads of the most complex and turbulent period of Caribbean history. For the closest parallel we would have to look at the Cuban Alejo Carpentier's great novel, translated into English as *Explosion in a Cathedral*, which has revolution in the Caribbean during this period as its theme and Victor Hugues as its protagonist. In Carpentier's work we are liberated (in spite of its depressing conclusion) as he ranges over time and space, nourishing the reader on the images of his baroque imagination. Naipaul's world, in contrast, is crabbed and confined; we are never allowed to forget the peripheral frontier society; the detritus of empire. The writing is low-keyed, matter-of-fact, passionless even; the imagination is not allowed to range but is tied to the horror of the stinking prison, the *cachots brûlants* with their decomposing Negro prisoners, of burning flesh and the rotting remains of quartered limbs. Descriptions are sparse, sentences staccato, comment terse but mordant.

It would seem from *The Middle Passage*, *The Mimic Men* and *An Area of Darkness* that Mr. Naipaul's essay at history is a further stage in a personal odyssey as he attempts to come to terms with homelessness. For intellectuals in newly independent countries history can be a therapeutic exercise. For Eric Williams *The History of Trinidad and Tobago* was an attempt to get out of his system the poison which politicians have to imbibe under colonialism. History becomes a 'manifesto of a subjugated people'; its function to provide a knowledge of the past which can be the essential guide to future action. In such countries a social function of historians may be to be the myth-makers of nationalism. But nationalists will not be able to draw much consolation from *The Loss of El Dorado*: there are no Aztecs or Incas to glorify; no founding fathers to whom to erect florid statues; no revolutionary traditions; no Maceo or Martí; no Toussaint l'Ouverture; no social myth to weld many races into a viable nation. And by becoming British, Trinidadians were finally excluded from El Dorado, unable to share the Venezuelans' identification with the utopian visions of Bolívar.

Whatever positive virtues emerge in the new state there is little inspiration to be derived from the past; nor, one would have thought, much therapy from writing its history. But by uncovering the roots of colonialism and by his insight into the complex attitudes engendered by exploitation Mr. Naipaul has helped us to comprehend its nature and perhaps, in some small measure, to decolonize our own imperialist way of looking at the West Indian past. It is a formidable achievement.

## (b) THE RAJ RETIRES

WAS PARTITION INEVITABLE? Did it lie 'in the logic of Indian history', or was it an impracticable and reactionary solution from which neither India nor Pakistan has yet recovered? In his short study, *The Break-up of British India* (a new volume in the 'The Making of the Twentieth Century' series), Dr. Pandey seeks an answer to these two questions and finds one in the proposition that the truth probably exists as it were in the no-man's-land across which the proponents of the two schools of thought still glare at one another.

His main preoccupation is with the origin and growth of the National movement and of Muslim separatism, and with 'the struggle of Indian Nationalism against Colonialism at the front and communalism at the rear', and it is difficult to imagine in so brief a form a clearer or more comprehensive study of these contributory factors to the creation of two independent dominions at the time of the imperial withdrawal.

Although one may judge that Dr. Pandey's sympathies are with the Indian National Congress in its stubborn attempts to stand as a body that spoke for all India, his partisanship does not extend to turning a blind eye to the mistakes Congress made, among which was the resignation from provincial office in 1939.

The elections of 1937 had gone some way to prove to Congress that it was what it had always held itself out to be—representative of all Indians—and that Muslim separatism was still a marginal movement, hardly to be taken seriously as an impediment to getting rid of the British. Dr. Pandey brings out clearly how the euphoria of the 1937 elections still persisted in 1939 and led Congress to disregard the dangers of resigning from office in protest against the involvement of India in Britain's war, without consultation and without guarantee of opportunity to fight Hitlerism as free men. The resignations left Jinnah's hitherto shaky Muslim League virtually in command of the political field until 1945; long enough to give credibility to the romantic dream of a separate Muslim state.

From *The Break-up of British India* we see in panoramic focus how much Anglo-Indian politics from the Mutiny onwards seem to have depended on advantages taken or missed. In the post-Mutiny period the Hindu upper class filled the vacuum left by British withdrawal of trust and preference from Muslims. Towards the turn of the century the Muslims took advantage of the Indian government's fear of a rising nationalist middle class which the government had helped to create and which was predominantly Hindu. The Indian government, of course, took advantage of whatever lay to hand, and there was by now plenty, in the form of growing communal jealousy and tension.

A prime cause of Muslim separatism was the tendency of upper-class Muslims—once they were back in favour —to cooperate with the *raj* against the restless Hindu middle class, a class typified in the minds of the British by the Bengali *babu* who seemed to have learnt more than was good for him. The British were not slow to respond to aristocratic Muslim overtures. The foundations were therefore laid for the separate electorates and 'weightage' which left most general administrative reforms looking far from hopeful from a national Indian point of view.

Throughout his book, Dr. Pandey emphasizes how closely the struggle for independence was linked with and hindered by what amounted to a class struggle within the various communities. Here, as in the field of western-style education, the Muslim community was backward in comparison with the Hindu. Until the Khilafat movement it could be said that there was no struggle among the

D

Muslims in India, but only an elite that cooperated with the British, and a vast artisan and peasant community that lived in comparative harmony with its Hindu counterpart.

The Khilafat movement died of inanition when the Caliphate was abolished, but its fruit in Muslim terms was much the same as that plucked several decades earlier by the Hindus, who had their history and religion rediscovered for them, mostly by European scholars. The fruit was the communalism that can hardly fail to follow a period of spiritual revival; but in the Muslim community this communalism was still an elite affair. In the established Hindu upper and middle classes, communalism already divided the westernized moderates and westernized political extremists from bourgeois Hindu reactionaries and terrorists. If the Hindu plot had long since begun to thicken, the Muslim plot still looked pretty thin. What was needed—if Muslim separatism was ever to amount to anything—was the creation of a vocal middle class. In 1937, as the elections showed, such a class did not exist communally within the Muslim community. That year, inspired by Gandhi, the Indian electorate spoke for the first—and last—time with an Indian national voice. The vocal Muslim middle class was created later by Jinnah, who seized the opportunity offered by the Congress resignations in 1939 to announce a day of liberation from a Congress Hindu *raj*.

\*      \*      \*

Just how far Hindu extremism, in two years of Congress provincial authority, made itself felt by the Muslim community as a whole is still largely a matter for conjecture. There is room for a penetrating and detached study of the effects in the provinces of the Congress ministries. Nehru obviously thought tales of 'Hindu' Congress tyranny over Muslim minorities so much eye-wash, the result of misunderstanding at best, of deliberate falsification at worst. Whatever the truth, Jinnah was not slow in 1939 to make the emotional point that heightened the political advantage of staying in power in those provinces where that was possible. For Jinnah, now, there was not only the opportunity of a separated Muslim authority but the explanation of its necessity. And to hand was a large, already separated electorate which if it did not actually represent a vocal middle class could be inspired by a member of the Muslim elite (Jinnah himself) to speak with a middle-class voice; which it did in the elections of 1945-46, when Indian independence was clearly visible on the horizon and the Congress had been in the political wilderness for four vital years.

The perpetually shifting ground upon which the drama of Anglo-Indian politics was played out is what both excites the imagination and interest and frustrates the instinct to plot a clear course to a logical conclusion. It may be that the question—was partition inevitable or an impracticable reactionary solution?—cannot be answered by concentrating on the internal politics of Anglo-India but by dismissing them as, in one sense, irrelevant, and looking to British home politics for a satisfactory explanation. Dr. Pandey is well aware of this other aspect of British involvement and responsibility. He accepts that Indian independence was an article of faith with the British Labour movement, memorably sums up the Mountbatten viceroyalty as being like a visit by a time-and-motion-study expert, and links the Indian independence movement to an internal social struggle that reflected a struggle of wider, international significance.

What he does not specifically do is examine the logic of these ideas. and this leaves him in a position of portraying the British almost exclusively in terms of the *raj*, of an administration—exiled from the political pressures and social changes at home—which, if it did not actually divide and rule its jealously held possession, did more to assist division than it did to encourage unity.

But was this *raj* the body-politic from which the Indians wrested their freedom? The situation is clearer if we ask what would have happened if in 1945 a British electorate—for the most part ignorant of or indifferent to the jewel in the old imperial crown—had voted Churchill back in? Perhaps then the guts and grit of the Indian independence movement would have been proved beyond doubt, and Nehru, Gandhi, and Jinnah (or more likely a successor to Jinnah, a man less publicly committed to the 'mad' dream of Pakistan) have joined forces to twist the archaic imperial arm. But the Indians were denied the opportunity of a real postwar confrontation with the *raj* by Smiths in Pinner and Browns in Bolton, who gave their vote to Attlee. From July, 1945, Indian freedom was merely a matter of careful arrangement, and for this both the Indians and the *raj* were sadly unprepared. But Attlee was determined; hence the sacking of Wavell (the last Englishman, surely, to have pondered the complex problem in purely Anglo-Indian terms?) and the appointment of the time-and-motion-study expert who came, saw, and

arranged. Through that glamorous viceregal figure, the methodical
Attlee cut through the Anglo-Indian complexity like a piece of wire
through cheese.

*        *        *

Dr. Pandey's book serves as an excellent introduction to *The Great
Divide*, in which the growth of nationalism and Muslim separatism
are dealt with comparatively briefly as a preliminary to a long,
detailed and impressive account of the Mountbatten viceroyalty and
Governor-Generalship of the newly created dominion of India.

Between 1941 and 1942, Mr. Hodson was constitutional adviser to
Lord Linlithgow. His assistant and successor was the late V. P.
Menon. He knew personally many of the men involved in the negotiations that led to partition, has had subsequent talks with several
of them, and full access to Lord Mountbatten's India papers. The
quotations from these papers, including some of those addressed to
the Sovereign, are of absorbing interest.

At the outset, Mr. Hodson warns us that his sources and outlook
are predominantly British. This is not to say that *The Great Divide*
is a phased rearguard defence of the *raj*'s reputation. The author is
well aware of its errors, opportunism and arrogance, as well as of
the devoted service given by many of its members. *The Great Divide*
does, however, sound a familiar note. It hardens the handed-down
image of the situation in which Mountbatten found himself as one
in which the *raj*, offering independence and finding Indian leaders
quite unable to agree the form in which it could be accepted, had to
exercise great self-control not to throw its hands up in paternal
exasperation.

Yet an historian must choose his parentheses. Those chosen by
Mr. Hodson enclose the negotiations to demit authority and the
consequences of demission (the migrations and massacres, the
Ruritanian tragi-comedies of Junagadh, Kashmir, Hyderabad, and
of the Indian princes in general); and in this context it is clear that
Mountbatten and his staff did marvels. Mr. Hodson rescues Mountbatten from the odium of Dr. Pandey's reference to him as a mere
time-and-motion-study man.

Like his predecessor, Wavell, Mountbatten cared about Indian
unity. He failed to conjure it. A charge often made against him is that,
anxious to deal efficiently, he dealt too hastily. What Mr. Hodson
proves, one may think beyond any doubt, is that the speed with which

the imperial company was wound up was a mark not only of Mountbatten's energy and grasp of essentials, but of his humane approach to a human problem. The steam was running out of the administration because the administrators knew their days were numbered. The great adventure was over. It would have been unkind as well as dangerous to prolong the agony. It was the decision to quit that dictated the pace. The decision, made in Whitehall, according to a mandate, revealed the extent to which 'unity' was a possibility and the extent to which it was illusory.

\* \* \*

Mountbatten went out with a brief to transfer power within a specified time, preferably on the basis of the Cabinet Mission plan, in which were embodied arrangements to allow for Pakistan while preserving a central authority that would reflect the 'real' legacy of the *raj*—an India which in spite of communal diversity had become, under imperial influence, a united nation. Mountbatten very quickly discovered that it was the diversity he had to deal with. We do not know whether in this he saw evidence of the *raj*'s failure or only of Muslim-Hindu intransigence. We do know, from Mr. Hodson's book, how manfully he struggled to create a 'centre'. In the Joint Defence Council set up to bridge the military problems of political separation he saw a chink through which consultation between the separated dominions might attract them back into each other's arms. He also made a melodramatic gesture which showed not only a fine theatrical sense of timing but a genuine desire to bring about, at the eleventh hour, a reconciliation.

At the close of the fatal meeting at which a 'moth-eaten' Pakistan was created on the nod (literally, Jinnah's—pre-arranged to save his face, and which implied he had the Muslim League solidly behind him), the last Viceroy threw on to the table copies of a paper prepared by his hard-worked staff, entitled, *The Administrative Consequences of Partition*. It was meant to bring the politicians back to their senses. It appalled them, certainly; but to the end the insular, as distinct from imperial, British failed to understand the Indian genius for accommodating itself to chaotic conditions.

Perhaps if the *raj* had ever exerted itself to solve and not use the communal problem, Mountbatten's gesture might have gone down in history as the one that saved the day. But the *raj* had not so exerted itself. The day was already lost. The gesture, although causing a sensation, fell administratively flat. Why?

The answer probably is that what Mountbatten actually had to attempt was a parenthetical situation of his own; one which detached all that Britain had done and failed to do from what Britain now devoutly wished should follow, and establish, in perpetuity, a monument to the noble aspirations that had supposedly always existed above and beyond the vulgarity of imperial pretension. Understandably, he failed. One does not, in a few emotional weeks, wipe out a century of cold, self-seeking appraisal of conditions that could be, and were, manipulated to imperial self-advantage.

All that is clear is that the creation of Pakistan nags at the British conscience. In this regard, Mr. Hodson makes two interesting statements which, granted their different contexts, still appear to be contradictory.

The question that the British people could address to their consciences was whether, in this transfer of power, their duty and their pledges to minorities and the weaker elements in Indian society had been discharged with honour. To the Muslims had been granted their supreme demand, separate nationhood. If this was not the best assurance for their future, the fault lay on Muslim heads, not British.

This passage seems unequivocal. But in his penultimate chapter he writes:

Could it [partition] then, have been rightly and reasonably created? The path to the answer runs through a jungle of ifs and buts. Perhaps the most certain proposition is that Britain's transfer of power came too late to avoid partition. How much is difficult to assess. Perhaps only a year, perhaps ten years or more.

Here there seems to be some confusion between what was honourable and what was timely; the hint of a suggestion that a pledge to a minority, honourably discharged in 1947 to appease that minority's insistence that it should be, either had not been made even as late as 1946 or could have been ignored, just as honourably, if power had been transferred then instead of twelve months later.

\* \* \*

It is probably useless to attempt to fix the date of the 'pledge' to the Muslim minority. The *raj* was too wily an old bird to commit itself in such terms. What it is more profitable to examine is Mr. Hodson's hidden persuasive connexion of the phrase 'weaker elements' with the word 'minorities'. In the context of the question of honourable discharge of pledges they cannot mean the same thing;

and indeed didn't, although in the quoted passage they have in common an appeal to the democratic and liberal impulse to see justice done.

The hard answer is that justice did not come into it.

Jinnah, the representative of the Muslim minority, could never be described as or even connected with one of 'the weaker elements'. He was a bulldozer; an irresistible force, strengthened by years of encouragement offered by the imperial wheelers and dealers; a brown-skinned de Gaulle who learnt the value of the word 'no'. The creation of Pakistan surely cannot be seen as a result of honourable recognition of the rights of a minority? If it can be, then the Christians, Sikhs, Eurasians, tribesmen and Princes must be seen as having been thrown to the wolves. Pakistan—the impression is overwhelming—was the political price exacted by an encouraged, stubborn and indigenous minority power from an alien power now intent on resignation and equally stubborn in pursuit of its ideals and aims.

It may be argued that the supreme factor in the creation of Pakistan was the gulf that separated the British at home from the *raj*-in-exile. Ignorance and indifference at home had always aggravated the instinct of the men on the spot to guard, preserve and possess. Increasingly, in the first four decades of this century, there was a notable lack of sympathetic correspondence between them. The Englishman at home was demonstrably of the same species as his counterpart in India, but the emotional and intellectual climates they enjoyed might have been those of two quite different planets. The one was natural to the English genius for social and political thrust, restlessness. The other was stultifying and encouraged nothing so much as the instinct to stand by old values by sitting comfortably on them.

It was the latter type of Englishman with whom the Indians were used to dealing and from whom they took their cue. Did Attlee realize this? Did he hope that the sudden confrontation with the kind of men Englishmen really were would sweep the Indians off their feet, hypnotize them into agreeing without argument to what these representatives of modern Britain proposed? It is doubtful whether he saw it in such terms, but there is evidence of his expectation of this effect if not of his understanding of what would have been its cause. But just as one cannot wipe out in a week or so of warm-heartedness and open-handedness years of cold calculation, neither can one in the same period superimpose one historical image of a ruling power upon another and more familiar image.

Mr. Hodson is probably right when he suggests that Britain's transfer of power came too late to avoid partition; but a line must be drawn between an explanation of what did happen and an excuse for what did not. Partition came, historically, when it did, with the granting of independence. The Britain that was determined to give independence was not at all the same Britain the Indian Congress had fought and the Muslim League (by and large) had cooperated with. Partition was inseparable, one may argue, from the determination of the now existing Britain to force independence upon the 'India' that also existed at that time. Partition, one may therefore continue to argue, lay in the logic of British domestic history, as a fortuitous creation of a Coronation Street electorate which did not and still does not know a Pakistani from an Indian, and—regrettably —now describes both as immigrants, if entrance into the headquarters of the Commonwealth is sought or effected by either.

*       *       *

One aspect of the situation which neither of these engrossing books pays much attention to is the secular approach to nationhood which excited the intellectual wing of the Congress and which was eventually written into the Constitution. Nehru was a statesman who existed above the melodrama of religious argument; Jinnah one who used the religious argument to gain political power. He had not always been. One of the biggest scares the old *raj* had was the 1916 Lucknow Pact between the League and the Congress when Jinnah, who had earlier left the latter for the former, with no hard feelings, attempted to awaken the generality of Muslims from 'the coma and the torpor' into which they had fallen to a sense of common national purpose. This could hardly have been what Minto had in mind, a decade before, when he responded to the request of a Muslim delegation (headed by the Aga Khan) for separate electorates in a way which Lady Minto described as 'the pulling back of 62 millions of people from joining the ranks of the seditious opposition'. Minto can only have seen the Muslim League as a bulwark against such 'sedition'. Fortunately, from the *raj*'s point of view, the League-Congress entente was short-lived; a situation which no doubt confirmed the *raj* in its abiding opinion that Muslim-Hindu unity existed only as a pious hope which had every so often to be expressed as central to their civilizing policy. Perhaps, truly, it never could have been made more than that; but it is difficult to point to any Anglo-Indian whose career was dedicated to the task of bringing unity about. Mountbatten, briefed at home to get rid of 'India', found that there was no such place. That there was not is the main charge to be answered by the nation that ruled the sub-continent for nearly 100 years, and influenced it for many more.

## (c) ENFANT TERRIBLE

'YOU LITTLE IMP!' Sir Reader Bullard tells in his memoirs how T. E. Lawrence was for once nonplussed when Gertrude Bell thus turned on him for making some *enfant terrible* remark during a serious discussion at the Cairo Conference of 1921. 'He went red to the ears and said nothing.' Impishness is one of the qualities that any writer about his life must try to analyse, both because it was part of his attraction and because it caused him to take an evil delight in baffling a world that loves a good romance. Indeed, he can be quoted to prove almost any theory: for instance, that he knew all along of British intentions of 'conceding Syria' to the French (to D. G. Hogarth, March, 1915), as against his 'No, Sir, I know nothing about it' (to Allenby, October, 1918); or his famous guilt-complex about Britain's swindle of the Arabs with promises of independence ('I had to join the conspiracy'), as against 'So we were quit of the war-time eastern adventure with clean hands'. The first task of any biographer is to explain why so mixed-up a kid was respected and loved by pundits as unlike one another as Winston Churchill and Thomas Hardy, Edmund Allenby and Lionel Curtis, Basil Liddell-Hart and George Bernard Shaw.

\* \* \*

In these two books, far the most perceptive discussion of this conundrum is that by Christopher Sykes in his short introduction to the 1969 reprint of Richard Aldington's biography—a book that caused delight in France and a furore in Britain when it debunked a British hero in 1955. Mr. Sykes is well versed in oddities (he is the biographer of Orde Wingate) and he knows how to recapture their attractive side. His preface rightly pinpoints by far the most sympathetic and endearing description of Lawrence's maddening ways that has yet been put on paper, which is that in the Peace Conference entries of Colonel Meinertzhagen's *Middle East Diary, 1917-1956*. Mr. Sykes also picks out from earlier biographies the most credible explanation of Lawrence's self-immolation after the First World War, which is that much as medieval penitents went into monasteries and put themselves under rule, so Lawrence chose to be borne along inside a moral package as a private in the services rather than trudge the open road.

Mr. Aldington came to dislike Lawrence and meant to be cruel; Mr. Knightley and Mr. Simpson meant to be just. At one point they label him 'likeable'. But they never succeed, as Meinertzhagen succeeded, in arousing affection for him. Rather the other way about. For the quotations they select from admirers as well as critics are on balance adverse: 'His motive [for an indiscretion] is solely to justify himself in the eyes of the people who helped to overthrow the Turks through his influence' (Hubert Young, 1919); '. . . his unfortunate love of drawing a veil of mystery over himself' (Air Vice-Marshal Sir Oliver Swann, 1922); 'Lawrence is not normal in many ways' (his idol, D. G. Hogarth, 1923); 'No, no quarrel, no unpleasantness. But he is such an INFERNAL liar!' (Mrs. George Bernard Shaw, undated). 'Poor tragic being', adds Lionel Curtis, but too late to arouse pity or compassion.

The new book is by the *Sunday Times*'s 'Insight' team of journalists, and the plural lives of its dramatic title are four (or six if one counts two that are blown up to life size on evidence that is distorted or misread). Only one of the four is secret. Three are familiar from earlier biographies and from the volumes of published letters; some new material is added by means of quotation from recently opened files in the Public Record Office in London and from private papers in libraries at Oxford to which the authors gained access; these dot a few 'i's, and are interesting to read, but add little of importance to the known story. The three tales retold are those of the relatively contented boy, undergraduate and medieval historian, turning his mind to archaeology and revelling in solitary travel, of the war and post-war hero during his years of power, and of the dedicated worker on R.A.F. speedboats during the last few contented years of his life.

In between falls the period (1922-29) that David Garnett called 'The Years of Hide and Seek'. About this 'life' the authors have discovered some wholly new material. It coincides with the years of self-abasement, part of which Lawrence himself described in *The*

*Mint*, and includes periods of indigence as a civilian which were quite unnecessary, since All Souls College had on his own showing given him 'leisure to write about the Arab Revolt'. The secrecy and novelty stem from the revelations of a brawny Scot who fortunately considered that his lips were sealed while Lawrence's mother was alive, but who after her death felt free to sell his story. This, here checked by a psychiatrist, is that when he was nineteen and Lawrence thirty-three, Lawrence hired his strong right arm to administer periodic birchings. This distasteful process, which lasted off and on for fifteen years, was carried out to satisfy the lusts of a family curmudgeon invented by Lawrence—'the Old Man'—who paid for the thrashings in order that Lawrence should expiate 'dragging the family name through the gutters', inter alia by insulting a bishop and the King.

Students of masochism will be interested in this part of the book. It also affords chances of discussing the possibility that Lawrence was homosexual, as well as the notorious incident at Deraa, where he sometimes claimed that the Turkish Bey had recognized him, raped him and let him go, and at others that this story was moonshine. (At this point the reader's heart warms to Bernard Shaw: 'I forbore to ask him what actually happened.') Anyway, research on behalf of the authors by an Arab scholar reveals that the Bey in question was a known womanizer, so that the conclusion is the usual one that nothing is proven, but that Lawrence, as some have said all along, was repelled by physical contact of all kinds.

\*　　\*　　\*

The two manufactured 'lives' are built up from single facts on to which wrong guesses have been tacked—wrong either because the authors lack a sense of historical sequence, and so produce war or postwar writings as evidence for prewar years, or because their researchers who galloped through the jungle of the Public Record Office photographed only papers mentioning Lawrence, so that his ideas are often judged out of context and in ignorance of those of other men and other Government departments. These failings lead to assumptions that stray as far from accuracy as does a computer into which a wrong digit has been fed.

To give examples: one 'life' is that of a prewar intelligence agent, 'trained for war' from 1911 by D. G. Hogarth (then the Director of the Ashmolean Museum at Oxford) and absorbing 'via Hogarth some of the precepts of the Round Table'—precepts which led them both to see a prewar 'vision that these ancient lands could be coloured red—not by conquest, but by example and persuasion'. It is well known that two archaeologists, Woolley and Lawrence, were in January, 1914, used by Kitchener, then British Consul-General in Egypt, as cover for a military survey of the Ottoman part of Sinai. This survey was conducted by Captain S. F. Newcombe, R.E., later famous in the Arab revolt, who found T. E. 'very observant' and therefore a valuable underling when he joined M.I. in Cairo after Turkey came into the war; but, wrote Newcombe, 'to suggest that either of them were secretly working for M.I. before that date is to me ridiculous'. Yet, for Mr. Knightley and Mr. Simpson, Newcombe is here 'off the mark'.

They base this stricture on their assertion, on evidence dated 1963, that the prewar work of the Round Table group 'has never yet been analysed'. This is, in 1969, untrue. Walter Nimocks's *Milner's Young Men* (1968) disposes of their assumptions because it shows that the Round Table group was until the war wholly absorbed in the task of trying to reconcile imperial unity with Canadian, Australian and New Zealand nationalism, and was a failure. To write of Hogarth as one of its knights in 1911 on the evidence of quotations dated 1918 and 1919 is to prove nothing. Other 'prewar spy' assumptions lead them to misuse or neglect evidence of Lawrence's own, including neglect of dates in his letters, and of the availability of the allegedly spy camera which is an archaeologist's contraption of its date that can be examined in a museum at Oxford.

The second 'life' that deviates from fact stems from the assertion that Lawrence, 'looking round for a trump card to play at Versailles', turned to 'a surprising quarter—the Zionists' as possible allies in wresting Syria from the French. Wider reading in the public records and in published books would have shown the authors that the notion was no surprise. It had been thought of in 1916 and pushed all through 1917 by a band that included several members of Lloyd George's secretariat, so that Lawrence merely jumped on to a bandwagon driven by Mark Sykes, Amery, Ormsby Gore and others. Advocacy of using the Zionists as a pawn against the French and getting them to help finance the Amir Feisal is surprising only in the light of hindsight.

*        *        *

Yet the book, though so full of faults, has its merits. It is immensely readable. When its authors are dealing with some circumscribed issue, and have no need of historical judgment, they do well. For readers with a taste for unravelling mystery dedications, they offer the most plausible solution yet produced of the 'S.A.' dedication to the *Seven Pillars of Wisdom*: they have written an excellent and moving chapter on the most straightforward of Lawrence's friendships— that with Bernard and Charlotte Shaw. They are honest; they put up many of the old Aunt Sallies, but only to knock them down and come to plain conclusions, such as that Lawrence was killed in an ordinary road accident. If they had no special knowledge of his life until the thrasher walked into their office in 1968, they have done a mass of research. But they do not know enough history to make the best use of their finds, and they are ungenerous to a degree to Lawrence's British seniors and companions in arms during the war. In this respect they have written the book of the film.

They will impress any uninformed reader with their footnotes and their access to research all over the world by people on the *Sunday Times* payroll. But they will irritate all scholars with their boasts of discovery in Israel of facts that have since 1949 been easily available in Dr. Weizmann's memoirs, with their undated footnotes, their unattributed quotations from secondary sources, their wrong facts and wrong references—one of them to a quotation as easy to check as is the Psalm of David that is on the arms of Oxford University. Instant history, like instant sauce and instant coffee, is fit for consumption, but not for connoisseurs.

# 5

# FICTION OF 1969

## (a) GRAHAM GREENE:

### *Travels with my Aunt*

In *Travels with my Aunt* Mr. Greene cunningly interweaves two stereotypes of English fiction: the Indomitable Old Lady and the Innocent Abroad. Henry Pulling is a prematurely retired bank manager, fond of dahlias and funerals. It is at his own mother's funeral that he meets his Aunt Augusta. She is in her seventies, he in his fifties; but the funeral is a beginning rather than an end. Its sequel is an entertainment in Mr. Greene's most stylish—and stylized —manner. His own never-quite-suppressed wordiness—a weakness for phrases rather than any slack syntax or redundant incident—is sheathed in Pulling's own middle-aged narrative voice:

My father had been dead for more than forty years. He was a building contractor of a lethargic disposition who used to take afternoon naps in all sorts of curious places. This irritated my mother, who was an energetic woman, and she used to seek him out to disturb him.

There is a pattern here, since Pulling himself is a morally sleepy fellow, and Aunt Augusta takes over the mother's role. A creatively disturbing mother figure is something new, although a good deal of Aunt Augusta's haughty patter is sheer Lady Bracknell ('No, no, my man. This is the Crescent.' 'You said turn *right*, lady.' 'Then I apologize. It was my mistake. I am always a little uncertain about

---

(*a*) GRAHAM GREENE: *Travels with my Aunt*. 319 pp. Bodley Head. 30s.

(*b*) VLADIMIR NABOKOV: *Ada*. 589 pp. Weidenfeld and Nicolson. 42s.

(*c*) PIERS PAUL READ: *Monk Dawson*. 219 pp. The Alison Press: Secker and Warburg. 30s.

(*d*) NORMAN MAILER: *Why are we in Vietnam?* 208 pp. Weidenfeld and Nicolson. 30s.

(*e*) BEPPE FENOGLIO: *Il partigiano Johnny*. 376 pp. L.3,000. *La paga del sabato*. 150 pp. L.1,800. Turin: Einaudi.

(*f*) MELVYN BRAGG: *The Hired Man*. 220 pp. Secker and Warburg. 30s.

right and left. Port I can always remember because of the colour—red means left.'). It is not the book's best kept surprise when she is finally revealed as Pulling's natural mother rather than his aunt. But by then she has effectively shaken him awake for life.

Curious places play a big part in this process. It begins with a modest trip to Brighton, where Aunt Augusta helped to run a Church for Dogs; moves on via Paris (revisiting a Feydeauesque affair set in those twin hotels, the St. James and Albany) to Istanbul and a botched attempt to sell a gold brick; and winds up in Paraguay, where Pulling finds an exile as complete and bizarre as the life-sentence of reading Dickens dished out in *A Handful of Dust*. But he is happy with it. Browning ('All's right with the world') rather than *Bleak House* summarizes his fate.

Mr. Greene's work has always been in part a plea against normality. Even his Catholicism is an appeal to un-Englishness: a minority within the country, a worldwide organization with many roots in the exotic outside. It is typical that Aunt Augusta (at seventy) should have a Negro lover, and typical of Mr. Greene's literary playfulness that he should be called Wordsworth.

Ar was working at the Grenada Palace. Ar had a uniform. Jus lak a general. She lak ma uniform. She stop an say, 'Are you the Emperor Jones?' 'No, ma'am', I say, 'arm only old Wordsworth'. 'Oh', she says, 'thou child of joy, shout round me, let me hear thy shouts, thou happy shepherd boy.'

It is equally typical that he should borrow Pulling's mother's funeral urn and substitute pot for the ashes. Mr. Greene of all English writers has most taken to heart Chekhov's dictum that nothing should be wasted, that if you describe a pistol on the wall in the first chapter it must be because someone is shot with it in the last. Even Wordsworth reappears in Paraguay, in most improbable circumstances; as does a C.I.A. man who happens to be the father of a girl met on one of Aunt Augusta's earlier trips. A final party reassembles the cast in a manner worthy of the West End stage, or Mr. Anthony Powell. Wordsworth's pocket-knife finds a Chekhovian function.

Mr. Greene is often charged with disrespect for the everyday. Certainly his American portraits tend to a lazy sketchiness. ('I was always taught that Yugoslavs were *good* Communists. We sell them strategic material, don't we?') But the life from which Pulling escapes is given its affectionate due. The attractions of suburbia, of dialling CHICKEN for a pre-cooked meal, of occasional sherries and meals out at the sparky Lesbian joint down the road, are almost sentimentally indulged. Aunt Augusta's world has its brutalities; so does the American girl's:

Her hand was on my knee, and the enormous wrist-watch stared up at me with its great blank white face and its four figures in scarlet, 12 3 6 9, as if those were the only important ones to remember—the hours when you had to take your medicine. . . . Most of the hours of my life had been eliminated from Tooley's watch.

Such melancholy directness is Mr. Greene's greatest strength. He can be mischievous: it is surely not an accident that the policeman trailing Wordsworth's marijuana is called 'Detective-Sergeant Sparrow John'. But even authority has a soul, and Sparrow is soon singing carols with boyish pleasure.

Indeed, the central contrast of the book is hardly a moral one. Aunt Augusta thunders sometimes at her nephew or son. 'You looked after people's money like a nanny who looked after other people's children.' She harshly urges him to let the dead bury their own dead: the only unsuccessful trip takes them to Boulogne, to Pulling's father's grave, which is tended by a devoted spinster whom he took on an unconsummated and fatal weekend. (Food-poisoning, rather than passion.) Aunt Augusta is scornful of that, though she reserves an equally dippy devotion for an Italian flame, a marvellous Autolycus of survival, whose smuggling business is Pulling's final destination. ('Mr. Visconti wants somebody he can trust to keep the books. Accounts have always been his weak point.') But her final appeal is to live dangerously for its own sake.

'My dear Henry, if you live with us, you won't be edging day by day across to any last wall. The wall will find you of its own accord without your help, and every day you live will seem to you a kind of victory. "I was too sharp for it that time", you will say, when night comes, and afterwards you'll sleep well.'

Exile in Paraguay can be cosy too. At one moment Pulling is a pure victim of nineteenth-century prissiness. 'If I had never known love at all, perhaps it was because my father's library had not contained the right books.' But when he finally decides to stay with his aunt: 'It was as though I were safely back in the Victorian world where I had been taught by my father's books to feel more at home than in our modern day.'

Some of his aunt's philosophy mixes with his own inherent

laziness. Of the C.I.A. man, he reflects: 'Anxieties in his case would always settle on him like flies on an open wound.' Better live dangerously, without anxieties; lose your security in order to find it. It is sentimentality, stood on its head, archness in a ruthless cause: a very proper entertainment for late middle age. Mr. Greene's skill, like Aunt Augusta's spirit, never flags, Whether one can stand being so lightly tickled over 300 pages is another matter. Pulling's obtuseness is sometimes no joke: he takes half the book to realize that Aunt Augusta has seen brothels from the inside, and it's only intermittently funny that she should have. 'Draw it mild' was a swell's phrase of the nineteenth century; 'draw it bitter' is a reader's message to Mr. Greene. *Travels with my Aunt* is drawn very mild indeed.

## (*b*) VLADIMIR NABOKOV:

### *Ada*

ANY AUTHOR worth parodying will sometimes achieve self-parody (*Sordello, Pericles, The Golden Bowl, The Kreutzer Sonata, Across the River and into the Trees*). Mr. Nabokov is no exception. *Ada* is the most Nabokovian novel ever, an idyll of aristocratic incest decked out with enough word games to stock an ocean liner. To appreciate it fully one should have perfect command of English, French and Russian, a working knowledge of botany and entomology, a flair for anagrams and a good deal of patience. (Well he's not writing for cretins is he?) If it ends in delight, it begins in hard labour. The book is clearly the author's Waterloo; it's less clear whether he figures as Wellington or Napoleon.

For a start, he has invented a new planet. Nothing so vulgar as science fiction, but an anti-Terra, the world as it should have been arranged. Mr. Nabokov has long been irked, it seems, by the inconvenient separation of his native and his adopted country. Why were there no Chekhovian house-parties in North America, or no enduring freedoms in Russia? The first problem drove Henry James to Europe, the second reduced Pasternak to years of self-imposed silence. Mr. Nabokov's solution is sprightlier: he sets his story in Estotiland, a stretch of North America largely settled by Russians. It is, in his own words,

that tesselated protectorate still lovingly called 'Russian' Estoty which commingles granoblastically and organically with 'Russian' Canady,

E

otherwise 'French' Estoty, where not only French, but Macedonian and Bavarian settlers enjoy a halcyon climate under our Stars and Stripes.

Its inhabitants also enjoy a pleasing kaleidoscope of anachronisms, like the Wellsian visions of a benevolent physics mistress: aeroplanes without bombs, duels and telephones, carriages and cars, all commingled (organically if not granoblastically) in a dream of 1890-ish cultured luxury. Mr. Nabokov's anti-Terra shows what God could have done if only he had had a little more education.

The stage exists, however, to be worthy of its characters: the Russo-Irish-American or Estoty family of the Veens, notably brilliant Van and his first cousin Ada. The Veens, like the Ptolemies, are too good for anyone but each other. Even as children they cast off a dazzling succession of erudite quips. Precocity is all. Their first meeting— Van 14, Ada 12—quickly develops into that familiar Nabokovian routine, shatteringly sexual first love. On Ada's parents' country estate they copulate like monkeys, tracked by a younger sister who threatens to spoil the fun. The adolescent's mixture of lust and idealism has never had such an outing. Narrator Van recalls every nervous sappiness; Ada, correcting his manuscript in old age, asks '*why* are you doing your best to transform our poetical and unique past into a dirty farce?' 'If people remembered the same', he replies, 'they wouldn't be different people.' On some anti-anti-Terra, maybe, Ada is composing a novel called *Van*, which might be an equally faithful reconstruction. There is much shadow-play with time, memory, and truth. ('On fait *son grand Joyce* after doing one's *petit Proust*', states another of Ada's marginalia, with more accuracy of aim than of italicization. The style is catching.)

So far, so good. It is easy to accept, and easier to enjoy, the celebration of this miraculous world, of Ada's and Van's sensual preenings, of their lifelong mutual obsession (and their lives, like their sentences, are very long). Two obstacles then intervene, or inter-Veen: their absurd self-admiration, and the constant drip of their creator's verbal ingenuity. To take the second first: it may be worth illustrating Ada's precocity with this neat little bilingual joke:

> Ce beau jardin fleurit en mai,
>   Mais en hiver
> Jamais, jamais, jamais, jamais, jamais,
>   N'est vert, n'est vert, n'est vert, n'est vert, n'est vert.

Render unto the Upper Fifth the things that are the Upper Fifth's (like some of Pound's Greek puns). But Nabokov throws them on to every page: 'the rose sore of Eros', 'Mexico or Oxmice', 'the sunglasses of the sung lasses', until the final effect is not lofty erudition but Victorian facetiousness. A trilingual Thomas Hood is still a dangerous bore.

Trilingual Scrabble is a characteristic Veen diversion. A few letters disappear from the board:

The missing *A* eventually turned up under an Aproned Armchair, but the *D* was lost—faking the fate of its apostrophizable double as imagined by a Walter C. Keyway, Esq., just before the latter landed, with a couple of unstamped postcards, in the arms of a speechless multilinguist in a frock coat with brass buttons. The wit of the Veens (says Ada in a marginal note) knows no bounds.

There is presumably a solution to this rebus (entries on a plain postcard). But the Veens' self-congratulation is a nasty warning. Van of course is not only brilliant in study but at all games, and performs miracles of maniambulation, combining a successful circus act with a career at Chose College, England. His asides might come from *An American Dream*: 'In my professional work, in the laboratories of pathology, I have devised myself many a subtle test (one of which, the method of determining female virginity without physical examination, today bears my name).' Ada's infidelities are grounds for high-style jealousy—though the duels are ludicrously side-stepped in a passage of microscopic comedy worthy of Quilty's last hours. But Van is permitted a broader, more seigneurial range. His heart remains true: 'those false romances soon fatigued him; the indifferently plumbed *palazzina* would soon be given away, the badly sunburnt girl sent back'. The explanation? 'His love for Ada was a condition of being. . . . He would have promptly plunged into boiling pitch to save her just as he would have sprung to save his honor at the drop of a glove.' It might be Lord Peter Wimsey.

'That precision of senses and sense', writes Van of his own feelings, 'must seem unpleasantly peculiar to peasants.' Haughty boy; and foolish, too, since so much of the precision is random synaesthesia or verbal roguishness. One can recognize in *Ada* the high point of a style, a stance, or a distillation of pedantry. If literature was invented for critics to practise on, *Ada*, like *Finnegans Wake*, might crown the arch of European writing. It is, like *The Golden Bowl*, a hard read. Perhaps for that reason, true Nabokovians should find it his masterpiece. The peasants may grumble.

## (c) PIERS PAUL READ:

### *Monk Dawson*

HIMSELF EDUCATED AT AMPLEFORTH, Piers Paul Read begins his story
with an account of a school called Kirkham, thus introduced by his
narrator: 'acting on mistaken principles of piety and snobbery, my
parents sent me to a boarding school in the English countryside,
which was run by Benedictine monks'. There is already something
unusual about the tone. He does not assume familiarity with the
system, so frequently mulled over by British novelists: there is a lack
of personal involvement, no warmth, whether indignant or defensive.

The second chapter begins: 'those of us who have had a private
education—a small but piquant part of the population . . .'. Mr.
Read is sketching in the necessary background, as if to inform
foreigners who may be expected to share the narrator's basic attitudes but are unlikely to know the details of Britain's strange
customs. The narrator explains why his friend, Edward Dawson, was
sent to this school, even though his widowed mother could not easily
afford it:

Mrs. Dawson knew, as we all know, that the sons of the rich go on to
become the rich of their day and that the rich not only have their money,
but the power that goes with it.

If her son failed to inherit his father's talents, his school would help
him in later life: 'he would have the friends and acquaintances to fix
him up with something respectable, rather than see him sink in
society to the level of a plumber or factory hand'.

It is the simplicity and certitude of these statements that distinguish
the novel's tone. There is no need for subtlety here: these are statements of the obvious. Yet the narrator seems to be a perfectly
conventional man, a successful journalist with no political commitment. He calmly, coolly accepts the idea that our society is organized
in the form of a conspiracy by the rich against the poor. Later in the
novel, when Dawson too has become a journalist, he meets a Marxist
shop-steward who takes much the same tone as the generally unob-
trusive narrator. Is there really, Dawson asks, 'a conspiracy to exploit
the workers and all that?'

'I don't know', said McKeon, 'I've never made up my mind on that. You
don't need many to preserve the *status quo* because most people just go
along. Its a matter of a small tap with a little stick to keep the ball rolling.

But there are people who make sure that the ball gets its small tap and you could call that a conspiracy.'

This conversation results in the total collapse of Dawson's attempt to come to terms with the world. A deeply pious boy, he had become a monk, remaining at his old school as a teacher; eventually, losing his faith, he had left the Church and turned to journalism, writing feature articles about political and social problems in a spirit of good will. Thinking of himself as a 'trouble-shooter', he goes to the scene of a 'crippling', 'wild-cat' strike at a Midland car factory. The shop-steward explains to this naive man the significance of the apparently trivial dispute—and assures him that this explanation will not be printed in Dawson's newspaper.

The liberal Dawson is confident that he can get the Marxist work-man's analysis published: he is wrong. His editor explains:

'If you'd been in it as long as I have, you'd realize that our so-called free-dom of the press is a tenuous thing. Newspapers with large circulations like ours have to be responsible if they are to retain respect; and if they lose respect, they'll soon lose freedom. . . . Now this question of the strike is very crucial because we're a trading nation. . . '

For a man like Dawson, with his passion for universal justice and his faith in other people's ethical consistency, this simple event—the rewriting of his article from the employer's viewpoint—is a punish-ing blow. Coinciding with two personal disasters, involving women, the normal, natural operation of censorship drives him back, out of the world and into the Church, accepting the severe discipline of a Trappist monastery.

As a 'story', this novel might be taken for a tale of an eccentric man warped by a quaintly antiquated education: those who think the Roman Catholic Church absurd may be able to read *Monk Dawson* in this light, as an illustration of the Church's failure to modernize itself, signalized by late-developing Dawson's failure to become 'normal'. The narrator has much of interest on these themes: the ex-monk's relations with women are particularly well described; there is a sound account of the effects of Pope John's benevolent policies. ('The Catholic Church in England was protected by its easy and insular situation. There was no competition for righteousness as there was, say, in Holland with its vital Protestantism and moral Socialism'.) But the novel is not in fact expressing a 'normal' point of view. The organization of Western society is considered with a judicial, foreign-seeming objectivity, recalling the way Mr. Read dealt with Nazi Germany in *The Junkers*. Neither Trappist monks nor Nazi S.S. men are presented as monsters to fascinate us. It is the conventional world, which we take for granted, that is made to seem strange.

## (*d*) NORMAN MAILER

### *Why are we in Vietnam?*

WHY INDEED *are* they in Vietnam? (The Americans are different from us. Yes, they have more money.) 'We', the British, are not in Vietnam —except in the metaphysical sense implied by the title of Peter Brook's show, *US*. Norman Mailer is not in Vietnam either; nor are the characters of his novel, they being young Texans engaged in a hunting expedition in Alaska. (Vietnam is not directly mentioned until the last page.) Presumably part of the novel's purpose is to try to explain the kind of young American who might be glad to fight in Vietnam.

We know, from Norman Mailer's more lucid book, *The Armies of the Night* (based on his personal involvement in anti-war activities in America), that this author tends to feel more natural sympathy with the concepts of 'manhood', discipline, patriotism and courage upheld by good soldiers and policemen than he does with the sloppiness of 'peaceniks'. He has identified himself, in the past, both with tough, comradely servicemen and with disobedient hipsters; but now these two life-styles are poles apart, and Mailer does not know where he stands. Jack Kerouac seems to be in similar difficulties.

On the last page Mailer commends himself for his inconclusiveness and obscurity. The narrator, D. J., after the hunting expedition with Tex, his buddy, announces: 'Tomorrow Tex and me, we're off to see the wizard in Vietnam.' He continues:

Unless, that is, I'm a black-ass cripple Spade and sending from Harlem. You never know. You never know what vision has been humping you through the night.

That is: we are not to know whether the author is in any sense celebrating the values and behaviour of Tex or D. J. or his father, Rusty, or whether he can claim to be consistently satirizing them, from the standpoint of a committed rebel.

The *International Times* published two years ago a couple of tape-recorded interviews with soldiers, a quiet young Glaswegian who had killed Communists in Malaya, and an American college boy on his way to kill Communists in Vietnam. The Scot had enjoyed himself, risking his life to kill others, and described his adventures, in a lively, straightforward manner, punctuated by colourful obscenities, without introspection or ethical considerations. The American was far more cerebral:

Today we tend to glorify the intellectual man at the expense of the physical man; and the war in Vietnam is a war in a totally physical world, a masculine world based on the kind of aggression that I want. I need to learn my capacity to run or crawl or punish my body in the mud and the slime and the dirt. . . . It's a way of proving manhood. I guess it was possible in the old West.

These two attitudes—spontaneous battle-lust, expressed with foul-mouthed glee; violence-in-the-head, expressed in cant about manhood—are present in Norman Mailer's book, but they are neither welded together nor kept separate: they are simply muddled up.

In *The Armies of the Night* Mailer congratulated himself on the style of this (earlier) book, remarking that he 'never felt more like an American than when he was naturally obscene—all the gifts of the American language came out in the happy play of obscenity upon concept'. The words which he labels obscene stud almost every paragraph, monotonously, which is a pity since he is also illustrating, quite seriously, the significance of some of them—the specifically American usages around 'ass' and 'butt', incest and oral copulation. Tex and D. J. leave the rest of the party and go on an expedition of their own, without weapons. They play with the offending expressions persistently, and the author comments:

Hey, hey, is this the way they really talk? And at sixteen and seventeen. . . . And all that pederastic palaver? Hell, yes. They is crazy about each other. They even prong each other's girls when they can, but fear not, gentle auditor, they is men, real Texas men, they don't ding ding ring a ling on no queer street with each other.

But then the author gets them under the same blanket and discusses, in the same style, what the boys would like to do to each other, and what is holding them back. The swear-words refer to incest, and oral and anal intercourse. No doubt it is possible to generalize about a nation on the basis of its favourite swear-words. But this is only a rough stab at such an attempt; and, surely, such a study does not help much in explaining why the Americans, rather than any other nation, are 'in Vietnam'.

The animals which the boys see are treated anthropomorphically. They are imagined to be issuing challenges (in the same foul-mouthed style, needless to say). There are descriptions, too, of the lovely countryside —with 'some sweet wine of old funk in the moss as well, some odor of dwarf's armpits wiped with velvet, thank you, milady'. Big Daddy Rusty has a page of interior monologue about his need to kill a grizzly bear, set out in terms of sexual fulfilment, racist patriotism and businessman's anti-communism. It is uncertain how far Mailer sympathizes with Rusty's stupid points. He has written elsewhere: 'You see, my mind wanders. It dissipates. I have no patience left for quiet exposition.' Yet he managed exposition very well in *The Armies of the Night* and it is a pity that this novel is such a miscellany of moods emanating from the private parts. To use a British vulgarism, he has a mouth like a vulture's crutch.

## (e) BEPPE FENOGLIO

### *Il partigiano Johnny* and *La paga del sabato*

TWENTY-FIVE YEARS AGO an event of little military significance but of great importance in the history of Italy's second Risorgimento took place in and around the small Piedmontese town of Alba: the Italian Partisans took it from the Fascists and kept it for twenty-three days, only surrendering it to the Germans after a heavy bombardment and a fierce battle. The town of Alba was soon honoured by the Italian Republic with the highest military decoration, the *medaglia d'oro*, and in 1969 on the occasion of the twenty-fifth anniversary of the siege, another gold medal was awarded 'to the memory of Beppe Fenoglio, Partisan and Writer'.

Beppe Fenoglio is not a name that many people know in this country, where another anti-Fascist writer from the same region, Cesare Pavese, has enjoyed and still does enjoy a great popularity. But if ever an Italian novelist deserved to be known and loved, by the British, it is Fenoglio, whose literary education was made on the English poets (his translation of Coleridge's *Ancient Mariner* was published by Einaudi in 1964), whose knowledge of the English language was such as to prompt him to use English expressions sooner and better than Italian ones, and whose native trust in British political wisdom and military power survived the most disappointing experiences of his life as a Partisan. Fenoglio was indeed a Piedmontese à la Cavour, and he looked to Britain as the great Mother of Parliaments and Protector of Exiles, the natural and providential friend of free Italy.

He was in his early twenties when he joined the Partisans in 1943. A native of Alba, he triumphed in its liberation and suffered in its surrender. After the war he went back to Alba and found employment in a wine exporting firm. But writing was his vocation, and in 1950 he sent the manuscript of his first novel. *La paga del sabato*, to the Turin publishing house which had specialized in Resistance literature: Einaudi. Although one of Einaudi's readers, Italo Calvino, was full of praise, the boss, Elio Vittorini, was less accommodating. Perhaps he disapproved of a book that did not try to hide or minimize the uglier aspects of the Resistance; the fact is that Vittorini persuaded Fenoglio not to publish *La paga del sabato* in its entirety, and Fenoglio dutifully complied.

He extracted from the novel a couple of tales, which were published in a collection under the title *I ventitrè giorni della città di Alba* (1952). A new novel appeared in 1954, *La malora*, and another in 1959, *Primavera di bellezza*. Soon after the author's death a short novel, *Una questione privata*, and another collection of tales under the title *Un giorno di fuoco* appeared in 1963. For a writer who had died at forty the output was already impressive, but there was more to come: *Il partigiano Johnny*, an immense novel published in 1968, and finally, in 1969, the book that Vittorini had condemned, *La paga del sabato*.

Apart from *La malora* and a few other stories, the perennial source of Fenoglio's inspiration is the Resistance. The conquest and defence of Alba is the central event that dominates everything, the background against which the individual characters stand out. Fenoglio's work is incomplete and repetitive but nevertheless it constitutes an epic of indisputable grandeur and also of historical value. The usual canonization of the Partisan as a Communist, and vice versa, which is the subject of so much Resistance literature, finds no grace with Fenoglio, whose hero leaves the red battalions of a Communist leader in disgust for the more traditional and better disciplined troops of a regular Army officer; and when the two factions come to blows, Fenoglio does not feel any embarrassment in telling the truth.

On the other hand, he is certainly sincere, and the effect is very moving, when he describes the new sense of solidarity and unity that Johnny, a student, experiences in fighting side-by-side with the workers: 'The humiliating feeling of class-consciousness had disappeared completely.'

*Il partigiano Johnny* was probably not meant for publication. The voluminous manuscript to which that title has been given by the 1968 editor was probably intended as no more than a rough copy for personal use and future development: indeed the story it narrates at great length is the same one which, with a few alterations to characters and names, had already appeared in separate shortened fragments in *Primavera di bellezza*, *Una questione privata*, *Un giorno di fuoco*. The great difference of style between these three books and *Il partigiano Johnny* confirms that they are revised editions of sections of this common matrix. Their language is polished, refined, very much à la Pavese in its realistic use of the Piedmontese dialect, but on the whole still subject to the Italian tradition of stylistic unity and linguistic purity. *Il partigiano Johnny* on the contrary is written in a personal language that owes much to English and has no regard at all for the purist's conventions: obviously the language that came naturally to Fenoglio when writing his first drafts.

The *Cruscanti* may well be shocked by the crude intrusion of English words in an Italian context ('quel *theatrical set-up* di fantomatici volumi', 'concluse Tito con triste *abruptness*', 'la chiesa chiusa, *nay*, sigillata'), or the bold italianization of others ('sensu*oso*', 'sogn*oso*', 'occhi *un*vedenti', 'acciughe ac*ride*'), but the effect is always one of great spontaneity and sometimes of great beauty. Not to mention the frequent quotations from English writers: Johnny marches into battle singing 'Sumer is icumen in'.

The spontaneity of the language corresponds perfectly to the true-to-life quality (Fenoglio calls it *truità*) of the characters. The men and women of *Il partigiano Johnny* are absolutely credible and convincing whatever they may do and whatever they may be: the young Partisan paralyzed by terror under fire for the first time, the other who behaves heroically without knowing it, 'inebriato dal suo stesso coraggio', the old woman who risks her life to shelter the wounded, the priest who acts as a go-between for an exchange of prisoners, the Fascists, the Germans, the peasants, all the people in this book are as they doubtless were in real life.

No other book by Fenoglio has in such degree this astonishing quality of sincerity and credibility, and none is so effective in the representation of the suffering, the horrors of war: you actually feel the mud in your boots and the cold in your bones, you see the little pool of blood under the fallen, you hear 'la grande *ouverture* della mitragliatrice'. No other book on the Italian Resistance is likely to survive, both as a document and as a work of art, better than this unfinished, unpolished, uninhibited, monumental 'rough copy'.

*La paga del sabato* is something different. It belongs to a time, in Fenoglio's career as a writer, when he was the victim, by his own admission, of a 'neo-realistic fever'. The effort to conform to the manner of Vittorini and Pavese is in fact clearly discernible and this is in itself a failure for an artist whose professed aim was an effortless style. But the artist is there, and his genuine gift for the representation of the hard life of the poor triumphs over the manner.

The hero of *La paga del sabato*, Ettore, is an ex-Partisan who cannot readjust to peace and normality. Not for him, who has been a leader of men on the hills, the common lot of working for a master: better to defy the law and join a band of former Partisans turned gangsters. Only when his girl tells him that she is pregnant does he realize that the time has come for him to settle down. He takes an honest job, but he soon dies, the victim, ironically, of an accident at work.

The story is rather naive and commonplace, but Ettore's mother, his father, his girl and her brothers, his fellow gangsters and workers, are portrayed with the admirable *truità* peculiar to Fenoglio. Ettore himself is a very convincing, very likeable character, and *La paga del sabato* for a first novel is a good start, full of promise. But, alas, not unlike Ettore, Beppe Fenoglio was struck down just when 'things were starting to go well'. The loss to Italian literature was a terrible one.

## (f) MELVYN BRAGG:

### The Hired Man

ONCE AGAIN Melvyn Bragg has written a novel about rural life in Cumberland, and once again it is earnest, worthy and sometimes a struggle to read. A country girl sees a farmer's son washing himself under a pump.

When he adopted a flamboyant expression of surprise at seeing her, she had smiled, recognizing the beer which leavened reactions to caricature: harmless, she thought, remembering the clumsy clutches at dignity of those she had seen drunk in her home village. When he parodied gallantry and filled the buckets for her then his attentions were excused, she thought, by her telling him who she was.

We are not meant to suppose that she used these words, that she said to herself: 'Beer leavens his reactions to caricature.' In what sense, then, did she 'think' these things? Surely she did not think in these terms. She 'recognized' the mood of a drinker, she 'thought' he was harmless, she 'thought' he could be excused. The rest is embellishment, the novelist telling us how he would have put it, had he been in that girl's place. But there must be a better way of telling us how that girl thought.

This is meant as a constructive criticism. Melvyn Bragg is a good novelist but his narrative is clogged by heavy phrasing, especially when trying to report the self-communication of his characters. When he tells what they said, what they did, how they and their environment appear to the author, he is consistently successful. There is a coal-miners' trade union meeting, in about 1913, excellently described, with the hero's fiery brother, Seth, trying to push his workmates a little farther than they are prepared to go towards adopting the 'closed-shop' principle, even towards a form of Syndicalism. Seth's fervour marks him out as something of a comic character among less committed pitmen: their different kinds of apathy and inertia are carefully set down. But here again comes the awkward 'he thought'. Seth's brother, John, listens uneasily to the ineffective oratory, 'the voice of Seth made raw by the cold response of his audience', and his concentration wanders:

These things should be put right. If only, he thought, he had the intelligence and the guts to see how they could be put right without recourse to actions in which he felt himself to be abandoned to the will of a mass less finely pointed than that of any of its members.

The over-subtle verbalizing of this 'thought' leads the reader to doubt whether John thought any such thing.

The story begins in 1898 when John aged eighteen and newly married, is walking to a Hiring, hoping to secure employment from a farmer. His grandfather gives him a piece of straw to stick in his mouth or under his hat, as a sign that he is for hire; but John is a little too proud to put up this sign. This novel is largely concerned with the changing attitudes among working men during this century

towards being 'hired'—or employed, exploited, used. John's grandfather had 'worked as if he was made for nothing else in the world:
he called by "sir" and "master" those "set above" him'. The movement of Seth and, later, John into the pits involves them in corporate
action against those set above. But there is another life-style hanging
over from older times, that of the third brother Isaac, who lives for
sport, like a free man—changing his job frequently, leaving his wife
for weeks on end, dealing with horses, dogs, fighting-cocks, boxing
and gambling.

Isaac has a harsh and witty tongue; further examples of his
humour would have been welcome in this often over-solemn novel.
He meets John at the Hiring, jeers brutally, and leads him to the pub
where Seth sits miserably with his whippet and a reprint of evidence
to the 1842 Royal Commission on the Mines. Much later in the story,
when Seth is in danger of being beaten up by a gang of anti-Union
miners, Isaac appears, and it is arranged that the vendetta should be
settled by a fist-fight, six men on each side. John finds it hard to
persuade Seth into this:

His persuasion was tempered by the melancholy realization that he was
urging his brother to a necessary action which with finer instincts Seth
wished to avoid. . . . Though such a flight seemed futile to Seth, such a co-
operative effort appealed to him.

Again the reader may wish that these thoughts had been put into
words which the men might really have used. If the author had
recorded their dialogue, which he can write so well, the situation
would have been enlivened. (Of course, this would have taken up
space, and Melvyn Bragg is determined to pack twenty-five years into
his 220 pages.) The result of the fight is important. John had been
planning to leave the pits but it is now 'impossible to think of working
anywhere in that town but with those he had fought'. It is a similar
sense of what is fitting that impels him to meet his brothers soon
afterwards and volunteer for the First World War. There is enough
in this theme to make a good novel; but Melvyn Bragg says a great
deal more, as if challenged by the largeness of his subject-matter—
the working class.

# 6

## TWO NOVELISTS

### (a) GÜNTER GRASS

WHERE TO BEGIN with *örtlich betäubt*? With the sense of anti-climax which even some of Günter Grass's harshest critics are bound to feel after a six-year wait for something to get their teeth into? (And does this mean giving unwarranted further publicity to Herr Kurt Ziesel, whose legal right, 'within the context of literary criticism', to call Herr Grass a pornographer was proclaimed by a Munich court in January of this year?) With the success which this relatively short, relatively fantasy-free novel, highly allusive and completely made in Germany as it is, is likely to have in the English-speaking-and-reacting world when the moment comes? (And is it too late to ask the translator—the book was printed, excellently, back in May—to omit and to Anglo-Americanize no more than he has to?) With the immediate topicality, the mixed-up messagizing, the unblinkered uneasy commitment which distinguish *örtlich betäubt* from its predecessors—*Die Blechtrommel* (1959), *Katz und Maus* (1961), *Hundejahre* (1963)—and which remind one that the weeks between publication day, August 14, and the West German elections have been weeks of some importance, not only to the Federal Republic?

There can be few story-tellers whose work loses more in the retelling—engenders greater reluctance to 'begin at the beginning'—than does that of Herr Grass. (Of his much adduced forebears,

---

(a) GÜNTER GRASS: *örtlich betäubt*. 358 pp. Berlin: Luchterhand. DM 19.50.

*Kunst oder Pornographie? Der Prozess Grass gegen Ziesel: Eine Dokumentation.* 88 pp. Munich: J. F. Lehmanns Verlag. DM. 7.

GÜNTER GRASS: *Speak Out!* Speeches, Open Letters, Commentaries. Translated by Ralph Manheim. 142 pp. Secker and Warburg. £2 15s.

WILHELM JOHANNES SCHWARZ: *Der Erzähler Günter Grass.* 149 pp. Bern: Francke. 8.80 Sw. fr.

GERT LOSCHÜTZ (Editor): *Von Buch zu Buch—Günter Grass in der Kritik.* 239 pp. Berlin: Luchterhand. DM. 6.

(b) JOÃO GUIMARÃES ROSA: *The Third Bank of the River and other stories.* Translated with an introduction by Barbara Shelby. 238 pp. New York: Knopf. $5.95.

Sterne might run him closest.) Those who are familiar with the writer's *Davor*—first produced, and coolly received, in Berlin last February, published in modified form in the April 1969 number of *Theater heute*—have a head start: the play of much of the book, it revolves around the plan of an uncouth seventeen-year-old schoolboy (Scherbaum) to burn his dog (Max) one afternoon on Berlin's Kurfürstendamm in full view of the cake-eating clientèle of a well-known café. The time: January, 1967. The idea is to shock the dog-loving public into an awareness of what is happening to human beings in Vietnam—for the petrol to be poured on Max, read napalm. (This is not the first of Herr Grass's two-in-one attacks on the use of napalm and the uselessness of impotent protest—see his poem in the volume *Ausgefragt* (1967) entitled 'In Ohnmacht gefallen'.) The boy has the backing of his Mao-mouthing classmate/girl friend (Vero Lewland)—the second-to-last in a now longish line of unpleasant young females from Herr Grass's pen—and is eventually dissuaded by . . . it's not clear what. He gets integrated, takes on the editorship of the school newspaper, decides to have his teeth fixed. The attitudes of the three oldsters in the piece—and even one or two of their arguments—may have helped bring about this change of direction: the young protesters' wistful, insightful, left-wing-liberal form-master (Starusch), his intrapunitive self-dramatizing colleague (Irmgard Seifert)—both, like the author at the time in question, pushing forty—and the confident no-nonsense middle-of-the-road dentist (a dedicated professional man, Seneca-oriented, nameless), who advises, lectures and treats the worried schoolmaster.

According to a melancholy report on the play's première in *Der Spiegel*, (17 February), Herr Grass and Starusch have much the same dental problems; according to Herr Grass as reported in the issue of *Theater heute* mentioned above, and to evidence extractable from a multiple of other utterances (notably the latest, paperback, edition of his *Über das Selbstverständliche: Politische Schriften*, Munich: d.t.v.), Starusch is not a self-portrait. Readers in search of the author will naturally start with Starusch and may be forgiven for looking no farther. After all, it's such a relief to find at long last a figure so representationally drawn, so readily equatable with so much that is known about its creator. And when, once there's room, in the novel, a number of clearly autobiographical details emerge; when even a dramatic right-handed slap—the stage Starusch coping with Irmgard—becomes an epic left-hander (Herr Grass, author of 'Die

Linkshänder', is reputedly himself one): then it's easy to forget that things aren't quite what they seem, that for instance the book's most outspoken condemnation of the use of violence comes not from Starusch but from the dentist, that the attempt to pillory the leader of West Germany's compromise government is made by Scherbaum —and that Scherbaum, too, leads with his left.

In among the Scherbaum story but mainly fore and aft (*örtlich betäubt*, like the earlier novels, is in three parts, though in this case the third part is nearer an eighth) Starusch presents an account, conflicting, imprecise, fitfully tentative accounts of his own career: this appears to have included a leading role in a gang of Danzig delinquents (a pity about the readers who do not remember Störtebeker of *Die Blechtrommel*), a year or two as the ineffectual fiancé of his former employer's warring daughter, Sieglinde (like Vero a bitch with a mission—and Starusch in the way), and the murder, repeatedly imagined, finally—could it be?—committed of the Amazon he failed. Starusch's ex-father-in-law-to-be is one ex-Field-Marshal Ferdinand Krings, a notorious Second World War-horse of the stick-it-no-matter-what brigade; and in Krings we are told in so many words—so many that 'Krings' is no disguise whatever—to recognize the controversial figure of that far from fictitious ex-Field-Marshal, Ferdinand Schörner. After being released by the Russians in 1955 Krings (civilian occupation: cement manufacturer) has one overriding ambition: 'to win', his daughter says, 'battles which others have lost'. The daughter's self-appointed task is to beat her father (N.B.: *Sieg*linde) 'on all fronts that occur to him', and she devotes herself to an elaborately organized macabre war-game with such single-mindedness that there is no real room for Starusch. She wins—and Krings determines to enter politics.

All this and more, much more, is presented in a manner which Herr Grass himself (in *Theater heute*) has attempted to summarize in part as follows:

the dentist has television in his surgery, facing the patient, and he [the patient, Starusch] tells his story all the time in fact onto the blank television screen or into whatever film is being shown, he projects it all onto the screen while undergoing treatment and he invents an inner dialogue between dentist and patient. It's hard to describe. . . .

It is indeed—and it's provocatively hard to read, even the second time round. Not that one can expect a conventional narrative technique from the inventor of Oskar and the *Hundejahre* trio:

but there are times when the inventiveness seems to get out of hand
and the result looks uncomfortably like gimmickry. In some respects
Herr Grass's new novel is a surprisingly controlled, calm composition
(*Katz und Maus* calls itself a novella, control is less of a surprise):
the linguistic exuberance—logorrhoea?—of six, ten years ago has
abated (not gone, thanks be), the floods of detailed out-of-the-way
information have receded (though we still learn rather more than
enough about caries and cement—cold comfort for those who have
been practising their Danzig place-names), and the repetitiousness
which threatened to swamp *Hundejahre* has largely subsided. But:
this 'inner dialogue' (Starusch's phrase, too) is a muddle, an ingenious
but irksome Heath Robinson device which, with all its 'telekinetic'
supports, barely manages to keep the whole together. Whether the
whole intriguing mixture of flashbacks, asides, allusions, daydreams,
hard facts and non-conversations *could* have been made to cohere still
further is a question best put, if at all, to the author.

Among the questions of more immediate interest to fans and foes
alike will probably be variants of the following:

First. What has become of Grass the shocker, the—roughly
speaking—'author of the worst kind of pornographic filth and [of
the worst kind of] denigration of the Roman Catholic Church'?
(The story behind the original words—'Verfasser übelster porno-
graphischer Ferkeleien und Verunglimpfungen der katholischen
Kirche'—may be read in and between the lines of *Kunst oder
Pornographie? Der Prozess Grass gegen Ziesel*: a remarkable and
anonymous piece of partisan reporting which has already reached its
second printing. Herr Ziesel and his fellow-feelers will find very little
to object to this time; picking out the dirty bits, the blasphemies—
admissible evidence-hunting in January—is now hard work indeed,
and if there's a case against *örtlich betäubt* it will scarcely be made
by the clean-in-thought-word-and-deed people.) Those who would
describe Herr Grass less colourfully but more accurately as the most
powerful, imaginative, free-speaking master of words Germany has
produced for a very long time—with a penchant, certainly, for the
grotesque and for what is commonly considered distasteful—will ask
in broader terms, will be more flatteringly disappointed: where is the
big belching Rabelaisian tour de force, where the profusion of
scenes, smells and symbols which we have learned to associate with
'a novel by Grass'? Could it be that *Davor*, written alongside *örtlich
betäubt*, has as it were taken the stuffing out of the story-telling?

F

Herr Grass's plays are comparatively lean affairs: is it that the
dramatist spoiled the novelist's appetite?

Second. Why, when displaying such—for Herr Grass, novelist—
unparalleled *engagement*, distort and trivialize the issue which is
arguably the work's principal concern? We know where Herr Grass,
citizen, stands. An ardent Social Democrat, advocate of constant
reform and eloquent campaigner for the resolution of conflict by
compromise, a self-confessed revisionist, 'living on productive
doubt', for whom tolerance is the supreme democratic virtue: his
readiness to stand up and be counted has been amply documented.
(A selection of Herr Grass's speeches, open letters and commentaries
has now been published in translation, with cuts, by Secker and
Warburg under the title *Speak Out!* All but one of the original texts
are included in full in the May, 1969, edition of *Über das Selbstverständliche.*) We see that citizen and writer are one in many ways—
and not merely when it comes to spreading the specific moral-cum-
electoral message 'For a number of compelling reasons a former Nazi
should not be Federal Chancellor'. But when it comes to the related
complex of problems which beset the young and their fortyish elders,
*örtlich betäubt* is oddly ambiguous, elusive if not evasive—'oddly' in
the light of past but unrecanted pronouncements.

Herr Grass has explained (apropos of *Davor*) that he deliberately
avoided setting his scene among *students* because that milieu is too
jargon-ridden, too fraught with frustration. And he has concentrated
his gaze on the liberals and the left, with little more than a glance at
their conservative and reactionary complement, because it is they,
he says elsewhere, who bear the brunt of 'this kind of problem and
unrest'—'this kind' meaning, reasonably enough, the kind which
afflicts the four or five characters in question and those they stand
for. These are two fairly fair comments, therefore, as far as they go,
but—like the play/novel to which they refer—a far cry from the
realities of the author's campaigning. For all his fervent moderation,
his tributes to 'the justified protest of youth, which is not only protest
by students', Herr Grass has singled out certain aspects of student
protest in his speeches and commentaries; has roundly condemned
the arrogance, the pin-up-worship, the fascist tendencies, the 'late
pubertal narcissism' of student radicals (in particular the SDS, an
organization with which democrats must nevertheless learn to live);
has paid so much publicized attention to the jargon-juggling, slogan-
shouting, left-wing extremist students, and to the reaction which

feeds on their antics, that the story of schoolboy Scherbaum and vacuous Vero, however interesting, however real, seems to fall flat. In the final paragraph we learn that Vero has married a Canadian linguist (it's a very funny book in parts) and that Scherbaum has become—a student, medical. The new milieu and his extra-curricular role in it are left to conjecture. The year, it appears: 1969.

Herr Grass has not confined his non-creative strictures ('arrogance', 'narcissism', &c.) to the young. On the contrary, his own contemporaries, and particularly those intellectuals who—sometimes actively—have egged the students on, have had quite a drubbing too. He and they belong to a generation which four years ago Herr Grass described as blameless by default (born too late to have incurred guilt under Hitler), a generation which, after a spell of postwar scepticism, had allowed itself to be corrupted by affluence: secure conformers squatting sulkily in front of the telly, dads who (this from a speech made three years later) try to wriggle out of the questions their sons are asking: 'Greece belongs to Nato, doesn't it, and Nato's meant to be defending freedom, isn't it? When the Americans use napalm, what's that if it isn't a war crime?' The age-group thus characterized is misleadingly under-represented in *örtlich betäubt*. Granted that speeches are not blueprints for novels, that some of the author's self-portrayal in Starusch's story is hardly speech material: if the conflict between the generations, between the juvenile utopians, the demolitionists of the left and their more temperate seniors, is as important as speeches and story make out, the avowedly negative roles of the older deserve far more fictional prominence than they get.

Take Starusch: basically a nice self-questioning well-intentioned chap with toothache and a sense of failure, 'a liberal Marxist who can't make up his mind', he sympathizes to some extent with Scherbaum's 'I-want-it-now' urge to change the world; but for the most part he dutifully and affectionately seeks to prevent the boy's projected protest and to give him less dramatic but constructive things to do, a local anaesthetic to stop the pain the world is causing him. (Starusch tries, he says, to be sad and indignant at the suffering and injustice which his pupil hopes to banish, glumly strives to communicate the experiences which have made him the evolutionist he is, and greets the news of Scherbaum's renunciation with a mixture of apparent scorn and relief—the reaction of a man who has himself adapted, been broken or at least broken in, and who half regrets the development he recognizes as right.) Ill-defined it may be, but the school-master's role in this presumably representative confrontation and in its outcome is not a negative one. And nor is that of the other two adults actively involved—the only other two.

The conscience-stricken Irmgard (sullied, as she sees it, by what she did and thought in her own late—'blameless', Nazified—teens) hopes for some kind of vicarious self-purification should Scherbaum do this thing. But such encouragement as she gives him repels, if only because of the turgid manner in which it—like most of what she says—is expressed. This crassly bombastic spinster, this flesh-and-cardboard schoolmarm is surely not spokeswoman for Herr Grass's culpable intellectuals? (Her subsequent engagement to Starusch, a man of some linguistic sensitivity, is one of the novel's implausibilities. *Davor*, in print, omits it.) And the preventive dentist? Again, a two-dimensional figure at most, he has little firsthand contact with the champions of 'demonstrative enlightenment' (Scherbaum's term for such schemes as the dog demo). Once contact is established, his commonsensical anti-demonstrative line somehow prevails; if there is conflict, as there could have been, we learn nothing of it. Whatever the dentist's trouble-free treatment of Scherbaum means (and irony is less foreign to Herr Grass than wishful thinking), he has no direct challenge to face from Scherbaum's kind either in the surgery or at home, where, as father of three, his controlling role might be harder to sustain. It might be, there's no telling, we never meet the family. So where exactly are the wriggling parents, the eggers-on-who-should-know-better? Virtually out of sight. And what, for that matter, of those to the right and far right of centre, of any age, whose function in 'this kind of problem and unrest' is significant and surely demonstrable? You can't have everything, it's true. But Krings and Kiesinger on the fringe are not enough.

First reactions to *örtlich betäubt* in German-language newspapers have been predictably mixed, luke-warm at best. In a note announcing the first of three reviews in *Die Zeit* Herr Dieter Zimmer points out: (a) that the more critical the review the more awkward for Herr Grass not only as writer but also as electioneer; (b) that it might have been wiser—and Herr Grass should have realized this—to postpone publication until after the elections. Just how to assess the effect of *örtlich betäubt* on the SPD vote is not clear, but in any case Herr Zimmer is perhaps over-apprehensive: Herr Grass's new novel, however received by the critics, will be read: and it scores points which on balance are unlikely to benefit any major party more than his own. The better the scoring the bigger the prize, but even a small score does not go unrewarded.

Post-election reading for those who wish to brush up on Herr Grass's earlier narrative work should include a recently published monograph by W. J. Schwarz entitled *Der Erzähler Günter Grass*; the author gives an interpretative summary of the stories, characterizes the characters and the form and the language, passes past critics in review, concludes with authoritative enthusiasm, and appends a very full bibliography—all in 140-odd closely printed pages. Professor Schwarz has assembled an impressive volume of skilfully processed information and well-founded comment which could be of considerable use on both sides of the desk. One welcome feature is the thirty-seven page survey of good and bad articles, essays, &c., the originals of which are often difficult to obtain—a valuable supplement in fact to last year's princely collection of primarily German reviews edited by Gert Loschütz (*Von Buch zu Buch—Günter Grass in der Kritik*). The survey draws quite heavily on material already reprinted in Herr Loschütz's volume; and it has only a short section on the drama and poetry critics. (Professor Schwarz's subject is the story-teller.) But criticism which has appeared outside Germany—mainly in English—is dealt with at some length and with some asperity. Among his concluding questions, Professor Schwarz puts one which has now been answered: where does Herr Grass go from here, that is to say from the massive performance of *Hundejahre*? He has gone to tackle problems which evidently and perhaps necessarily hamper his performance, which partly anaesthetize the otherwise dazzling performer.

It is to be assumed that one of the problems created by Herr Grass —how to convey the dazzle and the rest to an English-speaking public—is being worked out right now. Good luck to the translator. To do justice to *örtlich betäubt* will not be easy, and yet it sorely needs the fairest treatment. *Die Blechtrommel* was more robust.

# (*b*) JOÃO GUIMARÃES ROSA

A T  THE  BEGINNING of João Guimarães Rosa's novel, *Grande Sertão: Veredas* (translated into English as *The Devil to Pay in the Backlands*) the outlaw, Riobaldo, declares:

The sertão describes itself: it is where the grazing lands have no fences, where you can keep going ten, fifteen leagues without coming upon a single house, where a criminal can safely hide out, beyond the reach of the authorities. The sertão is everywhere.

'Backlands' is only an approximate English translation for 'sertão', a region of rocky, cactus-covered country in north-east Brazil, an area subject to wild fluctuations of weather and climate, to extreme drought and floods and edged by the *campos gerais* (the common lands), an area of cattle ranches across which stride scattered buriti palm trees. A prairie after rains, the sertão turns rapidly into a hot, arid desert during the dry season. But besides being a natural phenomenon, the area has close associations with Brazilian literature; its landscape was first described by Euclydes da Cunha in his classic, *Os Sertões* (Rebellion in the Backlands); it is the protagonist of dozens of novels of the north-east and, more recently, the setting for the novel and the short stories of João Guimarães Rosa.

Guimarães Rosa, who died in 1967, is one of Brazil's outstanding contemporary writers. He was born in 1908 in Cordisburgo, a small town in the cattle country of Minas Gerais province. For many years he was a doctor, first in a country practice, later in the army during the revolutionary war of 1932. Then, from 1934 to 1951, he served as a member of the diplomatic corps, living in Germany (where he was interned for a time during the war), Colombia and in France. Like Hemingway, he seems to have felt the need for periodic immersions in the wilderness, and after his return to Brazil in 1951 he almost immediately set out on an expedition to the Mato Grosso. The purpose of the journeys was perhaps not so much the newspaper articles which he afterwards published as the experience itself. Photographs show him crossing the sertão on horseback or sitting round the campfire with cattlemen, living, as it were, the myth of Brazil's Far West.

Though Guimarães Rosa's stories and novels are of the sertão, he is not a regionalist writer, any more than Cervantes was a regionalist novelist of La Mancha or Wordsworth a regional poet. Rather like them, he created a legendary country, in which geographical places and landmarks are stages in a pilgrim's progress or sites on an existential diagram. In his major work, his novel, *Grande Sertão: Veredas*, the sertão is analogous to the unknown 'other' which the individual comes to terms with on his journey through life:

Ancient sertão of the ages. One sierra calls for another and it is from these heights that you can discern how the sertão comes and goes. It is no use turning your back on it. Its border lies near and in far-distant places. You can hear its sound. The sertão belongs to the sun and to the birds— buzzards, hawks—which fly continuously over its immense expanse. A journey through it is dangerous, as is the journey through life.

*Grande Sertão* is structured round the journey/life analogy which is as old as literature, certainly as old as Latin American literature with its roots in quest and discovery. The novel harks back to the origins of the analogy in myth and epic. At the same time the primitive and archetypal elements thrust contemporary preoccupations about the nature of the self more forcibly to the surface. This juxtaposition of ancient and modern is disconcerting to the European reader but appropriate to Brazil where the *cantores* (troubadours) still compose ballads on the subject of Charlemagne and his knights in places not too distant from the futuristic towers of Brasilia. The form of the novel retains the archaic quality, for it is a monologue spoken by Riobaldo, the *jagunço* (outlaw), a monologue that has its roots in folk forms, in the *lenga-lenga*, the rambling, leisurely conversation of country people whose pleasure lies in telling rather than in finishing a story.

Anachronistic too is the plot, which is reminiscent both of medieval morality and of epic. It tells the story of Riobaldo and his friend, Diadorim, members of the bandit army of Joca Ramiro until he is treacherously killed by Hermógenes. Now Riobaldo and Diadorim seek vengeance first under the leadership of Medeiro Vaz and then with Zé Bebelo. When Medeiro Vaz dies and Zé Bebelo fails to make contact with the enemy, Riobaldo becomes chief of the bandit army, attempts to make a pact with the devil, and finally does battle with Hermógenes. Diadorim is killed in the encounter and is only then discovered to be a woman.

Such a plot could easily exist in ballad or in a novel of chivalry or in medieval epic. Certainly epic elements abound. There are catalogues of men and horses as they go into battle; there is the idealized and distant Otalícia whom Riobaldo loves, the Roland/Oliver-like friendship of Diadorim and Riobaldo. Signs and portents prefigure the tragedies and accidents of life and there are the great set-pieces of battles between rival bandit armies which recall Roncesvaux or the Cid's capture of Valencia. The language too has the solemnity of epic. Men's lives and deaths are raised to archetypal significance. Thus the exact place of Joca Ramiro's assassination is recorded, as if he were a Hector.

At a place on the Jerara, on lands belonging to Xenxerê, on the banks of the Jerara—there where the Jerara creek runs down the Vôo sloop and enters the Riachão—Riachão da Lapa, that is. They say it happened suddenly, unexpectedly. It was out-and-out treachery. Many of the ones who remained loyal died, João Frio, Bicalho, Leôncio Fino, Luís Pajeú, Cambó, Leite-de-Sapo, Zé Inocêncio, some fifteen altogether.

The style, indeed, is often deliberately portentous: 'Out into the wilderness we rode', 'It was thus we began our many hard marches and indecisive battles and sufferings, whose melancholy tale I have told you'; and at other times there is the sententiousness of epic and ballad: 'A master is not someone who always teaches but someone who learns swiftly'.

Nothing in the characters' psychology conflicts with this anachronism of style and language. Riobaldo's moral decisions, his vacillations and hopes are acted out as incidents in the larger struggle between the forces of good and the forces of evil, between God and the devil as conceived in popular lore. Thus as he rides to make tryst with the devil in order to secure victory over Hermógenes, he imagines the appearance of the evil one in a thoroughly traditional way:

Suddenly with a loud clap, or in a moment of dead silence, he could appear before me. Looking like the Black Goat? The Big Bat? The Xu? And from somewhere—so far and yet so close to me, out of the depths of hell— he must be watching me, a dog picking up my scent.

If the novel were simply medieval pastiche it would be of no interest, but of course it is very much more. Riobaldo's vacillations between good and evil may be translated into modern terminology. His struggle is the struggle for his identity, the different nicknames he adopts in the course of the novel representing different roles. And his adventures are stages in his growing self-awareness. Thus, for instance, he first faces his own nature on a dangerous river crossing after his first meeting with Reinaldo, the boy with the green eyes whom he later comes to know as Diadorim:

I was afraid. You know? That was what it was: I was afraid. I could make out the bank of the river on the other side. Far, far off, how long would it take to get there? Fear and shame. The brutal, treacherous water—the river is full of menace, deceitful ways and whispers of desolation.

On the other side of the river, on the other shore lies 'the promised land' which, in fact, turns out to be a place neither of rest nor of attainment. It is the journey that has been the significant psychological experience, the moment of self-awareness and transformation. But it is also a process in which there is no permanent goal, only the perpetual struggle. 'The imperfect is our Paradise', in the words of Wallace Stevens.

To the Brazilian public, *Grande Sertão: Veredas* was remarkable above all because it signified a linguistic revolution. The language was compounded from archaic Portuguese, from dialects and neologisms. New verbs were invented from nouns (the moon 'moons' for instance). Indeed, a large part of the pleasure of the novel is derived from the virtuosity of the style which is as individual and as inimitable as *Ulysses*. Unfortunately this aspect of Guimarães Rosa's work is the least accessible to the foreign reader. The English translation represents a valiant effort to solve the difficulties, but different styles jostle one another without fusing and without the unity of the original. Colloquialism and bits of slang stand out awkwardly. Even the title of the English translation, *The Devil to Pay in the Backlands*, lays stress on folksy aspects and conveys nothing of the mystery and poetry of the Portuguese title.

Fortunately, there is an alternative way: that is, to approach Guimarães Rosa's work through the collections of stories. There are three collections: *Sagarana* (1946), *Corpo de Baile* (Corps de Ballet, 1956), and *Primeiras Estórias* (1962, now translated into English as *The Third Bank of the River and other stories*), of which the last corresponds most closely to conventional conceptions of the short story genre.

In the first two collections, the stories have an epic spaciousness, and are something between novel and poetry, having the 'density of specification' of the former and the lyricism and intensity of the latter. Indeed, the title, *Sagarana*, means 'in the manner of the saga', *rana* being a *tupi* suffix. And as in *Grande Sertão: Veredas*, the framework is often reminiscent of medieval genres: hagiography in a story like 'Augusto Matraga's Hour and Turn' in which a bad man repents, becomes a saint and saves his native village from bandits; exemplary fable in 'The Return of the Prodigal Husband'; and animal allegory in 'The Little Dust-Brown Donkey,' in which the donkey of the title carries his load to safety in a disastrous flood.

The nearest that Guimarães Rosa comes to a more contemporary short story form in *Sagarana* is 'Mine Own People', a Chekhovian piece about a doctor who visits relatives in the country, woos his cousin, Maria Irma, and finally marries another girl. But even here

the main preoccupation is with self and identity, and again it is a
river which offers the analogy with human experience. The rapid
changes in the surface of the water in obedience to hidden forces
have their implicit parallels in the lives of the human beings of the
story. As the doctor observes:

All the streams here are mysterious—they suddenly disappear, in limestone
fissures, travelling for leagues in their subterranean beds, and bursting out
far away in a geyser or a canyoned cataract. But the most enigmatic of
them all is this river which at times rises, without rains, for no apparent
reason, and then suddenly dwindles in less than an hour. There is always,
at one spot or another, a gurgle, a liquid sucking, water swirling within
water; down below, over the stones, the stream runs, now fast, now slow,
but the sound is never the same as two seconds before.

The mysterious forces come dramatically to the surface as the doctor
fishes in the pool with his friend Bento—who is in love with a married
woman. The jealous husband appears and strikes Bento down with
a scythe, like the personification of death itself. But even this violence
is quickly forgotten, absorbed into the current of memory. In 'The
Little Dust-Brown Donkey', the donkey weathers the turmoil of
human passions and natural disasters because it can abstract itself
from these and perceive the essential, the flow of the current, the
strength of the river, its own possibilities.

In *Corpo de Baile*, the characters in most of the stories have similar
powers of abstraction and self-realization. Thus in 'Uma Estória
de Amor', Manuelzão holds a noisy celebration to mark the baptism
of a new chapel, but he and the rest of the gathering are suddenly
lifted out of the flux and passion of the event as an old story-teller
begins to relate a myth of the origins of things. In the stories both of
*Sagarana* and *Corpo de Baile*, the theme thus seems to call for complexity and space.

The stories of *The Third Bank of the River* are, in contrast, more
compressed, and they are more concerned with the 'essences'. The
title story gives a clue to the nature of the experience that most of the
stories gloss. A man builds a canoe and his family watch him paddle
away in it. From this moment onwards, he never again sets foot on
shore. The man's son grows up with a feeling of separation and guilt,
always aware of his father's lonely vigil on the river. Finally he offers
to replace the old man, but his nerve fails him at the last moment.
He stays on shore, conscious that 'it is too late for salvation now'. The
allegory expresses man's need to abstract himself from 'this shore'

and seek 'the other'. The penalty for failure is not hell but wretchedness, the impossibility of self-fulfilment.

The most explicit statement of the theme of self-fulfilment is to be found in 'The Mirror', the story of a man who tries to eliminate all non-essential traits from his countenance. 'I had to penetrate the veil, see through the mask, in order to express the heart of the nebula —my true countenance', he declares. By dint of concentration, he manages to block out non-essential and illusory characteristics, those that he has inherited from his parents, those which he has derived from limitation or from infectious passions. The result is a blank, a transparency, and he is forced to ask himself if

what I had supposed to be my self was no more than animal survival, a few inherited features, unbridled instincts, strange passionate energy, a tangled network of influences, all fading into evanescence?

A period of suffering restores a faint reflection of self, enough to bring him to the realization that the basic question of life is 'Do you exist *yet*?' To exist, then, is to find the real self, to abstract from the contingent and discover the authentic.

Authenticity is given a most striking symbol in the story 'Substance'. Sionésio, owner of cassava fields, falls in love with one of his workers, Maria Exita, who grinds the cassava root to make flour. At first Sionésio is repelled by the 'melancholy, sinister powder' in the 'wicked glare of the sun' and though fascinated by the woman and her apparent contentment, he is haunted by her unhappy heredity and the fact that her father had been interned in a leper colony. He watches her day by day unable to admit his love:

She ministered to the fine powder—the burning-hot, singular substance, limpid dryness, sandy material—the massiness of that matter. Sometimes it was still wet when it came, soft and friable, sticking to her beautiful arms and whitening them to above her elbows. Wet or dry, it shone like the sun's self, with a reflecting radiance that was too painful for Sionésio's eyes to bear. He might as well have stared the very sun in the face.

Only when he gives in to his feelings and declares his love are his eyes able to meet the dazzling whiteness of the flour. Then 'though only for an instant, he found there a power of greatness bestowed, a dilated repose that reduced to whiteness the tumult of ideas tormenting him'.

Guimarães Rosa seems to accept Spinoza's definition of identity as 'the power or effort by which a thing endeavours to persevere in its being'. Thus in 'The Thin Edge of Happiness', a child brought to a

strange environment intuitively perceives this power in a turkey and
feels an immediate sense of joy:

Lord! When he saw the turkey in the middle of the yard, between the house
and the forest! The lordly turkey imperiously turned its back on him to
receive his admiring homage. It had snapped open its tail like a fan, and
now it puffed itself up and wheeled around; the brusque, vigorous grating
of its wings on the ground was like a proclamation. It gobbled and shook
its thick buttoned armor plate of ruby-red wattles, and its head glinted with
flecks of rare light blue, the blue of the sky, tanager blue. The creature was
complete, sculptured, rounded, all spheres and curved planes, with metallic
green reflections on blue-black—the quintessence of turkey, beautiful,
beautiful.

But such moments of perception are fleeting. The turkey is killed.
The boy's sense of realization and happiness are as ephemeral as the
firefly he sees on the edge of the forest.

The view of life which Guimarães Rosa presents in *The Third
Bank of the River* is akin to oriental philosophy, and some of the
stories are, indeed, reworkings of oriental myth in Brazilian terms.
Such, for instance, is the pretentiously titled 'Nothingness and the
Human Condition' where Man'Antônio is a hero in the style of
the Rig Veda, in which it is the king who alone knows the rituals
necessary to gain favour with the gods. Towards the end of his life,
Man'Antônio distributes his lands to his followers:

The secret password was withdrawing—from himself toward himself
within himself. He no longer questioned anything—horizon or eternity—
peak or zenith. And so he lived, carrying the burden of years, erect, serene
and doing a doing-nothing with all his might, in acceptance of the emptiness, the ever-repeated inconsequence of his life.

When he dies, his house mysteriously catches fire and continues to
burn for days while the mourners become frenzied demons who
throw themselves on their faces in the dust 'imploring that they be
given something or nothingness, desperate to be at peace'. The
ending of the story is a beautiful evocation of Vedic belief:

And when the dead body had been consumed, in his ashes he, the lord,
began his journey through the earth, sepulchral sphere, and nothing more;
and all this as the sum total of a thousand acts, each a result and a cause.
He—became the Predestined One—Man'Antônio, my Uncle.

Though the tendency of Guimarães Rosa's stories is towards the
mystical, towards the revelation of truths which are hidden in the
daily flux of events, he does not always remain on a lofty plane.

There is irony and lightness too. One or two of the stories are little more than humorous anecdotes. 'The Horse that Drank Beer', for instance is an extended joke. Others are disturbing rather in the way that science fiction disturbs by allowing us to glimpse disconcerting possibilities. Of this type is 'Much Ado', in which a madman, mistaken for a Minister, shins up a palm tree and undresses in front of the crowd; and in 'Hocus Psychocus' a group of schoolboys rehearse a play but are taken over by a totally different plot when they come to perform.

Unfortunately, the stories do suffer in translation. The translator of *The Third Bank of the River* is aware of the difficulties and apparently consulted the author on some points. A better guide might have been her own ear, which would have prevented her calling a story 'The Aldacious Navigator', in an attempt to recreate a pun. Regretfully we must conclude that Guimarães Rosa's stature as a writer cannot yet be fully appreciated by an English public.

# 7

# OLD MEN REMEMBER

## (a) TOYNBEE AT EIGHTY

IT IS pleasant that the volume of essays Professor Toynbee has published to mark the occasion of his eightieth birthday, *Experiences*, is
decorated with two photographs by Lotte Meitner-Graf which show
what he has to give and what he has so persistently given. The profile
shows that kind concern for humanity, and the full face speaks of that
willingness to bear the yoke of office, which make the essays themselves so comforting, and so fully explanatory of the nature of the
comfort we receive and the means by which it has been bestowed on
us for such a lengthy period. Professor Toynbee's account of himself
has the great merit of leaving out almost nothing. The present
generation, which knows little of the English middle classes until the
time when they went gay and formed the Bloomsbury set, will have
an opportunity to see what they were like when they were serious
and industrious and, as Professor Toynbee points out, quite poor.

His own grandfather was a doctor who died young and left his son
with no chance to complete his education, with the result that he
became an ill-paid official of a philanthropic body called the Charity
Organization Society, on which Professor Toynbee is rather too
hard. It was not, as he suggests, merely, or even mainly, a society
which tried to impose on the poor habits of thrift actually beyond
the powers of any but the middle classes. We forget nowadays that
before the welfare state took care of the poor they were often compelled to ask help from the more prosperous; and as the rich were
well protected from them, they turned to people who were perhaps
only a little better off than themselves, and this gave an opportunity
to the professional beggar. One reader of *Experiences*, at least, feels
gratitude to the C.O.S. for having broken the link between a sentimental and needy grandmother and a bogus clergyman purporting

---

(a) ARNOLD TOYNBEE: *Experiences*. 417 pp. Oxford University Press. £2 15s.
(b) BERTRAND RUSSELL: *The Autobiography of Bertrand Russell*. Volume 3:
1944–1967. 232 pp. Allen and Unwin. £2 2s.

to be in ill health but proved by the Society to be robust enough to take a regular part in conducting a house of prostitution. Professor Toynbee's mother was a schoolmistress and a historian. These people and their kin believed in education and virtue of a public and private kind so ardently that they hardly noticed the austerity of their lives, and they brought up their children to continue in that state of pride in service which, as Professor Toynbee explains in suitable terms, became a dynastic tradition.

Through Edward, the Frankland family's abiding scientific ability has descended to a fourth generation. . . . His daughter, my cousin Helga Frankland, is now an officer of the Nature Conservancy. From her headquarters at Grange-over-Sands, she administers a region that is approximately coterminous with the Archdiocese of York and with the former Kingdom of Northumbria.

The early chapters, indeed, distress us with their recital of the hardships inflicted on the children of such dynasties to fit them for their tasks. The young Toynbee arrived at Winchester on a scholarship, and his account of its tribal laws terrify readers who have not had a like experience by the fullness and vividness of its recall. It seems odd that a man should be able after six or seven decades to remember that brown and not black boots should be forbidden for the first two years, and where it was that he must lift his hat because there had been, before the Reformation, a statue of the Virgin. Such trivialities can linger in the mind only because they are linked with its profundities, and it would take a Lévi-Strauss to judge why this link should be so specially strong in the case of Winchester men. In Professor Toynbee's instance the machinery, whatever it is, passed him over bound hand and foot to the slavery of an exclusively classical education. One has occasion to regret this throughout the volume, and there are, indeed, three pages in this book which sharpen this regret.

On these three pages Professor Toynbee declares that his faith can be summed up in the line, 'Homo sum, nihil humanum a me alienum puto', which he describes as a 'famous and moving sentiment', touching him because he writes, 'I am an inquisitive historian besides being an enthralled spectator of current human affairs and an eager participant in them'. These references are charged with emotion. But the line comes out of an adaptation of one of Menander's comedies by Terence; and can any good come out of Terence? It is in any case irrelevant to Professor Toynbee's warm-hearted virtue. Not a

beautiful line in itself, it is spoken by a busybody in reply to a
neighbour who has tartly asked him if he has so much time on his
hands that he has to meddle in other people's business, and that is
what it sounds like with its dull vowels and mumbling consonants.
That it should have lodged in Professor Toynbee's mind with this
false significance is disquieting.

It makes it appear possible that some gifted son of the future
civilization, speaking another language than ours, may be forced by
the prevailing educational system to study a play comparable, say,
to the current success, *There's a Girl in my Soup*, and should select
from it some such phrase as, 'I may be a Nosy Parker, but I do mean
well', and be deceived by a coarse and remote resemblance in seman-
tic outline into mistaking it for the apology of a sainted missionary
for some beneficent intrusion. The practical consequences of such a
misapprehension would only be minuscule, but it would add its mite
of increase to that imprecision of thought and perception to which
man is so gravely subject. Professor Toynbee's choice of Terence's
line does that damage by confusing us about his nature. For he
writes down as his creed something quite incompatible with that
line from Terence:

I believe that the dweller in the inmost spiritual sanctum of a human being
is identical with the spiritual presence behind and beyond the Universe,
and I believe that this ultimate spiritual reality is love. I have already
declared my two beliefs about love. I believe that love is not omnipotent
and I believe that love 'endureth all things' and 'never faileth'. If I am
committed to humanity, I am thereby committed to love and it is of the
nature of love that a commitment to love is unlimited.

There is implicit in this passage a recognition that there are all sorts
of human qualities from which the good man tries to alienate himself: greed, selfishness, cowardice, cruelty, and above all hatred.
He has chosen for himself from Terence a motto far poorer than he
deserves, enslaved by his education in the belief that a classical text
must be charged with dignity and significance.

Yet it is written on the tomb of Hafiz, 'Oh, heart, be a slave to the
king of the world and be a king', and slavery can be a form of en-
franchisement. There are pages in this book which describe how the
young Greek scholar enjoyed the freedom which his parents rightly
believed was not to be enjoyed by an unlearned man. Notable are
his descriptions of his walking tours in Greece. It would be interesting
to compile a list of those Greek scholars who did and those who did

not trouble to visit Greece, even when it had become fairly accessible. This scholar who had the fervour to be also a pilgrim tells how his feet became sore and swollen on the rocky Greek mountain tracks, and how the Greek villagers who had come home after some years in the United States talked of the sidewalks of Kansas City and Omaha as the most exquisite of luxuries. Thereby he was sharing in an experience which is to be detected in the simpler Byzantine frescoes and sculptures. There is a great emphasis laid on the male knee, for a peasant whose knees were free from arthritis could walk those cruel tracks and was not given up as old and helpless.

A continuing passion for the classical world burned in the young man's brain and was not to be extinguished by his other interests. At twenty-four the young scholar gave lectures to the School of Literae Humaniores at Oxford on the effects on Rome and her neighbours of the First and Second Roman-Carthaginian Wars. This is a subject which the English mind blankly disregards, although it is certain that because of these wars Rome brought on herself a calamitous period of revolution which deformed her development, and it is arguable that they created a Mediterranean problem not to be even partially solved for centuries, and that the destruction of an African civilization was a disaster for the whole world. Professor Toynbee at the age of seventy-six produced *Hannibal's Legacy*, two volumes which enchant any intelligent reader and build up a sense of the terrestrial process; and the germ of the book was contained in the lectures he gave in Oxford in 1913. This is good, obstinate, indefatigable, intellectual husbandry of which one must approve.

Yet there are still questions to be asked: notably whether eminence as a classical scholar has not led to an unfounded claim to the same sort of eminence in the field of international affairs. At the end of *Experiences* there are printed certain poems Professor Toynbee has written in Latin and Greek and, less happily, as he admits, in English. In one of these last he describes a boy,

> Unaware of the signs of the times—
>    an open book to me
> Who, thrusting forebodings aside, now
>    give myself up to the moment
> Tasting the joy of companionship.

Surely the signs of the times are an open book to nobody, and a former Director of the Institute of International Affairs should know this better than most people. It has been made quite clear from

G

time to time that the furniture of Chatham House does not include a crystal ball. This is not a really lamentable omission. The person who predicts the historical future is on the same plane as one who predicts the future of individuals: both are to be properly known by the not too honourable name of fortune-teller. Indeed, some belong to a class even more generally admitted to be prone to failure. At least one political pundit in the United States recalls the boastful cry, so often disappointed, of the late Prince Monolulu, 'I gotta horse. I gotta horse'.

The expert in foreign affairs who deserves respect is one who can make a valid analysis of an international situation in the shortest possible time, which shows a proper regard for the moral as well as the factual elements involved. This volume shows that Professor Toynbee enjoys a special advantage in fulfilling this role because his view of morality coincides with that held by the effective majority of the persons, even those much younger than himself, who take an interest in international affairs today. He carefully examines his own religious beliefs and finds that he has no difficulty in accepting the paramount value accorded to love by the Christian faith, and that he approves, and even welcomes with a warmth it can rarely have been accorded, the concept of original sin. But he feels obliged to reject the idea of an omnipotent God, on the ground that a divine being cannot be responsible for the suffering of the world.

He alludes sympathetically to the teaching of Marcion, who distinguished between the creator god who tumbled evil mixed with good pell-mell into the universe as he created it, and the redemptory god who through the ages purged the universe of its evil and would over the far horizon of eternity convert it into a fine manifestation of goodness. Professor Toynbee records these views as if they were the findings of an unusual man, but they have in fact been the motive-power of the idealistic left for the past half century and are today driving the young demonstrators into Grosvenor Square. One cannot make a good heresy lie down, history will always help it to its feet again. Manichaeanism and its allied heresies have never been knocked out for long. We must recognize in the intransigents of today a burning conviction that the human race is so wicked that the societies it forms are dedicated to crime, and that the virtuous and merciful force in the universe is in danger of defeat and must be aided by all people of good will.

These convictions must be respected. Were it not for their constant resurgence through the centuries society might indeed become wholly criminal; and Professor Toynbee's sense that original sin never sleeps and that the divine is in need of human cooperation has made him a most useful watch-dog to our own day. Nevertheless, it should be remembered that this rejection of the inconsistencies of orthodoxy does not leave Professor Toynbee and his allies in a satisfactory intellectual position. It appears illogical that God should have created pain and sorrow; but it is as illogical to think that a divine power of limited potency who is suffering from ills inflicted on him by persons made malevolent by original sin can be aided by persons also tainted by original sin. There are pages of *Experiences* which are puzzling in their suggestion of substantial aid afforded to divinity in difficulties unless some special arrangements were made to staff Chatham House with personnel immune from the consequences of the Fall of Man.

As it is, it cannot be said that the intellectual aid given has been always of the best. The blame called forth by original sin is too discriminate and too harsh. In an examination of the post-Christian ideologies Professor Toynbee names nationalism as the most dangerous. 'In 1969', he writes, with great concern, 'Nationalism is about ninety per cent of the religion of about ninety per cent of the whole human race.' This is not immediately convincing. It cannot be supposed that Professor Toynbee would be guilty of the illiterate practice of using nationalism as a synonym for imperialism; and one can think of little less mischievous than the nationalism of, say, the Baltic States before the Second World War. But the context discloses that Professor Toynbee has quite other arguments against nationalism, which are really too morally exigent, too hostile to what, by the end of this volume, one thinks of as poor old original sin. He writes:

In every country, whether Communist or Capitalist, in which the locally established ecumenical ideology has clashed with the country's particular national interests, these national interests have invariably been given precedence, and Communism or Capitalism—whichever it may happen to have been—has gone to the wall.

But this is dubious history. One can think of a number of countries which feel that national interests have been ignored by the pressures of communism and capitalism and can do nothing about it, though young men, European and Asiatic, set themselves on fire. But what startles is the impossible demand that a country should not give its national interests precedence. The world does well to ask of a country's government that it should make an adequate estimate of what its people need and how those requirements can be satisfied on the national resources. The information is needed. One could hardly ask for a better contribution to global well-being than that simple step towards self-preservation. What Professor Toynbee perhaps means is that sometimes a country is intellectually and emotionally unable to form a just and practical conception of its own needs; but surely we should remember that such inability may be the result not of any selfishness or pressure by greedy neighbours, nor to any ideological influence, but to natural environmental handicaps. There is really no occasion to blame anyone, and Professor Toynbee quotes a passage from a classical poet which might have reminded him of this.

> Ex ipsis caeli rationibus ausim
> confirmare aliisque ex rebus reddere multis
> nequaquam nobis divinitus esse creatam
> naturam mundi: tantâ stat predito culpâ.

The stars tell us, and much else bears witness too, that not possibly can divine providence have planned the universe for our convenience. It is not man alone that does harm to man; it is the whole of nature that shows him brutal indifference. These lines plainly mean much to Professor Toynbee, but there are often times when he fails to apply their lesson to facts which require to be considered in the light of Lucretius's warning that man is a part of nature, though nature is not the loyal ally that might be hoped.

The weak point in *Experiences* (which could also be said of some parts of *A Study of History*) is that Professor Toynbee treats man too much as a detached species, and at that singularly free from pressures other than those applied by man himself. To take a significant example, for a connoisseur of disaster he gives less attention to the population problem than might be expected, and he treats it as if it were contained by a framework established by the human will.

The cause of the population explosion is well known. The rate of premature deaths can be reduced sensationally, even in 'backward' countries, by simple measures taken by a small staff of public health officers, whereas the birth rate can be reduced only by the free choice of innumerable husbands and wives.

This is not a long-term view of human fertility. Sooner or later, the power of couples to reproduce themselves several times over would have produced a pressure on the food and space and general resources of society, even if the human mind had taken some turn that prevented the development of medical science. Infant care was not a star subject of our early kings, but the population is said to have increased from 1.5 million to 4 million between the time of the Norman Conquest and the reign of Queen Elizabeth I. Nor is the free choice made by the parents the only factor which raises or lowers the birthrate: this can be determined by an agricultural system which mutely, by the instrument of its crops and the conditions of harvesting them, determines whether men and women marry early or late. We must remember, if we are to get the feeling of terrestrial process that significant social changes, close parallels to the phases of our history, take place in the animal and vegetable worlds, in societies where there is no learning in our sense of the word, because words are not spoken, and even in many kingdoms where sounds are not uttered, and it is impossible to imagine that there is any equivalent of original sin, yet disaster and retrievement eternally recur.

Many of us can remember when seagulls lived up to their name; in our lifetimes we have seen them join peaceable communities on the Thames-side reservoir, and as they grew more crowded and less peaceful there were emigrations farther inland. In the same span we have known the malaria germ experience worse fortune than the British Empire, though the unending triumphs of dysentery make those of Alexander the Great and Napoleon look poor. There has been an invasion that has ravaged our land: the willow herb that was once a rare local plant now covers Great Britain with its flame and its inconvenient roots. Noble chestnuts rot, and so do elms, but nothing can stop the mediocre elder.

There is an essential similiarity between these zoological and vegetable ups and downs and our own, and it is the weakness of Professor Toynbee's picture of human history that it seems to be enacted solely by man in his limited capacity as a link in the chain of his culture. It is strange that Professor Toynbee should give us this denatured picture of man, for he himself owes his special distinction to a quality that surely would have survived if he had been born into another order of nature. He would have been the leader of the herd, or the tree standing tall against the skyline, to be seen for many miles.

## (b) RUSSELL AT NINETY-FIVE

With this volume Bertrand Russell brings his autobiography up to
1967, covering in it the period from his seventy-second to his
ninety-fifth year. The autobiography of a living man, published at
the end of the 1960s, could not very well break off in 1944, but this
should not be allowed to obscure the amazing achievement of having
something to write about at all in one's eighth, and ninth, decades.
It almost makes one feel that the publishers may have gone too far
in announcing, as they do on the dust-jacket, that 'this is the third
and final volume'. No doubt there have been some aged monarchs,
like Queen Victoria or Franz Joseph of Austria, who were as much
in the thick of events as Russell at such an advanced stage of their
lives. But this was a by-product of the institution of hereditary
monarchy, something devised before the modern idea of a retiring
age had got a grip. No private individual can have kept going so
notably for so long as the author of this autobiography.

In this period Russell was the spiritual and, to a considerable
extent, the effective leader of a large movement of public protest, in
whose physical activities he took a brave and prominent part; he
was involved in much-publicized correspondence with heads of state
about matters of the utmost human concern; he was active in a wide
range of libertarian causes, such as attempts to free political prisoners.
While all this was going on he contracted what seems to have been
an intensely happy and fulfilling marriage, survived an aeroplane
crash in Norway, published two of the most successful of his philosophical books (*Human Knowledge* and *The History of Western
Philosophy*), spent a short period in prison and, less arduously,
received the Order of Merit and the Nobel Prize. All this was done or
undergone after Russell's biblical span of life was complete and at an
age when most who survive so long are content to shuffle quietly
about.

As in the previous volumes there is a mixture here of narrative
text (ninety-five pages) and letters (one hundred and fifteen pages).
This method has a certain appropriateness. Russell is enough of a
Victorian for his life to be presented in a Victorian way. But the
interest of the letters in this volume is not as great as many of those
in its predecessors and they are themselves pieced out with long and
none too gripping matter about the assassination of President
Kennedy and the work of the Bertrand Russell Foundation.

The narrative itself, however, is superior to that of the second volume, which appeared to consist mainly of a resurrected manuscript of the early 1930s to which was appended a very perfunctory treatment of the later part of the period covered. The narrative here is more of a single continuous flow and gives equitably distributed attention to all parts of its period. All the main familiar events of Russell's recent history appear here in their natural biographical setting, and there is communicated to the reader a convincing sense of the unending flood of meetings, lectures, broadcasts, talks to visitors, and literary composition on which the more conspicuous events floated. But there is nothing fatiguing about this. Russell's lively and unencumbered prose perfectly expresses his own marvellous vitality. The rather sombre aspects of his personal life at this time (always with the exception of his marriage to Edith Finch) are not allowed to depress us because they do not seem to depress him. Throughout he displays a wonderfully civilized gift of laughing at himself and even of gently mocking some of the pieties of his own strenuous libertarianism.

The story begins with Russell's return to England from the United States in 1944. For the next five years he was once again a lecturer at Trinity College, Cambridge, after a quarter of a century away from it. In 1949, he crisply observes, 'my wife decided that she wanted no more of me', referring here to his third wife, Peter Spence. The happiness of his marriage to Edith Finch some time later was clouded by the emotionally extraordinary and practically catastrophic behaviour of his eldest son. At Christmas, 1953, when Russell was about to have a serious operation and the rest of the household were down with flu,

my son and his wife decided that, as she said, they were 'tired of children After Christmas dinner with the children and me, they left, taking the remainder of the food, but leaving the children, and did not return.

This meant that he had three grandchildren to support at a time when he was paying alimony to two wives as well as providing for the expenses of his younger son. On top of this he had to pay the income tax his elder son had omitted to pay for many years.

Yet before this dismal state of affairs can really sink in we are swept away on Russell's first serious involvement with the dangers of nuclear warfare: the manifesto he and Einstein produced, the Caxton Hall meeting at which it was presented, his part in the Pugwash conferences, his correspondence with Khrushchev and Dulles, all of this culminating in 1958 with his leading part in the foundation of the Campaign for Nuclear Disarmament. After a time he came to believe that protest against the Bomb must take the stronger form of civil disobedience. He parted from Canon Collins and the more orderly majority of the Campaign's supporters, a course which led to the formation of the Committee of 100 in 1960, the sit-down demonstrations of 1961, and prison for the second time in his career. He resigned from the Committee of 100 after the Cuba crisis of 1962. The extremism and dispersal of aims of the new movement which caused him to abandon it might seem a natural consequence of the stronger style of protest for whose sake he had joined it in the first place.

Since then, his main public work has been carried on within the framework of the Bertrand Russell Peace Foundation, whose aims are by no means limited to what is directly connected with the preservation of peace, but include also the freeing of political prisoners and the defence of oppressed national minorities. To most people who know of the Foundation, it probably appears as an agency for anti-American propaganda which benefits from the prestige of Russell's name but which is actually run by his younger ideologically committed associates. Russell is aware of this opinion and combats it with spirit.

In so far as the Foundation is anti-American, it is because he believes that since Stalin's death the United States has been the main threat to world peace. He lays much stress on the fact that it was Khrushchev who gave way over Cuba. 'Journalists and commentators', he observes with justified acidity, 'are apt to deal with me personally by saying that I am senile . . . if the charge is true, I fail to see why anyone troubles to remark on my babblings.' To this criticism, at any rate, there could be few more conclusive replies than this book.

The incidental pleasures of reading Russell on the subject of himself remain as great as ever. There is a fine exchange with George VI, who said after bestowing the Order of Merit: 'You have sometimes behaved in a way that would not do if generally adopted.' There are some shrewd observations about how to ingratiate yourself with young academic audiences: they like 'to hear liberal or even quasi-revolutionary opinions expressed by someone in authority . . . also any jibe at any received opinion, whether orthodox or not'. Magnanimity is shown to Lord Hailsham who alone failed to take part in an ovation to Russell at a meeting of scientists. 'He was present in his capacity as the Queen's Minister of Science. He was personally, I think, friendly enough to me, but, weighed down by office, he sat tight.' Russell has a good memory for the absurd: an Indian who insisted that Russell should watch his daughter dancing (he 'did not welcome having all the furniture of our sitting-room pushed back and the whole house shake as she cavorted in what, under other circumstances, I might have thought lovely gyrations'), and the 'small, bird-like lady', who, as he walked down a corridor on the way to give a broadcast, 'leapt from one of the huge red plush thrones placed at intervals along the wall, stood before me and declaimed, "And I saw Shelley plain", and sat down'.

The most touching thing in the book is his coming together again, after forty years of separation and silence, with his first wife, Alys. There is a poignant letter in which she blames herself for never having been able to surmount the disaster of the breach between them. There is a gentler pathos in the fact that his daughter married an American episcopalian missionary in Uganda. Smiles, he recalls, greeted the famous atheist when he went to the Bank of England to arrange a transfer of money that would help his son-in-law to become ordained. The police exhibited more self-control when the first major exponent of the sitdown in this country called on them to remove an actress who, for the purposes of publicity, deceitfully insinuated herself into his house and refused to budge. 'Their behaviour', he says of the police who came in answer to his call, 'was impeccable. They did not even smile, much less jeer.'

Now that Russell's autobiography is, seemingly, complete, it is right that something should be said of it as a whole. From a literary point of view its most obvious defect is also its most serious: its haphazardness of structure. The distribution of attention to different tracts of his life seems very arbitrary and does not appear to correspond either to the comparative significance of these tracts in his outward achievement as a whole or again to their internal, emotional significance for him. Some outwardly important things are thoroughly described, for instance, the long and painful struggle which lay behind the writing of *Principia Mathematica*. Others, like his return to philosophy in the late 1930s, are passed over very sketchily.

It is difficult not to feel that, like nearly everything that he has written since he set out to live by writing after the First World War, it has been put together in a brisk and hasty fashion and so, for all

its merits, is not as good a book as he could have written. He owed it
to himself to make a better, more coherent job of it. It is witty,
invigorating, marvellously candid, generous in spirit. It manages to
combine passionate involvement with moral and social issues with a
fine freedom from petulance and obsessiveness. But it lacks a final
unity of design and has something of the air of a task carried out in
time taken from other more pressing preoccupations.

On the other hand, this underlying attitude is a proper expression
of Russell's genuine selflessness, of his truly modest valuation, of his
own importance as a person, rather than as the servant of knowledge
and peace. The man who is described in these autobiographical
volumes could not have written the sort of autobiography that would
have required a comprehensively reverential attitude to the fine
texture and detail of his experience. The particular imperfections of
the work are the natural outcome of the very special integrity of his
life.

# 8

# THE STUDY OF FOLKLORE

IN MANY PARTS OF THE WORLD other than the United Kingdom, but notably in Russia, Germany, Scandinavia, France and the United States, the study of folklore long ago achieved a status of thoroughgoing academic respectability. The chief practitioners are full university professors of high international prestige who conduct their jargon-loaded semi-mathematical debates with the taut incomprehensibility of astrophysicists discussing the structure of outer space. Anyone who doubts this need only take a look at *FF Communications*, issued from Helsinki, or the Folklore Series of Indiana University Publications. But in this country folklore remains what it has always been, an intellectual entertainment for muddle-headed amateurs, a mixture of scholarly curio-collecting and crack-pot fantasy. Certainly, there are exceptions; some years ago the University of Oxford had the good sense to award honorary degrees to Peter and Iona Opie for their first-hand researches into the lore and language of schoolchildren, but in most respects the British Folk-Lore Society is at least fifty years behind the times.

One symptom of this ossification is that apart from a reduction in size—325 pages against 572—Volume 79 (1968) of the journal *Folk-Lore* is barely distinguishable from Volume 22 (1911). A piece entitled 'Easter Eggs', contributed by Mrs. Newall, the present Honorary Secretary, conforms closely to a long-established orthodoxy. Starting from the premise that, 'For most people, in England especially, an Easter Egg is a pretty triviality provided for a child', the author develops a random and far from exhaustive catalogue of customs and stories which feature the use of eggs as symbolic objects. The geographical distribution of her inquiry is world-wide, stretching (literally) from China to Peru and from ancient Egypt until modern

---

RICHARD M. DORSON: *The British Folklorists: A History.* 518 pp. £4 4s.

RICHARD M. DORSON (Editor): *Peasant Customs and Savage Myths.* Selections from the British Folklorists. Vol. I. 402 pp. Vol. II. pp. 403–751. £3 3s. each. Routledge and Kegan Paul.

times. The underlying hypothesis is that all parallels to our egg-giving custom must provide insight into its historical origin and its original meaning. The scholarly diligence is obvious, but somehow, with the lapse of time and blindfold repetition, the logical structure of the curio-hunt has become quite obscure and is now dissociated from any general theory—such as that of the unilinear development of human thought—which might once have given it rational coherence. The fact is that the English study of folklore has gradually worked round full circle so that it ends up where it began as the antiquarian collection of customary oddities.

But here is Professor Dorson's expensive labour of love to serve as a reminder that, for a rather brief period around the turn of the century, things were very different; as indeed they might be again if ever the officers of the Folk-Lore Society were to get around to reading Lévi-Strauss on the theme of *La Pensée sauvage*.

The term folklore itself was an 1846 coinage of W. J. Thoms designed to replace the earlier expression 'popular antiquities', which was in turn simply a euphemism for 'quaint and amusing customs of the uneducated classes'. The educated gentry had long been accustomed to entertain themselves and their children by reading scrapbook anecdotes about the superstitions of their less privileged contemporaries. Significantly, the earliest of these collections, published in 1586, was written in Latin. But by the end of the eighteenth century snobbery was moving down the social scale, and the literate middle-class whose members could take comfort from the stupid inferiority of their neighbours was expanding very rapidly. In this context, the massive Brand-Ellis compendium *Observations on Popular Antiquities: chiefly illustrating the origin of our Vulgar Customs, Ceremonies and Superstitions* (1813) which was itself a summary of many earlier publications, had an enormous success. It was repeatedly reprinted throughout the nineteenth century, the last revised edition appearing in 1905.

From this point of view folklore is simply a rag-bag of anything that seems eccentric to those who claim to be sophisticated. The prospectus of the first volume of *Folk-Lore Record* (1878), the precursor of *Folk-Lore*, declared that it would contain 'those scattered notes on the popular superstitions, legends and ballads, which are almost the only traces of the primitive mythology of our islands', while the *Handbook of Folklore* (1890, revised 1914) has a definition running for half a paragraph:

Folklore is . . . the generic term under which the traditional Beliefs, Customs, Stories, Songs and Sayings current among backward peoples or retained by the uncultured classes of more advanced peoples are comprehended and included. It comprises early and barbaric beliefs about the world of Nature, animate and inanimate, about human nature and things made by man, about a spirit world and man's relations to it; about witchcraft, spells, charms, amulets, luck, omens, disease and death. It further includes customs and rites as to marriage and inheritance, childhood and adult life, and as to festivals, warfare, hunting, fishing, cattle-keeping, etc.; also myths, legends, folk-tales, ballads, songs, proverbs, riddles and nursery rhymes.

The significant words in all this rigmarole are *backward, uncultured, early* and *barbaric* which, as can be seen, are treated as synonyms. This provides the clue to our cyclic fashion. The period during which folklore was accepted as a subject of at least approximate academic respectability in this country was almost exactly coincident with the currency of unilinear theories of social evolution among the professional anthropologists. Tylor's *Primitive Culture* (1871) sets the style at the beginning, the twelve-volume edition of Frazer's *The Golden Bough* (1915) marks its close. Basic to the whole epoch is the assumption that a rationalist agnostic monogamous society, backed up by late Victorian technology and a paternalistic Pax Britannica, is the final culmination of human destiny, which provides a standard of moral superiority against which all other value systems may be judged and found wanting.

The Folk-Lore Society did not go into dissolution along with the British Empire, but it lost its ethical basis and it also lost contact with the anthropologists. At its foundation in 1878, it had been the creation of a group of men (Andrew Lang, G. L. Gomme, E. S. Hartland in particular) who felt themselves to be disciples of the great anthropologist E. B. Tylor; their purpose was to rescue their 'science' from the romantic eccentricities of Max Müller (of whom more anon). For many years liaison between the folklorists and their anthropological contemporaries was very close, and as late as 1911 no fewer than twelve of the officers and Council of the Folk-Lore Society were simultaneously on the Council of the Royal Anthropological Institute. Today there is not a single individual who serves on both these bodies. And this perhaps explains the whole business. The modern folklorists have carried on staunchly in a tradition established by anthropologists nearly a century ago, but contemporary anthropologists are now sailing in quite different seas, and the study of English folklore has lost all sense of direction.

But even in the hey-day of evolutionist social theory the anthropological and the folklorist attitudes were by no means identical. The anthropologists imagined that they could reconstruct the details of a once universal primeval human culture by piecing together the historical residues which survive in the customs of contemporary peoples, but they paid most attention to customs associated with very primitive technology; they only turned to contexts of literacy as a matter of last resort so as to illustrate the principle of 'cultural survival'. But folklorists of the Gomme-Lang school tended to start at the other end; their primary concern was to explain the existence of quaint (i.e. 'primitive') superstitions among 'advanced' communities; interest in 'savage custom' was secondary.

The two groups shared a common body of evolutionary theory which reduced all contemporary primitive tribes to the status of social fossils, but the difference of emphasis was substantial. Mrs. Newall's article on Easter eggs is fully representative of the folklorist style. The initial question is: Why do we give our children coloured eggs at Easter? To seek an answer the author chases up egg symbolism on a world-wide basis. But the questions which the evolutionist anthropologists asked themselves were concerned with much more grandiose categories of supposedly primeval custom, and if they ever got around to a discussion of Easter eggs, it would have been by derivation. In point of fact, we do encounter quite a large part of Mrs. Newall's material in the pages of *The Golden Bough*, but it is tucked away into sections concerned with the survival of tree worship and of fire festivals in nineteenth-century Europe!

Either way, all this seems a very long way from the current interests of British academic anthropologists, and if it had been left to local endeavour it seems most unlikely that anything resembling these three formidable volumes would ever have got into print. This is specialist work, and not many people are going to pay ten guineas for a serial biography of twenty-five British folklorists plus a two-volume anthology of their writings, but the whole adds up to 1,260 pages, and for the enthusiast this is good value for money. Professor Dorson himself is unquestionably an enthusiast. He has been working on this project ever since he first visited London on a Guggenheim Fellowship twenty years ago. Meanwhile he has become President of the American Folklore Society and Director of the prestigious and well-endowed Folklore Institute of Indiana. At all times he seems to have had unrestricted access to the library and archives of the Folk-Lore Society of London, and this is his primary source.

As an historian, Professor Dorson is pedantic and narrow. His theme is the folklore of the British Folklorists—who they were, and what they thought and wrote about their subject and about one another—nothing else matters. So his heroes emerge as dummies living in a world without context. The manner is very transatlantic, and this has odd consequences for an English reader—a book published in 1813 is described as 'timely for non-academic Victorians', Gladstone (who resigned from the Folk-Lore Society in 1896 because of the advanced agnostic opinions of the president, Edward Clodd) appears as 'ex-Prime Minister William E. Gladstone'—the style is heavy with cliché (Scotsmen are 'dour', efforts are 'monumental', erudition is 'uncanny'), and every page is a clutter of authors' names and the titles of long-forgotten publications. Even so, this story of the rise and fall of a semi-academic fashion deserves a minor niche in the history of late nineteenth-century thought.

In order to get things straight, Professor Dorson's readers need to put his laboriously extracted details back into their original social setting. For the main period the clique of gentlemen (some rich, some poor) who were the mainspring of the whole folklore enterprise only numbered a dozen or so all told. They all knew one another intimately, yet they engaged in printed polemic of the most embittered sort. The issue whether two stories, one from South America and the other from India, were to be regarded as accidentally similar or historically connected was debated with a venom appropriate to a discussion of the theories of Charles Darwin in the backwoods of Tennessee. Professor Dorson offers no comment on this peculiarity, but the heart of the matter is surely that the dry-as-dust controversies between the Evolutionists and the Diffusionists aroused passion precisely because they tied in directly with some of the most deeply felt political issues of the time, particularly those of European colonialism. For example, the 1891 International Folklore Congress was used by J. S. Stuart-Glennie as a platform from which to advance the view that

in the origin of every civilisation of which we know anything there was a conflict of either racially or culturally higher or lower races, and, particularly in the primary civilisations of Egypt and Chaldea, this conflict was between white and coloured or black races.

This is duly reported by Professor Dorson but he does not remark that at this precise period in history the governments of Great Britain, Germany and France were busily exchanging treaties designed to carve up the world of 'coloured or black races' into colonial spheres of interest.

Indeed, Professor Dorson is altogether too detached; he not only fails to discuss the relations of his heroes to their social world, he also avoids all comment either on their relations with one another or on the merits of their respective intellectual positions. Any reader who is not himself a folklore addict is likely to feel like a shipwrecked mariner with water water everywhere nor any drop to drink.

The chronology is so scrupulously balanced that it takes 187 pages to get even as far as Tylor's *Primitive Culture* (1871). But this diligent rescue operation is not likely to have much effect on received opinion. Among the evolutionist writers of the 1876-1914 period, only the versatile Andrew Lang shows up as having any significant originality; the antiquarians of the previous century still retain their status as collectors of scrapbook anecdotes; discussion of post-1918 British folklore is tactfully reduced to a two-page epilogue.

However, one long-tarnished reputation does recover a little of its pristine gloss. The famous Oxford Sanskritist, Professor Max Müller, was responsible for the doctrine that mythology should be regarded as 'a disease of language' and that all traditional stories of the Indo-Aryan language zone had originated as part of a solar mythology among pre-Rig-Vedic Aryans. However improbable such a thesis might now appear, it had the attraction in its own day that it carried the implication of an innate Indo-European intellectual superiority. One of Müller's main tenets was that the myths of a great literate civilization such as that of Ancient Greece could not possibly have been derived from stories current among primitive savages. The evolutionist theories of Andrew Lang and his associates were based on precisely the opposite proposition.

A new look at Max Müller's arguments do not make them any more plausible than before, but Müller himself shows up as a much more hard-headed intellectual than his woolly-minded amateur opponents whom he criticized on precisely the same grounds as did the functionalist social anthropologists of a much later generation, namely that the exponents of the comparative method in anthropology relied on information collected by travellers and missionaries who had not mastered the native languages, that the invention of universal categories such as 'totemism', 'animism', could not be justified, that details of custom can only be understood in context, and so on and so forth. In retrospect, Müller and Lang both seem equally effective in their destruction of the opposition, but nothing much from either side has survival value for the present day.

The modern 'theory' of folklore studies in other countries depends in every case on some kind of technique of structural analysis. The significant cross-cultural similarities in traditional materials are now felt to reside not so much in content as such as in the way the content is ordered, and interest in this ordering stems from the thesis that, in the last analysis, there must be some correlation between the structural organization of cultural products and mental structures in the brains of those who produce them. In the 1930s A. M. Hocart and Lord Raglan did begin to develop the framework of a structural theory of this kind, but they never got very far, and they do not fall within the ambit of Professor Dorson's survey, As the author himself seems to recognize, his enterprise is a funeral rite rather than a revivalist meeting. Perhaps the Opies can do something about it!

# 9

# VICHY AND AFTER

## (a) THE RESISTANCE IN FOCUS

A GENERATION AFTER THE EVENTS, the history of French resistance is coming into focus, as the principal movements and personalities emerge from the clouds of misrepresentation and myth. New perspectives are being opened up by new research, and some old ones now look different. The time must be near when an academic historian, perhaps a participant in what was done, will be able to resolve the worst remaining muddles, and put the whole glorious, tragic, heroic, almost unbearable, almost unbelievable tale into a single book.

That historian will rely largely on the collection of monographs, edited by Henri Michel, entitled 'Esprit de la Résistance'. Sixteen of these have already appeared, decked out with the scholarly virtues of accuracy and conclusiveness; though some are touched as well with the scholarly vice of aridity. The latest, *La S.N.C.F. pendant la guerre*, is only dry at first glance; through the formalities and the formulas indispensable for railway work there shines a bright flame of patriotic effort. After all the press puffing of heroes and heroines of the secret war, some of it undeserved, it is refreshing to read an

---

(a) PAUL DURAND: *La S.N.C.F. pendant la guerre*. 666 pp. Paris: Presses Universitaires. 40 fr.

HENRI MICHEL: *Vichy année 40*. 461 pp. Paris: Laffont. 24.70 fr.

HENRI NOGUÈRES and others: *Histoire de la Résistance en France*. Volume 1: June, 1940 to June, 1941. 510 pp. 24.70 fr. Volume 2: July, 1941 to October, 1942. 736 pp. 32 fr. Paris: Laffont.

MICHEL GARDER: *La Guerre secrète des Services Spéciaux Français (1935–1945)*. 523 pp. Paris: Plon. 25 fr.

EBERHARD JÄCKEL: *Frankreich in Hitlers Europa*. 396 pp. Stuttgart: Deutsche Verlags-Anstalt. DM 28.

ROBERT ARON: *Histoire de l'Épuration*. Volume 1: November, 1942 to September, 1944. 661 pp. Paris: Fayard. 23.85 fr.

PETER NOVICK: *The Resistance versus Vichy*. 245 pp. Chatto and Windus. £2 2s.

DAVID LAMPE: *The Last Ditch*. 219 pp. Cassell. 36s.

(b) LOUIS-FERDINAND CÉLINE: *Rigodon*. 320 pp. Paris: Gallimard. 20 fr.

DOMINIQUE DE ROUX: *La Mort de Céline*. 190 pp. Paris: Union Générale d'Editions. 4.40 fr.

undoubtedly authentic account of some of the outstanding feats of resistance in which hardly any of the actors are named at all.

M. Durand relies primarily on the French national railway archives, and on a great many questionnaires sent out to railwaymen with a resistance record. According to the picture he paints, the S.N.C.F. was always devotedly anti-German; not only were individual railwaymen good resisters, as has long been known, but the entire organization worked, as a corporate body, to serve French interests rather than German so far as it possibly could. His book is well designed. He discusses in turn the mobilization, the catastrophe, and the armistice, with its injection of a Wehrmacht-transportleitung and a series of Eisenbahnbetriebsdirektionen into the high command of the railway system; then turns to traffic, material, and money; and then to men. Nearly half his long book is taken up with a series of splendid hair-raising stories of what *cheminots* could do to counteract the occupation; culminating in the insurrectional railway strike of August, 1944, that immediately preceded liberation. This is a valuable contribution to the history of transport and of war.

M. Michel himself wrote *Vichy année 40*, a penetrating study of the origins of Pétain's regime; because it has little to say about resistance, it does not appear in the same series. The author puts his finger on Pétain's fundamental motive: saving France, not from the transient perils of military defeat, but from the secular dangers of a democratic constitution. The aged marshal thought that, under his guidance, France could yet be reborn; he felt, at eighty-four, that he had many years to live (in which, after all, he was quite right: he did not die till 1951); he saw himself as the long awaited saviour of a once-great country that had gone astray. And he was too old, or too little of a politician, to appreciate the enormity of one main consequence of his 'national revolution': that it divided the French people, officially, into two categories, good and bad, just at the moment when the French had most need of unity. And while the old men at Vichy toyed with their senile dreams of greatness, multiplying rules and orders to deprive the 'bad' French of their legal rights and rescinding the constitutional guarantees built up since 1789, those ordinary French people who were neither exiles nor prisoners of war had an agony to face in their own homes: famine. The population of the Vichy zone, swollen by hundreds of thousands of refugees from the panic exodus of June, and deprived of the labour of hundreds of thousands of farm hands already deported to Germany, had far too little to eat. Their government, in M. Michel's view, never recovered from two original errors: the belief, shared by Hitler, that England had 'essentially' been beaten already, and so would soon give in; and the belief, which Hitler did not share, that the Germans with whom the armistice had been signed were reasonable beings, who would make further concessions if defeated France suffered too much. Hitler's Germans never cared at all for the sufferings of the peoples they defeated. Neither what the author calls 'la douloureuse affaire de Mers-el-Kebir'—might that, he asks, simply have been due to 'un malentendu'?—nor the replacement of Laval by Darlan in the seat of chief direction of detail at Vichy made any vital difference; but those two cardinal mistakes did.

There is only one, quite minor, complaint to be made about *Vichy année 40*; the reference notes are put, exasperatingly, at the end of each chapter, instead of at the foot of the page or in one gathering at the back of the book. The same fault is repeated by the same publisher, in Colonel Noguères's big *Histoire de la Résistance en France*, of which the first two volumes have so far appeared. But the difference between the two books is much more striking than this minor resemblance. One is by an analytical historian; the other is by a team of journalists. Each is an accomplished work of its own kind. In the six months they both cover there are few points where their subject-matter, and fewer still where their points of view, coincide.

Colonel Noguères had a distinguished career underground, as did both his collaborators; M. Degliame-Fouché was prominent in the large movement 'Combat' (from which he did his best to hide his communist sympathies), and J.-L. Vigier, who worked on an escape line over the Pyrenees, survived an attempted suicide after arrest. They have constructed a chronicle of resistance activity, arranged month by month, which will be valuable to future historians; and they have attached to it a scholarly apparatus more imposing in appearance than in reality.

For British activities, they rely largely on M. R. D. Foot's *SOE in France* (in the original edition—the corrected second impression, of July, 1968, presumably came too late). For Gaullist activities their main source lies in Colonel 'Passy's' and Colonel 'Rémy's' many volumes of war memoirs. They also make extensive use of interviews and of books; they have plenty of photographs—some acknowledged, some just borrowed—and they make occasional telling use of French security service documents not hitherto published. The main interest

of their book is that they interleave tales of sabotage and subversion
with the exploits of the main French intelligence *réseaux* of which
particulars are known; and the main slant is that they are determined
to give the communist resisters a full share of the credit. Many of
these communists were excellent men, and excellent Frenchmen, and
died horribly; it is no real service to their memory to leave out of the
story everything that tells against their party.

*La Guerre secrète des Services Spéciaux Français* deals with resistance from a quite different angle. In a lengthy narrative, little
supported by notes, based mainly on personal experiences during the
war, Michel Garder's study describes the prewar and wartime
adventures of the French army secret service, located in the 1930s at
2 bis, avenue de Tourville, behind the Invalides. That service and
the army's Deuxième Bureau translated Guderian's *Achtung Panzer*,
and sent a copy to every garrison library in France; a provincial
tour in the winter of 1937-38 revealed that the pages of not a single
copy had been cut. M. Garder's chief heroes are Colonel Rivet,
the prewar head of the Service Renseignements—who was eventually,
in a charming phrase, 'nommé général de brigade, le 13 avril 1944,
et admis à faire valoir ses droits à la retraite'—and Colonel Paillole,
his counter-espionage expert. Rivet's deciphering teams had the
melancholy satisfaction of establishing, by the third week of May,
1940, the order of battle of the armoured avalanche that was about
to sweep away the Third Republic.

Paillole hung on, at Vichy, and set up through the Travaux
Ruraux—ostensibly, road and bridge-mending gangs—a valuable
intelligence service on German dispositions in France; but to whom
was the intelligence of use? He had tons of archive material hidden
at Marseilles. Vichy's naval staff refused to send it, early in November, 1942, to North Africa: 'Il n'y a aucune raison que sous le
prétexte d'échapper aux Allemands les secrets de notre contre-
espionage tombent aux mains des Anglais!' He got out to Algiers
himself, as did Rivet; both were swallowed up in the Free French
secret service empire where 'à côté de héros authentiques, un lot impo-
sant de personnages douteux, d'aventuriers ou de simples profiteurs
s'assurent des postes de commande ou des planques rémunératrices'.

*Frankreich in Hitlers Europa* makes a necessary, even a welcome,
complement to Jacques Delarue's *Trafics et crimes sous l'occupation*
(reviewed in the *TLS* on July 4, 1968); it is, indeed, far its superior
in method and comprehensiveness. Inspired by a French friend, and

by Heine's remark in 1834 that things would happen one day in
Germany that would make the French revolution look like a harmless idyll, Dr. Jäckel has settled down among the archives of the
Third Reich and found out what the Nazi government's wartime
French policy was. Half his book (which is the fifteenth volume in
the 'Quellen und Darstellungen zur Zeitgeschichte' series) deals with
the first year of occupation; and he treats collaboration between the
Vichy regime and Hitler's government as having broken down
altogether in the winter of 1941-42. He is able to treat dispassionately
subjects about which older writers easily get excited; he gives an
honest, careful, historian's appraisal of what actually went on.
When German troops or police behaved cruelly, he does not hesitate
to say so; but he does not let himself be drawn away from his tasks of
narrative and analysis by any desire to make a sensation. He produces an explanation for the Marseilles atrocity that baffled M.
Delarue: Himmler ordered it, and more as well: he called the Vieux
Port a 'Saustall' that must be rooted out, if necessary with 100,000
deportations.

It is clear, in fact, that the Germans were their own worst enemies,
creating the resistance that helped to throw them out wherever it did
not occur spontaneously. And yet—were not the French their own
worst enemies as well? Two books about the purge that accompanied
the liberation of France in 1944 suggest it.

Robert Aron has already written two long books, and a collection
of essays, on the history of France during the war of 1939-45; his
*Histoire de l'Épuration* looks as if it may equal the other two com-
bined for bulk. He begins with the 'Torch' landings in French
North-West Africa, in November, 1942; pictures Algiers as a test-
bench for purges in the late summer of 1943; and gets into his stride
when he discusses 'la période insurrectionnelle' in the summer of
1944. He attributes to de Gaulle the role that a senior British officer
in France in 1943 applied to the French communist leaders: sorcerer's
apprentice, conjuring up powers he cannot properly control. 'Le
peuple justicier a été d'une cruauté sans pareille.' He contrasts, for
example, the peaceable hand-over of power in Lille, where the retiring
Vichy regional prefect signed the warrant for his own arrest, and the
brutal chaos at Nîmes, which culminated in a mass execution of
*milice* in the old Roman arena. Mothers took their children to watch
such spectacles of rough justice; and of course many people seized
the occasion to pay off old personal scores.

This is an interesting, indeed in places an exciting book; but unsatisfactory for the historian because the author seldom gives the sources for his many quotations—half of the 10 reference notes in his first 100 pages refer to his own books. Professor Novick, treating the purge of collaborators in liberated France from a constitutional historian's angle of sight, is much more careful in *The Resistance versus Vichy* to cite his authorities, and has constructed a book quite as interesting if less dramatically worded. 'In the minds of résistants', he says, 'the purge was intimately and inextricably tied to their chiliastic vision of a "new France"; it was to be the first step in the construction of a "République pure et dure" . . . The inadequacies of the purge became the symbol of all the disappointed hopes of the Liberation period.' He is fair to the judges, and is satisfied they were doing their best; he is also fair to the judged.

As a footnote to this survey of what became of occupied France, we might well consider for a moment what would have become of occupied England, if Hitler had managed after all to cross the Channel. Would we have done any better than—would we even have done half as well as—the French? Speculating about who would have been our collaborators and who our resistance leaders is hardly more than a parlour game; but *The Last Ditch* does provide some useful nuggets of historical fact. David Lampe describes the arrangements made for 'left-behind parties', saboteurs of German communications who were to hide as the battle flowed past them and then to emerge to do what they could. They were certainly brave, but we have too few data to be sure how effective they would or could have been. Many of them subsequently had distinguished careers in S.O.E. under their commander, Colin Gubbins.

He also publishes in facsimile the Gestapo's list of wanted British subjects, to be arrested when found. Among many surprising names in it, we may single out that of a former contributor to these pages, Virginia Woolf.

## (b) CÉLINE AND THE APOCALYPSE

ONE OF CÉLINE'S MORE RELIABLE GRIEVANCES was the assumption of critics that prose as scathing as his must be spontaneous, and that he was therefore a reckless, artless writer. He timed his death to prove them wrong: he finished the extensive rewriting of *Rigodon* in the morning and died the same evening, a tamer but more moving abdication than that of another writer, Ernest Hemingway, which followed a few hours later. In the newspapers it was Hemingway who hogged the necrologies, or what Céline himself, always bucked to be in at a noteworthy death, called the 'courrier des Parques'. In his last years he had, if anything, stepped up the self-contempt that kept him young, and his final revenge on France for its neglect was to anticipate his own patriotic bones being tipped anonymously into the 'fosse commune'. He would have been endlessly gratified to have foreseen the coincidence of his own death and Hemingway's, with even Paris's homage being spent on the jazzy tourist of the 1920s rather than a born and beleaguered native like himself.

In a testamentary aside in *Rigodon*, Céline provides against any betrayal of his last manuscript by underwriting it down to the last comma, and refusing to have it edited with mere common sense, 'the death of rhythm'. As a result two lawyers, André Damien and François Gibault, had to put in seven years of their spare time before *Rigodon* could be published. The text hardly repays their scrupulous services to it. But Céline's œuvre is a major one and any *nachlass* well worth salvaging, especially now that it looks as though there can't be any more: according to the foreword to *Rigodon* all his souvenirs and manuscripts were burnt in a fire at his old house in Meudon in May, 1968, a month of more conflagrations than we had realized.

Yet however croaky a swansong it may be, *Rigodon* will last, for, along with *D'un château l'autre* and *Nord*, it makes a spectacular trilogy of Céline's experiences in Germany in 1944-45, after he had prudently decamped from Paris and the incipient nastiness of the *épuration*, fomented in his own case, or so he boasted, by murderous anathemata broadcast from the Free French in London. With his wife Lucette (Lili), an actor friend Le Vigan, and the cat Bébert, Céline went first to Baden-Baden, then to Zornhof near Berlin (both settings are astonishly realized in *Nord*), to Sigmaringen, the Bavarian asylum of the Vichy government and scene of *D'un château l'autre*, and finally to Denmark, where he spent two years in prison on melodramatic charges of collaboration and from where he only returned to Paris after the amnesty of 1951.

There, on the slopes of Meudon, behind his doctor's brass-plate, his barbed wire and his mastiffs, and with a view—it seems too good to be credible—of M. Dreyfus's Renault factory, Céline wrote two books, *Féerie pour une autre fois* and *Normance*, feeble enough to re-assure critics, understandably inhibited from admiring anything new by the anti-semitic prophet of the prewar years, that he was finished, that he had nothing worth adding to *Voyage au bout de la nuit* and *Mort à crédit*. Fittingly, it was to collect some of his substantial royalties on these two books that Céline had tried to get to Denmark, having banked them in Copenhagen in the typically flimsy belief that Danish neutrality would be proof against any holocaust.

The loss of his money, and of six years of his life in Denmark, left Céline with a specific rancour that he milks tirelessly in his trilogy. A single pun which he ought to have found but did not would epitomize his sense of victimization: 'galèremard'. With a ball-point pen for an oar he sits sweating away like a galley-slave, for the reward not of himself but to settle his debts to his wealthy and aged pub-lisher, Achille Brottin (or Gaston Gallimard of the rue Sébastien Bottin, whose firm had once turned down *Voyage au bout de la nuit* then snapped Céline up later, a repetition of its inglorious coup with Proust).

The trilogy, therefore, is stridently self-conscious: Céline's hard-ships are constantly rolled out into public view item by item and the narrative of his past halted for imprecation against his poverty, the intrusions of journalists and others still out to pillory him, and, above all, against the 'literary' life of Paris, trifling and fiddling while Céline burns. Anyone with power or disciples is a necessary target and an excuse for torrents of overwrought abuse, slightly modified at each repetition so as to sound more like a litany than a tic. Jean Paulhan, who treated Céline quite honourably, appears as Norbert Loukoum, the impresario no longer of the *N.R.F.* but of a *Revue Compacte d'Emmerderie*; Sartre is simply Tartre or sometimes, more intestinally, Taenia; Aragon is L'Harengon.

These elementary lampoons, however, are not the main business of the trilogy, which is offered as a 'chronicle' of the last months of Nazi Germany. To be present at the ruin of a regime and a nation was a favour due to Céline as a writer, not as a man; no addict of that monstrous but tasty sedative, 'la nostalgie de l'apocalypse', was ever granted such a definitive dose. Much of what went on around him in 1944-45 was momentous and disorderly enough to meet even Céline's requirements for a general insecurity of physical existence. In peacetime he had known he was an anachronism, a man of the middle ages, condemned to live in a state of perpetual anxiety—a

'Hamlet of the leekbeds' was his last picture of himself in Meudon—
and threatened in his insecurity by the real or imagined complacency
of everyone else.

As a chronicler of war he sees himself released by history from any
narrow obligations towards the truth; catastrophe surrounded him
with a genuine if unholy poetry of extremes that solicited his skills as
a writer: life at Sigmaringen, for instance, he recognizes as poised
temptingly between the two orders whose trained intermediary he
was, 'ni absolument fictive, ni absolument réelle'. The Vichy bosses,
many of whom Céline attended as a doctor, stumble uselessly about
their Hohenzollern château, waiting on extinction amidst the derisory
bric-à-brac of ten centuries of rapacious devotion to inessentials.
The rhetoric of their lives, whether it emerges as a political slogan or
a military uniform is worn down daily, and Céline's own anti-
rhetoric reminds them of it: 'Donau blau! . . . mon cul! . . .' is a
typically crude synthesis which antecedes Zazie's similar treatment
of the Emperor Napoleon by some years.

Particular scenes of degradation in Céline's last books are every
bit as cruel and nightmarish as those in the early ones. In *Nord* the
Célines and Le Vigan live among a grotesque community in Zornhof:
a Junker Rittmeister of eighty and his family, including his legless,
epileptic son, gangs of conscientious objectors hacking coffins out
of the forest, Russian and French prisoners of war, a Nazi doctor
with a fabulous cache of smuggled delicacies, prostitutes taken off
their beat in Berlin to be treated for V.D.

The grisly life of this community is nothing compared with its
deaths: the Rittmeister rides ridiculously off, sabre in hand, to turn
back the Russian hordes single-handed and is eventually found
pinioned in a ditch with the whores sitting down to dine off him;
his son is dumped into a pond of fermenting beetroot juice during a
concert by his giant Russian attendant. These warped and passionate
inventions, registering an anarchist's glee at the undoubted vulnera-
bility of any social order, as well as a nostaglia for the heroic and
futile gesture of an aristocrat too grandiose for the world he lives in,
are an indispensable part of Céline's vision.

Men are only themselves, he once wrote, on the w.c. or on their
deathbeds; the rest is histrionics. This being so, it is quaint that one
of his companions on the rout should have been a professional actor,
with, perhaps, a head start over the rest of us. Friend or not, Le
Vigan is not spared Céline's judgments as 'a man from nowhere'

(rootlessness was a most serious crime for Céline), with a deplorable facility picked up on a pre-war film set, for playing Christ.

Céline's own definition of the 'chronicle' is as a form concerned with the 'movement of peoples', and *Rigodon* is the victim of its own perpetual motion, as Céline, Lili and Bébert track across Germany on their way to the Danish border. The book is a trying sequence of swarming railway compartments, littered platforms, cascading bombs and burning buildings. There are only a few moments when the strenuous pursuit of hallucination crystallizes into something memorable: an elderly, paralysed Englishman being wheeled through the wreckage of Hanover on a porter's trolley, or the mixture of pomp and dereliction at Rommel's funeral in Ulm.

The Célines' journey, moreover, has been rather slackly universalized, compared with the more modest journeys in the two previous books, largely through a telescoping of the seasons, which change in the time it takes to pass through a tunnel. And in the end, to glue the allegory firmly to the page, the children must be brought aboard, so that the mingled generations can draw away from the platform together. In *Rigodon* it is Céline who gets in with the children, rather than the other way about, smuggling himself into Denmark in style, as passenger on a well-stocked mercy train operated by the Swedish Red Cross. The conjunction of hope with youth is not explicit, but it is a measure of Céline's inability to see any trajectory in life but the downward one of the body.

His is the a-metaphysical world-view of the doctor; he does not deny the speculations of other, more transcendental minds, yet he implicitly discounts them by turning his anguish and disgust at physical decay and ugliness into literature. And one of the mannerisms that becomes more apparent in his later books than the earlier ones is his mock obsequiousness in conversation, the instant surrender to anyone with abstract opinions; the surrender is an insult, and an insinuation that only Céline, unable to detach himself so glibly from what is actual, is a truly serious man.

Read as the work of a doctor who made a brief and often bloody-minded career in social medicine, Céline's books mellow and also reveal more of the care with which they are put together. The movement from reality to hallucination may even be exposed by him as a movement from health to sickness, as with the vision of the antiquated *bateau-mouche* as a ship of death in *D'un château l'autre*, ascribed to a chill caught on a visit to a patient; the nightmare pays him out for his charity. The ambiguity of Céline's own position, a healer in real life and a scourge in his books, is reflected in some of his characters, especially by the Nazi epidemiologist Harras in *Nord*, constantly flying off to Lisbon to confer with specialists from the Allied side and lamenting the absence of pestilence in the modern world.

Yet the name of Harras is an inescapable reminder of how sinister a fatalism Céline's concern with biology could become when exercised on a wider scale: 'haras' is the French word for a stud-farm, and Céline hangs on to his demented visions of the coming mingling of the races throughout his trilogy. The last of the bogies he raises to scare us into greater life is not the Jews any more but the Chinese, who will one day be arriving in Brest and clapping the effete whites into the shafts of their rickshaws. (Was it to put more weight behind this warning that *Rigodon* was written on yellow paper?) But Céline also hedges against a possible reluctance of Mao's men to cooperate with him, by invoking another menace which, in those days, before D.N.A., he gleefully deemed irresistible—the 'gametes' ball', a sort of genetic Paul Jones that must sabotage all attempts to keep the races apart.

These crackpot updatings of the forms of western Europe's doom show Céline up as an opportunist, ready to swap *bêtes noires* in mid-stream. Such a facility makes him a more complete prisoner of his times than his defenders have often allowed, but it also makes his own defence of his anti-semitic pamphlets, written, according to him, to warn Europe of the coming war, less offensively naive. In his postwar books he attributes the hostility to him not to *Bagatelles pour un massacre* but to *Voyage au bout de la nuit*. Was this simply guilt and an attempt to deflect antagonism in a way that would flatter his vanity? It could well have been an unconscious evasion of far greater subtlety than that, as Dominique de Roux implies in his combative tribute, *La Mort de Céline* (first published by Christian Bourgois in 1966): a weird identification between himself as scapegoat for an immovably superficial society and the Jews as traditional scapegoats for Christendom.

# IO
# THERE WAS AN OLD FELLOW

IT MARKS, one supposes, some kind of epoch when a respectable London publisher gives us a collection of limericks, including many of the most obscene, in the form of a sort of small coffee-table talk— *The Lure of the Limerick*. Even the series of short essays preceding the main bulk of the material—or rather, short ruminations punctuated by lines illustrating, or vaguely fitting, the points—are appropriately light-hearted.

In these Mr. Baring-Gould develops both the historical and the aesthetic approaches. The scholarship of the literary origins of the limerick is a complex inquiry and one which has often been performed. Here we once again follow the trail through 'Sumer is i-cumen in', Tom O'Bedlam, and so on. Most unforgettable is the devotional co-limerick attributed to the Rev. Patrick Brontë:

> Religion makes beauty enchanting
> And even where beauty is wanting.
> The temper and mind,
> Religion refined,
> Will shine through the veil with sweet lustre.

Brontë's daughters figure indeed in a later vignette, not quoted in this collection, which gives something of the other side of Victorian attitudes:

> Charlotte Brontë said, 'Wow, sister! *What* a man!
> He laid me face down on the ottoman
> Now don't you and Emily
> Go telling the femily—
> But he smacked me upon my bare bottom, Ann!'

Reaching Edward Lear, we are on the threshold of the true limerick. The selection from him here—eleven in all—only demonstrates that,

---

WILLIAM S. BARING-GOULD: *The Lure of the Limerick*. 143 pp. Rupert Hart-Davis. 25s.
HUGH DE WITT: *There was a Young Lady* . . . 155 pp. Tandem. 5s.
*The Bagman's Book of Limericks*. 100 pp. New York: Collectors' Publications. $1.95.

like Brontë, he had not truly grasped the form and that, in the rather different one he contrived, it was only occasionally that he achieved a memorable effect. In general, the question of origin is not a very compelling one, and greater interest resides in the nature and structure, in the aesthetic of the genre.

It has been described as the only original verse form in the English language. Mr. Bernard Levin, writing to *The Times* recently, suggested himself as candidate for the Oxford Chair of Poetry, on the grounds that he had composed one about Mr. Tariq Ali. Whatever the merits of that particular work, it is at least not fantastic to say that a successful limericker must be regarded as a better poet than many writers of modern free verse. The shortness of the artefact is not to the point—the Greeks put Sappho only just after Homer, and in our own culture a comparison between Emily Dickinson and Walt Whitman is relevant. Nor is, surely, the fact of the verse's 'lightness'. (Belloc makes it an accusation against women that they 'confuse levity with frivolity', but if that is so there are many effeminate men.) *Don Juan* is widely recognized to be one of the greatest poems of its period. And while 'greatness' in this sense may have some relation to size, clearly goodness does not. (The argument will be familiar to followers of the various controversies about haiku, and is perhaps not worth pursuing too far.)

Poets have indeed liked the limerick form since it came up in the middle of the last century. From Tennyson, Swinburne and Rossetti to Auden, Conrad Aiken and Dylan Thomas, they have provided a considerable corpus between them (though one attributed to Dylan Thomas, starting 'The Postmaster General . . .', is to the personal knowledge of this reviewer, who told it him, not his). Prose-writers too, like Arnold Bennett, have contributed. A piece attributed here to Bertrand Russell is highly competent. One said to have been much used by Woodrow Wilson ('My face, I don't mind it/Because I'm behind it') is more often heard of rather as the favourite of Coolidge: on the other hand, if Wilson did indeed compose the celebrated 'When out with the Duchess to tea . . .', a surprisingly human side of his character is revealed. Mr. Baring-Gould agrees with the American pornologist, Mr. Gershon Legman, that limericks are 'the folklore of the educated', while the working man prefers such songs as 'The One-Eyed Riley' and 'The Good Ship Venus'. Mr. Legman specifically says that this is true 'for either Britain or America'. But one cannot go the whole way with him, so far as we in

Britain are concerned. Limericks (including bawdy ones with the last line mumbled) were sung on music halls until quite recently. And they were heard in sergeants' messes during the Second World War—sung with a 'connective' between them different from those mentioned by Mr. Baring-Gould and Mr. Legman, in being far more obviously genuine 'folk' (and including the only hostile reference, though merely in passing, to the German Army ever come across in such songs).

The definition given here, that essentially the limerick is an anecdote in verse, is much too limiting. The alternative qualities of the limerick—though it is true that there are occasional blends—are wit and fantasy. And the wit is almost invariably less a matter of story than of situation. (How much of the wit still surviving in English verse in these days when real satire, like real lyric, is scarcely to be met with, seems to have become concentrated in the limerick?) The *TLS* is quoted as commenting:

The form is essentially liturgical, corresponding to the underlying ritual of the Greek tragedy, with the *parados* of the first line, the *peripeteia* of the second, the *stichomythia* of the two short lines . . . and the *epiphaneia* in the last.

You can say that again. But it applies to only one style of limerick. And the attempt, especially in American limericks, to work up to a kind of explosive revelation at the end, is not the only structure available—the civilized comment on what has gone before (even the Latin tag) being an equally valid ending. (The frequency of 'Mens sana in corpore sano', 'Vox et praeterea nihil', &c., may incidentally be felt to show, though the point is a small one, that 'dactylic', rather than, as is so often said, 'anapaestic', is the truer description of the form.

The limerick is specially welcome nowadays as a genre in which success is unfakable. While under the protection of portentous apologetics the meaningless and the structureless can now pass for serious verse, the limerick remains a voice of craft and common sense. 'The Fellow of Wadham', given by Mr. Baring-Gould, though adequate enough in his own right, cannot be compared with the variation, or rather different limerick, which may be taken as illustrating some of the problems of the form in general. The true rhymes (in this case) are clearly confined to Wadham, Sodom, Modom. The solution was:

> There was a young Fellow of Wadham
> Who asked for a ticket to Sodom.
>     When they said, 'we prefer
>     Not to issue them, Sir,'
> He said, 'Don't call me Sir, call me Modom!'

the 'prefer', arising as a rhyme from 'Sir', which is, in turn, produced by 'Modom', is style at its most brilliant. And we may note here how this limerick, like many others, lends itself to (or rather demands) a specially skilled oral recital. The appreciation of skill properly speaking is (as has often been pointed out) an inextricable element of aesthetics. Even the skill of rhyme alone is not to be slighted, though in a limerick this may be, as here, the effective use of the expected word, like Corneille, or of the unexpected, like Racine. An example of the latter might at random be the middle lines of the Young Lady of Bude:

> A young fellow said 'What a m
> agnificent bottom!'

The selection in *The Lure of the Limerick* consists at a rough count of sixty-nine limericks which are very bad, twenty-three which are good, and ten which would be good if they had been got right. Those not put into these categories, that is 400 odd, may be regarded as ranging from those which are barely passable to those which have some slight merit. It is interesting to see how, in oral tradition, a work may suffer 'degradation', in the thermodynamic sense. That is, a line often seems in the course of transmission to meet the loss or deformation of its best tropes. Time and again in this collection such a process is visible. One might think that this would not occur, that after all the good version is still in some sense in existence, and would tend to drive out the bad, but this would only be true in conditions of a perfect market: if the nexus of accessibility were immediate and complete.

The point at which many of the present collection have been netted is often an unfortunate one. The scansion, even, seems to have gone wrong here and there as with the last line of 'The Young Lady Named Bright', given as: 'And returned the previous night'; one can see no way of making this fit the rather rigorous metric required—surely the common reading is 'came back'? Some seem to have gone wrong on being transmitted through people unaware of specific British connotations. 'A Young Parson Named Bings' should, of course, be 'A Young Fellow of King's', while the last line needs the indefinite article before 'jelly', and hence a monosyllabic substitute for 'bottom'. The second line, since a 'fellow' is not automatically a parson, should revert to 'Who cared not for whores and such things'. Similarly, 'A mathematician named Hall' is better as 'A Wrangler of Trinity Hall'; and the last line, in an attempt to jazz things up, here departs fatally from the mathematical rigour of the original, or better version.

While it may be true that bawdy is a great limerick quality, no serious advantage is gained by transforming the barmaid who was originally 'tattooed with the price of brown ale' into a prostitute advertising her wares, while the last line, as well as containing a misprint, falls to pieces with inappropriate words like 'embroidered'; it should run, 'Was the same information in Braille'. Again, no improvement whatever is effected in a version of the 'Young Lady of Crewe', which has her finding in her stew not a 'large mouse' but 'an elephant's whang'; moreover the last line given here as 'The others will all want one too', is much more awkward than 'Or the rest will be wanting one too'. It is even the case that the perfectly 'clean' limerick published originally in *Punch*, which ends 'I'm James Winterbottom Esquire', has gone wrong: in order to have him come from the in any case mispronounced 'Eire', he ends up as the jarring combination of formal and informal 'I'm Pat Winterbottom Esquire'. The young girl of Kilkenny—and her youth is evident from the whole context, though she is given here as 'old'—garbles the very fine last line, which should be 'An economy practised by many'. Even 'The young fellow named Skinner'—one of those, incidentally, which have been done on television music-hall with instrumental substitution for the last line—has suffered, as so often, an alteration from 'a quarter to nine' to 'half past nine' simply in the interest of speeding Skinner up, at the expense of both rigour of metre and aptness of apposition. Nor can minor solecisms like the complaint of the 'young lady of Padua' who had only been paid a 'peso', or the rhyming of 'Torquay' with 'day', really be countenanced. (A few other slips: a transposition between east and west on page 54; on page 58 a slightly awkward 'There once was an old man of Lime', which does not take the scansion as well as the conventional 'There was a young fellow . . .'—or 'There was an old fellow . . .'; an Anglo-French version of 'the young plumber of Leigh' which has him coming from Pau, rhyming this with 'bois' and 'moi'—he must surely have come from Blois, or some such town; and on page 74 it

I

is surely barrels of pork rather than port that are going to Boston?)

Mr. De Witt's much less elaborate (and modestly asterisk-ridden) collection, *There was a Young Lady . . .*, has some extraordinary lapses even of basic scansion—and of spelling, at least in the Latin. On the other hand, it gives us the Fellow of King's almost untarnished (as well as a Bings—here unaccountably 'Binns'—version); it rightly attributes the 'vice that is foul and unsavoury' to the Master of Balliol and not, as Mr. Baring-Gould does, to an anomalous 'Bishop of Wessex'; and it gives us an excellent variation of the Young Man called Macleod—so promising yet finally so anticlimactic—as a Young Fellow of Bude. The Young Man of Australia, too, is far closer to its optimum than in the Baring-Gould collection. So, in spite of its many and equivalent faults (and, for example, neither collection has more than the crudest adumbration of the Young Girl of the Cape—moved here in part to Dundee), this is better value as a five shilling paperback than its competitor is for five times that amount, unless you have a coffee table, and no Mabel.

Another collection, *The Bagman's Book of Limericks*, is now obtainable (with a vast mass of old-fashioned pornography such as *The Pearl*) in the ordinary paperback racks in America. Its versions, too, sometimes conflict with Mr. Baring-Gould's, on the whole for the better, though it makes no pretence to be a critical edition. As for *The Pearl*, recently reprinted by the Grove Press, its prose is reasonably imaginative and erotic, but the limericks, of which there are a fair number, are almost uniformly tedious, having no virtues but the inadequate one of form alone. This is not the case with the various ballads and other metres which are also given. Taken in conjunction with the similar lapses in the three other books under discussion, it does seem to imply that a taste exists simply for the formal structure, the fact of rhythm and scansion being able to provide enough of the element of wit for a large number of hearers. This is a surprising conclusion (to which a faint parallel may be seen in the rhymed epitaphs to be found in provincial newspapers), and one worth taking into account in any sociology of aesthetics.

But perhaps the low quality of many of the versions given here is after all the result merely of accident. They seem, often, to have entered the written literature in debased form in the first place, and have been perpetuated by a scholarship insufficiently attentive to oral research. The identity of the versions of a number of cases in these books implies derivation from the same earlier printed sources, to which Mr. Baring-Gould's bibliography refers. And it is, incidentally, worth making the point that Norman Douglas's much touted selection is not of very high quality (and that his celebrated footnotes are in the most tedious style of mock-erudition).

'Wherever there's an art', a writer remarked testily the other day, 'there's a talentless but trendy creep who has missed out on the barbarian invasion of the other artistic territories, waiting to carve out a barren fief, like the Suevi in Galicia'. He had just returned from an admittedly loopy science fiction convention marked by the enthusiastic intervention of people uninterested in the genre itself, but keen on new lebensraum for the non-arts. The limerick has long been defended from this by its—almost invariable—obscenity, which used to guarantee at least unprintability. But this has now gone. Here we have books of the bawdiest kind calmly printed on white paper with sharp type. Does this mean that the last Alsatia of untrendiness is lost? Fortunately there are good reasons for thinking not. Not only is it true that if you 'free' the limerick it is no longer a limerick, but it also seems intrinsically to resist trendification. Try writing 'There was a Young Fellow from Brooklyn', and with the best will in the world it will bounce him back, pretensions and all, up his own exit.

For in our present condition, when obscenity is presented to us in solemn—perhaps it would be appropriate to say 'po-faced'—guise, as having a significance and relevance comparable to the work of the great philosophers, the limerick may stand for that deep-set, often underestimated, element of good literature and good sense which resists trends—upon which indeed, the trends are merely the phosphorescence, not always unputrid, on an old and deep ocean.

A year or two ago a sociologist read out passages of *Eskimo Nell* to a conference up in Scotland, and maintained that it was an expression of self-indulgent fantasy and phallic sadism. But, of course, it is something far more subtle—a skit or satire on these things, a piece of humane self-criticism. And Mr. John Calder, it is interesting to note, has similarly attacked Mr. W. H. Auden for his sacrilegious attitude to pornography. Auden, appropriately enough, had expressed this in limerick form, thus compounding the offence:

> The Marquis de Sade and Genet
> Are most highly thought of today;
>    But torture and treachery
>    Are not my sort of lechery,
> So I've given my copies away.

Yes, the limerick, bawdy or otherwise, clearly has more in it of the human condition than is to be found in all the frigid and tedious obscenity of these presbyterian priapists. Their products, it is true, will affect only the most nose-led and fashion-bound of the reading public, those who would in their times have been saga-followers, sheikh-fans, social-realism-fodder, and are now becoming a pathic market for the new obscenity.

# II

# REFRESHMENT AND RELIEF

## (a) THE GAELIC WATER OF LIFE

THE REPUBLICATION of Alfred Barnard's magnificent—one is tempted to say, sacred—work is more than welcome. For the numerous admirers (not all of them Gaels) of the Gaelic 'water of life', the mere names of the great distilleries and the great whiskies are a most potent stoup of madeleine—if one may so mix literary metaphors. Mere words like 'Talisker' are magic. The names of the seven great Glenlivet distilleries have been described, improving on Rossetti, as 'Seven sweet symphonies'. And there is much economic and social history hidden in the story of the conquest of the Saxon market by whisky.

By the time this reverential pilgrimage by a mere Englishman was made in 1887, the barbarous contempt of the Southrons for what makes a Scotchman happy was over. There is, in Dr. Johnson's famous remark, something of the condescension of an Infidel tourist in the Maghreb, eating sheep's eyes to show sympathy and toleration for the natives. If the English drank whisky at all, it was Irish whiskey. (Readers may be referred to *The Diary of a Nobody* for this now surprising truth.) But, as the learned editor asserts, phylloxera helped by making good brandy scarce and dear, and perhaps the Good Queen's fondness for the drink that made John Brown happy, if it shocked Mr. Gladstone, gave 'tone' to what had been a proletarian drink, inferior, even at a low level, to gin and rum.

The decline of Irish whiskey is rather surprising, for one of the great technical innovations was the invention of the ingenious Mr. Coffey of Dublin, and most of the Irish distilleries mentioned here are out of business today. True John Jameson flourishes and is

---

(a) ALFRED BARNARD. *The Whisky Distilleries of the United Kingdom.* 457 pp. Newton Abbot: David and Charles. £6 6s.

DAVID DAICHES: *Scotch Whisky.* Its Past and Present. 168 pp. André Deutsch. £3.

(b) CLAUDE MAILLARD. *Les Vespasiennes de Paris ou les Précieux Édicules.* 138 pp. Paris: La Jeune Parque. 37.40 fr.

immortalized by a mention in 'Father O'Flynn', and we are glad to learn that the solemn Ulstermen who produce Old Bushmills started as illicit distillers, but there is no doubt that, in spite of Swift's patriotic plea for Scotia Major, it was Scotia Minor that in this, as in other ways, carried off the balm, or dram. Innovators like Coffey, and the need for cheap, quickly produced booze, led to the dangers of blending and to the production of whiskies that were better but not much better than the worst poteen and possibly at the level of modern pub Beaujolais or the products of 'les côtes du Berkshire'.

Barnard was interested, indeed fascinated, by the technical processes of distillation. He knew the importance of water (not its colour but its purity) and of good peat for drying good barley. But he was too tactful to do more than hint that not all distilleries, even traditional distilleries, produced really good whiskies. There is no discussion of the spreading of the power—or tentacles—of the Distillers' Company and no prophetic vision of the great whisky plants of Glasgow. But we are given plenty of information: figures of production; the normal destination of the product; transport problems.

There are hints of other problems. As Miss I. A. Glen's admirably judicial and learned introduction makes clear, many famous distilling families started as what Americans call 'moonshiners'. Sensible changes in the revenue laws made legal whisky economic to manufacture, sell and drink. One still finds romantic stories of the wonderful whiskies made by such romantic figures as the Orkney illicit distiller who was formally a zealous U.P. elder. If there are readers who don't know that U.P. means United Presbyterian, they don't deserve to drink good whisky. That will not prevent their drinking whisky. There is Japanese whisky (bad); there is Australian whisky (worse); there is German whisky (a descendant of Hamburg trade gin with a tartan label). There are also the fancy brands made for Americans, the kind of Americans who import Loch Lomond water to mix with the ice in their sophisticated Scotch. (There are readers who think that the advertisements for Scotch and Bourbon are the best fiction *The New Yorker* publishes.) One is glad to note here some of the respectable and not overpriced whiskies which Scots drink at home and which are now beginning to win favour with people who don't want excessively ornate prose and preposterous art, but a reliable whisky.

Apart from being a most valuable document for social history, sociology, daydreaming, a preparation for the terrible American weekend, Barnard produced a book of great charm. Even the illustrations have charm, though the drawings of distilleries have a certain grim Presbyterian monotony even when the distillers belonged to great Catholic families like the Macdonalds (of Fort William), the Peter Dawsons, and the Calders. Barnard toured more than mere distilleries. He was fond of verbal landscape painting and some passages recall the corresponding efforts in the novels of William Black. He gives due tribute to the great steamers Iona, Columba, the Hebridean—part of the childhood memories of so many Scottish children still alive who learnt why their father had gone down to 'see the engines'. There is an account of the Good Queen at Balmoral worthy of McGonagall. There are fond memories of the past that sadden the people who can remember the great days of Campbeltown, when the most beautiful waters (barely rivalled by the Bay of San Francisco) were covered with ships from douce Highland towns (each with at least one distillery) on their way 'to Glasgow of the Steeples'. The compliments paid to Edinburgh are more conventional, but justice is done to Aberdeen and injustice is done to Perth in its pre-Dewar days.

There is a great deal of very bad verse in Barnard, far inferior to that poetic equivalent of the Douanier Rousseau, the great bard of Dundee. There is a good deal of middling verse by Burns. But Robin struck the right note.

> Freedom and whisky gang thegither
> Tak aff ye'er dram.

Poor Burns! The infernal powers that avenged Scotch humbug in him deserved and deserve to be immured forever in the great bleak gaol at Peterhead (which Barnard tactfully does not mention in his account of that interesting town). What a fate! Worse than Dante could have invented for his worst Florentine foes, to make the great poet of whisky die an Exciseman.

When we turn from the late Victorian prose of Barnard to the more stripped and scientific prose of Professor Daiches, we are in a new world. It is not that Professor Daiches is not a worthy *laudator temporis acti*. He knows that the blessings of the popular blends, created for the English and American markets are very mixed. He knows a great deal more about the chemical and bacteriological problems of the manufacture of whisky than did Alfred Barnard, who had never heard of an enzyme. The triumphs of the Distillers' Company do not evoke unqualified rejoicing, and years of self-deprivation in the United States have made him sceptical of American taste and American advertising prose (the disquisition on the ambiguity of the adjective 'light' in America is a masterpiece of polite debunking). There is near tragedy in the story of how, having praised a real whisky on the air, he found he could no longer buy it for himself, since Macy's had been sold out.

There are stories of the ups and downs of the booming trade. The fall of the House of Pattison, if not as great a disaster as the collapse of the Darien scheme, nearly rivalled the failure of the (Glasgow) City Bank. We learn of the rise of the soda siphon and its failure to conquer the United States. We have the magnificently bad picture by Sir David Wilkie of whisky being presented in Edinburgh to a slenderized George IV. (The photographs by Professor Daiches's son, Alan, are magnificent.)

There are one or two signs of the Edinburgh origins of Professor Daiches's book. There is nothing about the curious and not totally edifying history of the relations of the Glasgow dockers to the greatest of British export trades. The religious problem behind the original story of *Whisky Galore* is lightly passed over. It was no trivial matter that Eriskay is a Catholic Island, rather indifferent to the rigours of the Presbyterian Sabbath. Professor Daiches repeats the nineteenth-century Edinburgh superstition that 'Scotch' is a vulgar adjective for everything but whisky. It was good enough for Sir Walter, and if Professor Daiches were a little older, he would have received proof of his fitness to enter the Town's College from the Scotch Education Department. And the name Stein is neither Dutch nor German. It is a good north-eastern Scotch name, borne by distinguished members of the distilling mystery. Its most famous bearer at the moment is the manager of (Glasgow) Celtic Football Club.

## (b) VANISHING MONUMENTS

THE PISSOTIÈRE, a more permanent monument of the Paris scene than the pig-snouted bus, or the G7 taxi or the 'agent à double barbe' of the Porte Saint-Martin, and a tribute to the steady architectural conservatism of the ironwork poets of the Voierie, is likely soon to be a museum piece, *classé monument historique*, and no doubt disconnected from its base: an object of aesthetic satisfaction, but no longer the sought-after terminus of needed relief, a poor, tame edifice in cast-iron, deprived of its pungent smell which, for the specialist—the *renifleur*—constitutes more than just an *hors-d'œuvre* to the wealth to come.

Yet what long and faithful service have these round, welcoming, artistically perforated chapels of fraternity rendered to the Parisian male, from eight to eighty (most of those questioned in the present work date their first visit to the temple to eight, ten or twelve), and to the foreign tourist! From the 1890s no Paris landscape could be complete without the obtrusive *théière*, the old-fashioned, two-storeyed edifice, pushing to the front, like a sentinel—there is one bang outside Notre-Dame, one outside the Bourse, one outside the Morgue, one, often in the cruder, more basic, lean-to variety, at the entry and against the wall of each cemetery, one outside the Biblio-thèque Nationale. The Panthéon, the mausoleum of *les Grands Hommes*, suitably gets two, twin guardians at the national shrine, each railway station is flanked by two or three, each little square is given unity by the *édicule* placed in its centre, so that the needs of religion, travel, tourism, scholarship, speculation and reverence are immediately satisfied with the rigorous impartiality of a secular, stone-eyed Marianne.

They form the central motif in the golden age of the post-card, standing out at the tram termini, Porte de Montreuil, Porte des Lilas, Porte de Clignancourt, or under the shadow of the Sacré-Cœur or the Moulin de la Galette, or competing with the harmon-ious façade of the Monnaie, or merely breaking the fearful monotony of the boulevard Voltaire and of the *boulevards extérieurs*. Near their narrow, odorous entrance linger the usual over-dressed, hieratical post-card figures: the boy in the sailor outfit with outsize hoop, the bigger boy in knickerbockers, the nurse, the *gavroche* in peaked cap, the *apache* in a loudly checked cloth one, the top-hatted *cocher*.

They stand out like scattered urban lighthouses, above the waters of the Venetian streets of the 1910 floods. And they are never far from the dread cross-flagged proclamations: *Mobilisation Générale* of August, 1914; they must have been much in demand during those hot nights. Between 1914 and 1918, the *vespasienne* is the light that did not fail for so many poor *poilus*, the symbol of a longed-for leave and of a lost civilian paradise. They figure weirdly, palaces of mystery, temples in the night cults of Dada and surrealism.

   This was the Imperial Period of the *vespasienne*, firmly rooted in the
'pavé de Paris', tied to the sewers by a multitude of pipes, witnessing,
on its outer walls, for apéritifs, medicines and for the varying brands
of political extremism (their political message is never moderate,
corresponding no doubt with the urgency of need of the user), and,
in the secrecy of the inner temple, after relief, to the sad boastings or
to the lonely, humble hopes of sexual deviation. Their round pale
globes light up the velvet night for Utrillo or for Van Gogh. They
have acquired *droit de cité* among the politicians of the Conseil
Général and can be used as mute, but convincingly odoriferous
apparati of sighing blackmail, outside a restaurant (preferably *avec
terrasse*) or a theatre or a private residence (they are so easy to move).
   For the hidden armies of pederasty—antique-dealers, dress-
designers, sailors, waiters, grooms, jockeys, valets, coachmen, boots,
actors—they are the free equivalent of the 'gros numéro', places of
rapid pleasure, stimulated by the pungent smell of urine and put to
music to the sound of waterfalls. And so they constitute too, with
their narrow entrances and their three confined, stand-up cubicles,
admirable murder traps; those placed on a treed square or at the end
of a long dark road or amidst the Siberian silence of the wintry
*boulevards extérieurs* are closely watched by *apaches*, themselves
watched by Casque-d'Or. At a favourite moment these will spring,
with the stealthy feline grace of the Désossé and, then, instead of a
pair of feet facing inwards, the passer-by might have the surprise of
seeing a hatless head, at urine level, in the space between the bottom
of the decorated ironwork and the pavement.
   How many lives were thus terminated, after a copious banquet,
like that of the bourgeois depicted in *L'Assiette au Beurre*, in June,
1901, his corpse splayed out at the entry to an *édicule*, a cloth-capped
figure with a face like a skull and his girl stooping over him? As
recently as Christmas Day, 1957, September 4 and October 24,
1959, commercial travellers were quietly knifed to death in *pisso-
tières*, their bodies left standing in the act of relief, wedged forwards
into the compartment, like those New York gangsters shot, with
their stetsons pushed forward over their noses, in telephone boxes.
   In the autumn, the season at which they become blocked with the
falling leaves, one or two, particularly located on lonely streets,
blackened Martian edifices, their slits dark with squinting, menacing
eyes, seemed, before their destruction, to issue warnings of a violent,
silent and smelly death, amidst green piping and blocked-up gurgling

drainery. There was one such black Bastille, darker than the night, squatting expectantly at the end of a long straight road that cut through the cimetière du Montparnasse and that, in the 1930s, was credited with half a dozen victims.

The Golden Age ended some time in the 1920s; the Decline set in during the early 1930s. In 1930, there were still 1,200 *urinoirs*, catering for every taste, with the armies of *la pédale* concentrating on certain favoured spots near les Halles (rather like the lady from the XVIe who explains: 'je fais mon marché aux Halles, c'est tellement plus économe'—it has, for her, other advantages too), much to the indignation of *les forts*, as conservative sexually as they were politically. By 1939 the number had been almost halved, to 700. This was reduced to 561 in 1954, 347 in 1965, and 329 in 1966. Two more years of Gaullism have no doubt added further to the holocaust of these ancient symbols of anti-clericalism, *le pot de vin*, heavy drinking, the habits of the boulevardier and of the *apache*, of objects that have contributed so richly to popular slang, and that have been such consistent invitations to the inventiveness and candour of popular literature. There could—and should—have been a Prix Pissotière to cater for this sort of talent.

Since the turn of the century, the enemies of the *urinoirs* at the Hotel-de-Ville have tended to be—or at least have proclaimed themselves as such, for realization has dragged far behind promise —the partisans of underground lavatories and of *châlets d'aisance*, more banally *châlets de nécessité*, Switzerland's leading contribution to Paris topography, hidden in decent foliage in the gardens off the Rond-Point. Of the former, there were ninety-three in 1920, ninety-seven in 1940, and ninety-six in 1963, hardly an effort to meet the expanding needs of a masculine population increasingly faced with the disappearance of familiar and well-liked points of relief above ground. For forty years, *les édiles* have talked much of grandiose underground establishments—they even sent over a commission to report, very eulogistically, on the facilities provided at Piccadilly Circus Underground Station—but, characteristically, only the Communist members have ever pressed hard for something to be done.

Each year a few more *vespasiennes* are removed to the chagrin and discomfort of the elderly—a group as much neglected by the Fifth Republic as by its two predecessors—while nothing is put in their place. Men are clearly to be reduced to the unhappy, furtive status so long experienced by women, very much the underprivileged in this important matter, and to be driven into an enforced *consommation* in order to benefit from the existence of some wretched contrivance among the telephones. It is, of course, understandable that banks, great corporations, embassies, theatres and cinemas should be anxious to remove the curved sentinels placed so often on their thresholds. But some other place must be found for them: the slaughter-houses, the markets, the cemeteries (the dead at least are not going to complain), the churches (with their long services), the hospitals, the railway stations have always cried out for need.

Just what does happen to these monuments of a considerate and artistic past? One can imagine some junkyard, to the north-east of Paris, full of uprooted and once useful edifices, in strange, jumbled companionship—the *théière* next to the lean-to, the rotund up against the rococo or the neo-classic—awaiting the hammer of the *ferrailleur* or the visit of the American collector (for we learn that they are already in the market), in Les Lilas of Montreuil, a lesser-known *puces*, near those secret places where the round, snout-nosed buses of the 1920s decay amidst rank grass.

So *Les Vespasiennes de Paris* is more a record of things past than a guide to the living geography of Parisian relief. Many favourite palacettes have disappeared: that on the corner of the Pont Neuf, that at the entrance to the Luxembourg, rue Guynemer, that opposite the Thermes. And most of those with the best views have gone. Even the 'Liste Noire' is largely of retrospective interest and those of a certain inclination would be sadly disappointed if they treated it as a guide; even the construction on the Place Saint-Sulpice has been pulled down. The Liste is rather a reminder of the geographical distribution of the active public centres of *les amateurs* in the early 1960s: a heavy concentration in the XVIe and the XVIIe, as in the Ier (les Halles) and in the XVIIIe, representing the convergence of the highest and lowest classes in the democracy of deviation.

There is an interesting appendix, based on a series of questions put both to habitual users and to the underprivileged of the other sex. From this it emerges that feminine opinion is remarkably tolerant towards the existence of these noisy temples from which they are for ever excluded but the scent of which they have to share. There are some small gems of social observation: one questioned states he is 'Pour', with the proviso: 'A condition qu'on voie à travers. Le soulagement semble meilleur à voir les autres continuer à s'agiter.'

A taxi-driver is likewise in the 'Pour' camp: 'Nécessité publique, surtout pour nous chauffeurs de taxi'. Another appendix contains a standard *procès-verbal* for 'outrage à la pudeur'. Perhaps the numbers are being reduced in order to release the police for more important duties.

The book is copiously and acutely illustrated, often by the author himself who, at some risk, has photographed the passing customer, both before and after. There is little trace of vulgarity, 'la pompe à merde' is not quoted (but there is something for the *amateur* on page 119) and M. Maillard has on the whole succeeded in avoiding the earthy *poujadisme* of Gabriel Chevalier and Dubut and the cruel, unfunny 'humour' of 'le cocuage'. This is not a funny book, but a melancholy one. It will be appreciated, nostalgically, by all those who have known what it was to experience relief in fraternal, cascading surroundings, with an outlook on chestnut and plane tree, on tiny, intimate squares, alongside one's fellow-men likewise engaged and with politics briefly forgotten. The politics are for outside, inside is for *soulagement*. The most endearing, most reassuring view of Paris is that seen, or rather surprised, through the starred or heartshaped slits, from inside. It is better to look out than to look in.

# 12

# POETRY OF 1969

## (a) JOHN BERRYMAN

### *His Toy, His Dream, His Rest*

IF THE CONTENTION is accepted that an excess of clarity is the only kind of difficulty a work of art should offer, John Berryman's *Dream Songs* (it is surely permissible by now to call the complete work by that name) have been offering several kinds of unacceptable difficulty since they first began to appear. It was confusedly apparent in the first volume of the work, *77 Dream Songs*, that several different personalities within the poet's single personality (one doesn't suggest his 'real' personality, or at any rate one didn't suggest it at that stage) had been set talking to and of each other. These personalities, or let them be called characters, were given tones of voice, even separate voices with peculiar idioms. The interplays of voice and attitude were not easy to puzzle out, and many reviewers, according to Mr. Berryman and their own subsequent and sometimes abject admissions, made howlers. With this new volume of 308 more dream songs comes a rather impatient corrective from the author pointing out how simple it all is.

Well, the first book was not simple. It was difficult. In fact it was garbled, and the reviewers who said so and later took it back are foolish. *His Toy, His Dream, His Rest*, this new and longer book, is simpler, with many of the severally-voiced conversational devices

(a) JOHN BERRYMAN: *His Toy, His Dream, His Rest*. 308 Dream Songs. 317 pp. Faber and Faber. £2 10s.

(b) PETER PORTER: *A Porter Folio*. 70 pp. Scorpion Press. 25s.

(c) W. D. SNODGRASS: *After Experience*. 92 pp. Oxford University Press. 15s.

(d) DOUGLAS DUNN: *Terry Street*. 62 pp. Faber and Faber. 15s.

(e) DONALD DAVIE: *Essex Poems, 1963–67*. 53 pp. Routledge and Kegan Paul. 25s.

(f) SEAMUS HEANEY: *Door into the Dark*. 56 pp. Faber and Faber. 15s.

(g) ROBERT DUNCAN: *Selected Poems*. Vol. I. *The First Decade, 1940–1950*. 136 pp. Vol. 2. *Derivations, 1950–1956*. Fulcrum Press. 35s. each.

abandoned. Its difficulties are more of texture than of structure: the plan is less schematic but the indulgences are proportionately greater, eccentricity proliferating as the original intellectualized, constructional gimmicks fold up under the pressure of released expression. There are passages that are opaque and likely to remain so. Some of the language is contorted in a way designed to disguise the platitudinous as a toughly guarded verity. The range of reference is very wide (the *Dream Songs*, like dreams in sleep, draw freely and solidly on the cultural memory) but there are some references which go well beyond the legitimately omnivorous curiosity of the poetic intelligence and achieve impenetrable privacy through not being, like most of the rest, explained by their general context.

This last, the general context, is the true structure of Berryman's complete book of 385 individual, but not isolated, lyrics. It is not wise to contend that the ambitions of structure (with a capital S) can go hang, the individual lyrics being all that matters. In fact, the lyrics mostly explain each other's difficulties—sometimes across long distances—by tilting themes to a different angle, revisiting a location, repeating a cadence or redefining a point. It was Yeats's way and for that matter it was Petrarch's—the long poem as an arrangement of small ones. One proof that this is the operative structure in the *Dream Songs* is that the work feels more comfortable to read as one gets further into it. But if it is not wise to say that the structure is nothing and the individual lyric everything, it is still less wise to say that the work is unintelligible without a perception of its grand design. It is unlikely that a clear account of such a grand design will ever be forthcoming, although the chances of several bright young academic things building a career on the attempt are unfortunately 100 per cent. It will probably not be possible to chart the work's structure in the way that the *Divine Comedy*, for example, can be charted out in its themes, zones and stylistic areas. The development of the *Dream Songs* is much more a development by accretion: Ezra Pound and William Carlos Williams are the two obvious models. An indication of this is the already mentioned fact that the multi-voiced interplay of *77 Dream Songs* is in these later ones not so much in evidence: as a device it has yielded to ideas more productive, especially to the unabashed elegiac strain, sonorous as lamenting bagpipes, which in many ways makes this new book a convocation of the literary ghosts. One feels at the end of this new volume that there is no reason, except for the necessary eventual loss of inspiration, why the work shouldn't go on literally for ever —just as the *Cantos*, whose material is *un*digested information (Berryman digests his) could obviously go on to fill a library. The work has no pre-set, confining shape to round it out, and one doesn't see why the 385th song need absolutely be the last one; not in the way one sees that the last line of the *Divine Comedy*, for many previously established reasons, must bring the poem to an end.

In brief, with the *Dream Songs* Berryman has found a way of pouring in everything he knows while still being able to tackle his themes one, or a few, at a time. Attacking its own preliminary planning and reducing it to material, the progressive structure advances to fill the space available for it—a space whose extent the author cannot in the beginning accurately guess at but must continue with the poem in order to discern.

The *Dream Songs* are thus a modern work, a work in which it is possible for the reader to dislike poem after poem and idea after idea without imagining that what he likes could have come into existence without what he dislikes. It is particularly worth remembering this point when one comes across gross moments which make one feel like kicking the book around the room. And it is particularly worth making this general point about the *Dream Songs* having the title to a work (rather than just a trendily labelled grab-bag) in view of the virtual certainty that the weirdball academic studies will soon be upon us, bringing with them the inevitable reaction into an extreme commonsensicality which would deny the existence of a long poem rather than have it 'studied' in brainless terms.

It was a brilliantly asserted, overwhelmingly persuasive version of commonsensicality which enabled Croce to liberate the *Divine Comedy* (the case is again relevant) from an inhumanly attentive *wissenschaft* and release the poetry within it to immediate appreciation. But of course the Crocean case was over-asserted. The poem *does* possess an informing structure, a structure which the reader must know in detail, though better later than sooner and better never than in the first instance. Berryman's *Dream Songs*, on their much smaller, less noble scale, likewise have a structure, and will continue to have it even when the scholars say they do. That is the thing to remember, that and the fact that the structure is inside rather than overall. Especially when a long poem is such a present to the academics as this one is, the humane student is engaged in a fight for possession from the very outset: he needs to remember that to be simplistic is to lose the fight. He must admit complication: certainly here, for the *Dream Songs* are extremely complicated, having almost the complexity of memory itself. They depend on the perception that the mind is not a unity but a plurality, and by keeping the talk going between these mental components, by never (or not often) lapsing into a self-censoring monologue, they convey their special sense of form. It's even possible to say that the poorest sections of the work are the sections where the poet's sense of himself is projected into it as a pose—where an attitude is struck and remains unquestioned in a work of art whose unique quality is to question all attitudes through the critical recollection of their history and a sensitive awareness of all the clichés attendant on the concept of the creative personality. And the personality in play is, of course, the creative one: the central motive of the *Dream Songs* can be defined as an attempt by a poet to examine himself without lapsing into self-regard. 'The poem then', Berryman writes in his prefatory Note,

whatever its wide cast of characters, is essentially about an imaginary character (not the poet, not me) named Henry, a white American in early middle age sometimes in blackface, who has suffered an irreversible loss and talks about himself sometimes in the first person, sometimes in the third, sometimes even in the second; he has a friend, never named, who addresses him as Mr. Bones and variants thereof.

Not the poet and not me. But obviously, in what is mainly the story of a poet who is currently writing a poem which sounds remarkably like the one the reader is reading, the poet *is* the hero, a fact readily ascertainable from the amount of autobiographical material being used, some of which would be embarrassing if not rendered neutral by the poem's universalizing mechanisms, and some of which is not rendered neutral and consequently *is* embarrassing. The question is always being turned up, as the reader ploughs on, of whether the author *knows* that every so often a certain insensitivity, a certain easily recognizable 'creative' belligerence, is getting through unqualified to the page. Here and only here is the central character 'me' in the raw sense: in the refined sense the 'me' is representative of all artists and hence of all men in their authentically productive moments. The embarrassments are probably best accepted as a contributory quality, a few turns of the stomach consequent upon the many thrills. The poem's devices of voicing are not meant to distance personality but to reveal it: the doubts begin when we suspect that attitudes are reaching us which the poet has not analysed,

K

that he does not realize he is being revealing in a crude sense. But really there are bound to be these. The important thing to say here is that the personality in the poem, manifold, multiform and self-examining in an obsessive way, keeps all one's attention. The language never settles into anything less than readability, and even when the restlessness becomes a shaken glamour in which one can see little, it is evident that something is being worried at: we are not just being dazzled with an attempt to churn meaning into existence. There is not much fake significance, though quite a lot of blurred.

Thematically, these new songs are first of all a disorderly, desperate and besotted funeral for Berryman's literary heroes, who might be called, following the author's own terminology, the 'lovely men'. Of these, Delmore Schwartz is easily the star. His decline is convincingly (one hopes fairly) illustrated. There are sketches towards blaming this writer's collapse on society at large, but there is also a more powerful evocation of a sheer inability to cope. 'Admiration for the masters of his craft' was one of the emotions Edmund Wilson picked out as characterizing *77 Dream Songs*. In the new book the simple admiration for the masters continues, but in Schwartz's case (and to a lesser extent in Randall Jarrell's) it goes a long way beyond admiration, and a good deal deeper than craft, into a disturbed exploration of the artist's way of life in America now—and this concern again, through the internalizing way the poem has, is referred back to the condition of the poet-narrator, a condition of physical crack-up and a fearful but no longer postponable facing of the unpalatable truths. Some of the evocation of Schwartz's life seems a trifle cheap, like all those Greenwich Village memoirs conjuring up the less than compelling figure of Little Joe Gould: here, as in the sporadic scenes of Irish pubbing and loosely buried claims to a hairily abrupt way with the ladies, the underlying ideas of bohemianism sound a touch conventional, the reactions provincially American as opposed to the acutely modern, prolix Western intelligence of the work's usual tone.

Exemplified by the poet's cacophonous admiration of Shirley Jones, the supposedly 'genuine' identification with the straightforward and simple reads as hick gullibility and sheer bad taste. Another thumping example of bad taste is the insufferably patronising farewell for Louis MacNeice. A lack of 'good taste' is one of Berryman's strengths, in the sense that he can range anywhere for images without a notion of fitness barring his way. But positive *bad* taste is one of his weaknesses. His tough, anti-intellectual line on the American virtues, for instance, echoes the screenplays of 'Spig' Wead: ideas like this can bore you in an instant by the insensitivity of delivery alone. There are moments when Berryman writing sounds a bit like John Wayne talking. For all his absorptive capacity for the fine details of life, Berryman's conception of America and of civilization itself seems cornily limited, and even the book's elegiac strain, its congested keening for the gifted dead, edges perilously close to an elementary romanticism whose informing assumption is the withdrawal of support by the gods. Waiting for the end, boys. But at its best the *Dream Songs* is a voice near your ear that you listen to, turn towards, and find that you must turn again; a voice all around you, unpinnable to a specific body; your own voice, if you had lived as long and could write in so condensed a way; a voice not especially prepossessing, but vivid and somehow revivifying. A solitary quotation makes an appropriate finale:

. . . I can't read any more of this Rich Critical Prose,/he growled, broke wind, and scratched himself & left/ that fragrant area.

## (b) PETER PORTER

### *A Porter Folio*

THE MOST PROMINENT and gifted of the literary ex-Australians to date, Peter Porter has no Nolan-style Ned Kelly figures to provide a tunnel home. 'Phar Lap in the Melbourne Museum' (a poem which would incinerate most of the stuff in the proliferating anthologies of contemporary Australian verse) and a few other works devoted directly to the homeland are by now years behind him. Also behind him is the giddy period known to every Australian writer who makes the break and which ought to be called the Transfer Lounge. 'Who is Peter Porter?' asked Stephen Spender testily upon the appearance of *Penguin Modern Poets 2* (Amis, Moraes and our man) as if the answer might be that he was some chap who picked a peck of pickled pepper.

Meanwhile and until recently Mr. Porter was busily overasserting his own corruption as he waded deeper into the British experience—Chelsea, the ad agencies, the Jensen set—which the world has since come to recognize as the Scene. Poems half-confessed complicity while half-celebrating the luxurious. He could have been the prophet of the new thing (indeed *Oz*, likewise an ex-Australian happening, invited him in, but in those pages his work looked ill at ease, what with its long words) except that his cultivation was working against him as a success, and for him as a poet. 'It's a Condé Nast world' he wrote, accurately; but he did not have a Condé Nast mind, he had a contemplative one. Since which time the real Condé Nast poets have moved in. The Australian alienated by a European intelligence arrives in Europe in time to find the European inheritance being shouted down by a volunteer militia of variously clad trendies marching faultlessly in formation.

It is a rich situation for satire, and it is quite possible that the desperation induced is the real reason for the streaks of dreadfully careless writing which continually turn up in Peter Porter's work, otherwise the product of a man with a genuine formal sense. There is something in the poetry which believes that the poetry is reaching no one, that it has no future. The Fit City, Mr. Porter's Audenesque pleasure dome, is not even Audenesque; not imagined or even willed, not believed for a possible future, and certainly not extrapolated from anything or anywhere in the present. To find an illuminating parallel to his use of the past, especially his debt to the heritage of European music, you would have to go to the Montale of the years between the wars—and find even more acutely in the Anglo-Australian than in the Italian the sense that the tradition is failing and that the old assumption (I will refer to those gone and those to come will refer to me) is no longer tenable.

Mr. Porter parades his culture in every sense, so that England may take a last look. The role (Eliot's role) of the visitor who knows the place better than the inhabitants retains its power. Cold comfort for the hip, bad news for the mandarin, the resulting poetry, even at its most clumsily rushed, pulls off the trick of staying in contact while conveying no sense whatsoever of belonging. Mr. Porter should realize, incidentally, that he *has* an audience and provide notes to his allusions and epigrams from now on—never mind what Robert Graves says. The scraps from Auden (the Adversary has a walk-on part) are all too readily notable but the book is stiff with unidentified Germans. The density of reference is functional in nutty games like his 'Metamorphoses' but elsewhere the reader would surely like to take down the relevant books.

## (c) W. D. SNODGRASS

### *After Experience*

A POET in a country where anything can be turned in for a new one, W. D. Snodgrass stays loyal to his unpoetic surname, and the essential claim his poetry makes is that it is necessary to write beautifully in spite of circumstances. Reading his list of acknowledgements (they have already been quoted by British reviewers, to whom names like the Corporation of Yaddo will always sound as if a homeward-bound Dickens is contemptuously pronouncing them) and remembering earlier awards and fellowships from the Ingram Merrill Foundation and the *Hudson Review*, the reader is more than mildly put off, as by the abstractly unimpressive multiple rows of fruit salad on the chests of American generals. But the crucial point is that all this information is available: Snodgrass does not cover up. It is nowadays very difficult for an American poet of manifest talent to be put out of business by want or by neglect. Snodgrass does not pretend otherwise. Hemmed in by endpapers and wrappers proclaiming his jobs, honours and awards (naturally the Foundation will bear your expenses), his poetry steers clear of the poet's condition, which is obviously in A1 shape, and concentrates on the personal condition, which seems to be in a fruitful state of permanent confusion.

If 'confessional' poetry exists at all (and if it does, Snodgrass and Lowell are still the two best Americans writing it), its basic assumption is that the time-honoured separation of the private man and the public artist can now be closed; the pose is over, and all the masks can be put away. The trick is worked, when it works, not by lowering the universal to the level of personality, but by elevating the vicissitudes of private life to the level of the universal. Insofar as the poet succeeds in convincing the reader that his personal suffering has an impersonal resonance, his work will chime: insofar as he does not, it will grate. Snodgrass grated badly in passages like this from the title poem of his first book, *Heart's Needle*:

> In their smooth covering, white
> As quilts to warm the resting bed
> Of birth or pain, spotless as pages spread
> For me to write,

Or this, from the same poem:

> Like nerves caught in a graph
> the morning-glory vines
>     frost has erased by half
> still crawl across their rigid twines.
>     Like broken lines
> of verses I can't make.

Years later, in the work collected in *After Experience*, the same slate is scratched:

> Now I can earn a living
> By turning out elegant strophes.

The reader's first and sound reaction is that he does not want to hear this: just read the news, please. The reaction is sound because this new habit of calling attention to the practical business of putting words on paper is the trivialization of what for some centuries has correctly been regarded as a divine act, an act which no decent practitioner should regard as his own preserve. The effect is childish, even in a poet of Snodgrass's abilities: he is joined in this to those academically-environed hordes of giftless poets who utterly fail to realize that man is not the measure of art. But before we come to that general point, it can be put beyond doubt that Snodgrass is a poet capable of extraordinary effects. His acute, sparely employed (in fact under-indulged) metaphorical sense can put an era into an image:

> This moth caught in the room tonight
> Squirmed up, sniper-style, between
> The rusty edges of the screen;

Faster and neater than that you don't get: a whole background comes over in a flash. The well-known virtuoso effort 'The Examination' (once 'the Phi Beta Kappa ceremonial poem at Columbia University', save the mark), detailing the ghastly victimization of a generalized Otherness and recalling the eery dismemberment of angels in the film by Borowczik, has an exquisitely schooled timing in its local effects that creates for the reader a nightmare he cannot stop.

> Meantime, one of them has set blinders to the eyes,
> Inserted light packing beneath each of the ears
> And calked the nostrils in. One, with thin twine, ties
> The genitals off. With long wooden-handled shears,
> Another chops pinions out of the scarlet wings.

You can see how each line of the stanza infallibly brings something worse to life, and how, after the qualification 'wooden-handled' has placed your own garden-shears in your hands, the jump across the gap to the next stanza tells you that the next thing is the worst of the lot. In an age of fake rough-stuff turned out by those youngish poets who seem fascinated by greased hair and high boots this poem, and another called 'A Flat One' about an old man dying, are evidence that Snodgrass is capable of genuine tragic power—a power that the fashionable preoccupation with violence tends to dissipate. And it is not accidental that in these two instances the view-point is impersonal: the crippling assumption that one man can be a world is not in evidence.

Of those poems referring to a life meant to sound like his own the best are those in which the experience has a general applicability to a time, to a culture.' What We Said', a gently singing reminiscence of estrangement, is a good example. When he tries extra hard to supply the specific detail which will give the sense of a particular life (this is really *me* talking) he tends to be in the first place flimsy ('Mementos I' fades right out beside Larkin's poem using the same properties, 'Lines on a Young Lady's Photograph Album') and in the second place dishonourable, since the theme, reduced to the loss of happiness, seems to assume a *right* to happiness—which for sound reasons has never been counted among an artist's legitimate expectations. Betraying themselves technically by a prevalence of shakily cantilevered rhymes (bringing the reader as near as he will ever get to groaning at poetry of this accomplishment), such poems demonstrate that a necessary consequence of abolishing the distinction between private life and public life is that ordinary privacy ceases to exist as a concept; characterized with a ruthless hand and unable to answer back, the true sufferers in 'confessional' poetry are the poets' wives.

The contradiction inherent in 'confessional' poetry which goes beyond its scope is damagingly evident in Snodgrass's attempt at a poem about Eichmann, 'A Visitation'. Technically very interesting, it creates an effect of jammed dialogue by interlacing two monologues, one by Eichmann, the other by the poet. (This exceedingly difficult trick of stereo voicing is used by Snodgrass elsewhere in 'After Experience Taught me . . . ' and he may be said by now to hold the copyright on it.) But examined close to, the poem reveals itself to be dependent on all the usual weary banalities that would trace the phenomena of mass-murder to tendencies in the artist's own soul, provide the illusion of debate and flatter the pretensions of the liberal spirit towards a forgiving generosity. In view of this it is particularly unfortunate that the poem should carry as an epigraph a quotation from Hannah Arendt, who has certainly declared (in the very book from which Snodgrass quotes) that these events can be understood in the long run only by the poets, but who equally certainly, and as long ago as the appearance of her monumental *The Origins of Totalitarianism*, made her views known about those who thought 'that inner experience could be given historical significance, that one's own self had become the battlefield of history'.

'Confessional' poetry has taken a small, previously neglected field among all the possible fields of poetry and within that field pushed on to a new adventure. It becomes absurd when it usurps the impersonal fields with the language of the personal—when it fails to recognize its limitations. Eichmann's crimes, for example, were in the public realm; they are not to be traced to the sadistic impulse which is in all of us or to any other impulse which is in all of us; they can be understood only in history. When the poet pretends to contain, mirror or model history within his own suffering, his talent gives out for just as long as the folly lasts; the better he is, the worse the work he does; and even a first-rate talent like Snodgrass's produces the smoothly 'distinguished' work which is the bane of our age and to which we do not normally expect a man of his powers to contribute.

## (d) DOUGLAS DUNN

### Terry Street

DOUGLAS DUNN has a beat covering Hull's Terry Street and its environs. He has been in there, like a Disney cameraman parked up a palm-tree with his head disguised as a coconut; he has shot the stuff and he has got it out. The results are distinguished in a prize-for-reporting kind of way. It is a distinction of a fashionable kind. The problem the publication of his book poses Mr. Dunn is to go on from it before time repudiates it. Tireless in its microscopic observation, remorseless in the scrupulosity of its language, the work is about as close as a patently gifted poet can go to the banal. This is poetry attempting to survive on a determined honesty alone: the no-poses principle is carried through to the point where it becomes itself a pose:

Yet there is no unrest. The dust is so fine.
You hardly notice you have grown too old to cry out for change.

Who you? This is the clinching couplet from 'New Light on Terry Street', but the light is not all that new:

> Up terraces of slums, young gum-chewing mothers sit
> Outside on their thrones of light.

Cf. Larkin, *passim*. Meanwhile the following kind of ability is largely going to waste:

> The children bounce balls
> Up into their dreams of sand

—which is a step up in ambition and (probably consequently) in language from just flatly describing everything that has novelty value as a fearless observation. It is quite obvious that Mr. Dunn's gift of language lies in this direction and not the other, but he cannot go in that direction because for the moment he is not allowed to. No D.T.'s please.

> The ball I threw while playing in the park
> Has not yet reached the ground.

That is Dylan himself. Mr. Dunn's is the same gesture, the same feeling for the language, but in a period so different that he cannot allow himself to travel even a tiny way towards a language creating emotion through its own plasticity. Instead, a relentless application to fine detail, a retrograde Grierson-style documentary in a language as flat as faded film is grey:

> In small backyards old men's long underwear
> Drips from sagging clotheslines.
> The other stuff they take in bundles
> to the Bendix.

Look at Life again soon. And in 'Sunday Morning Among the Houses of Terry Street' we are given a rhapsody on a windy night without the night, the wind or the rhapsody, but with the same confidence (misplaced in this case) that the detail will add up and with a really quite serious underestimation of how thoroughly this kind of thing has already been taken care of:

> On the quiet street, Saturday night's fag-packets,
> Balls of fish and chip newspaper, bottles
> Placed neatly on window sills, beside cats.

In poems a page or more long he feels compelled to disperse Panorama-style comment among his descriptions, but a few very short poems show the landscape unadorned with captions or voices-over. We just hold it for a long shot and leave the audience to draw its own conclusions:

> Recalcitrant motorbikes;
> Dog-shit under frost; a coughing woman;
> The old men who cannot walk briskly groaning
> On the way back from their watchmen's huts.

This poem is alive in the first line because bikes refusing to start often kick back at you, so 'recalcitrant' is a good word. But you would need to go a long way into the bad lands of Poundian theory ('congeries of minutely observed particulars'?) to make sense of the selectivity exercised in the rest of it. Poems like these pass only negative tests: no, they do not pose; no, they do not stunt; no, the language is not inflated. They arise out of a determination concerning what poetry should not be. Yet everywhere there are hints of a pull towards lyricism, of form transmitting delight by its own concern with itself. The last stanza in the book's last poem is a clear echo of James Wright ('Suddenly I realise/That if I stepped out of my body I would break/ Into blossom'), but it is a satisfactory distance from Terry Street and shows the way Mr. Dunn's poetry could go.

> The back of my hand
> With its network of small veins
> Has changed to the underside of a leaf.
> If water fell on me now
> I think I would grow.

One is sure that he will, just as one is sure that this book is out a shade too early for its author's good health and a shade too late to set any new marks for the fashion is exemplifies.

## (e) DONALD DAVIE

### *Essex Poems, 1963–67*

THE THEMES of Donald Davie's new collection are Nature and civilization, peace and death, love and spiritual emptiness—curiously metaphysical concerns, one might think, for so studiedly reticent, stringently pragmatic a poet. A new note seems to have entered Davie's poetry with this volume, as its final lines suggest:

> The transcendental nature
> Of poetry, how I need it!

> And yet it was for years
> What I refused to credit.

'Need' is the crucial term, with its stressed emotional urgency. It points, throughout the book, to a withdrawal from a felt blankness in ordinary life: a withdrawal at once so total and so indiscriminate that it can only reach the outer edge of articulation. The firm, coolly wrought obliquity of style which Davie has come to practise so expertly still holds; but now its poise seems maintained against the pressure of an isolation and rootlessness too undermining to be effectively transmuted in the poetry itself. That process of transmutation is still seen as the necessary and redeeming work of art—

> The practise of an art
> is to convert all terms
> into the terms of art

—but the sense of absence at the heart of the volume seems, nevertheless, resistant to any complete expression. When it breaks fully into the open, it emerges as stark statement or cryptic notation, in symbols which are offered rather than critically examined:

> Resignation, oh winter tree
> At peace, at peace...
> Read it what way you will,
> A wish that fathers. In a field between
> The Sokens, Thorpe and Kirby, stands
> A bare Epiphany.

It might be said that the peace of which the poems speak is so ultimate that hint and symbol are its only proper expressions; yet the oppositions around which some of the poems turn—silence against discourse, Nature and death against society—are, when fully exposed, unfocused and even naive, for such a finely intelligent poet:

> Thanks to industrial Essex
> I have spun on the greasy axis
> Of business and sociometrics...
> I know that what they merit
> Is not scorn, sometimes scorn
> And hatred, but sadness really.

The limpness of this amounts, in the end, to a wearily conventional Romantic wisdom, at odds with the still alertly discriminating technique. It is the blank disjunction between the placed local details of 'The Sokens, Thorpe and Kirby' and the mute, inscrutable Epiphany, which discloses the essential slackening of engaged intelligence in the poems. Or, to put it another way, it is the lack of relation within a single poem between a characteristically fastidious, self-consciously literary gesture—

> And the Soke of Peterborough
> Is one long arm of the cold vexed sea of the North

—and the authentic, vulnerably emotional impulse a few lines later:

> Pacific is the end of the world,
> Pacific, peaceful.

In these poems from four years' work, the gap between what can be effectively said and the intricately accomplished technique available to say it looms disturbingly large. It is disappointing, and ominous, that one of English poetry's most experienced practitioners should come, at this stage, to the point where all that can be offered, against a discerned loss in social and personal life, is really no more than a different kind of blankness.

## (f) SEAMUS HEANEY

### *Door into the Dark*

OF ALL THE NEWER tight-lipped poets Mr. Heaney is the hardest case, and the tight-lipped critics whose praise is not usually easy to get have been sending quite a lot of approbation his way. His technique is hard-edged: a punchy line travels about two inches. The subject matter is loud with the slap of the spade and sour with the stink of turned earth. Close to the vest, close to the bone and close to the soil. We have learnt already not to look to him for the expansive gesture: there are bitter essences to compensate for the lack of that. *Door into the Dark* confirms him in his course, its very title telling you in which direction that course lies. I will show you fear in a tinful of bait. It should be said at the outset that poetry as good as Mr. Heaney's best is hard to come by. But it is all pretty desperate stuff, and in those poems where we don't feel the brooding vision to be justified by the customary dense beauty of his technique we are probably in the right to come down hard and send our criticism as close as we can to the man within. The man within is at least in some degree a chooser. If he chose to be slick, to let his finely-worked clinching stanzas fall pat, there would be a new kind of damaging poetry on the way—squat, ugly and unstoppable.

But first let us demonstrate the quality of the poetic intelligence with which we have to deal. This is the first stanza of his two-stanza poem 'Dream': it should be quickly apparent that his virtuoso kinetic gift can find interior equivalents in language for almost any movement in the exterior world, so that the mere act of sub-vocalizing the poem brings one out in a sweat.

> With a billhook
> Whose head was hand-forged and heavy
> I was hacking a stalk
> Thick as a telegraph pole.
> My sleeves were rolled
> And the air fanned cool past my arms
> As I swung and buried the blade.
> Then laboured to work it unstuck.

All the correct chunks and squeaks are caught without being said. But where does it get us? It gets us to the second stanza.

> The next stroke
> Found a man's head under the hook.
> Before I woke
> I heard the steel stop
> In the bone of the brow.

He had a dream, you see, and his skill brings you close to believing it —but not quite. This deadfall finish is really a conventional echo of the professional toughies, 'realistic' about violence, who have been giving us the jitters for some time. Most of the other symptoms in the syndrome are manifest somewhere or other in the book. Human characteristics tend to be referred back to animals and objects. As with Ted Hughes, it takes a visit to the zoo, the game reserve, or an imaginary dive below the sod before the idea of *personality* gets any showing at all. The people themselves are mostly clichés disguised in heroic trappings. A stable vacated by a horse ('Gone') offers more character than the smithy still occupied by the smith ('The Forge'). This latter poem, surely fated to be an anthology piece for the generations to come, can usefully be quoted in full:

> All I know is a door into the dark,
> Outside, old axles and iron hoops rusting;
> Inside, the hammered anvil's short-pitched ring.
> The unpredictable fantail of sparks

Or hiss when a new shoe toughens in water.
The anvil must be somewhere in the centre,
Horned as a unicorn, at one end square,
Set there immovable; an altar
Where he expends himself in shape and music.
Sometimes, leather-aproned, hairs in his nose,
He leaps out on the jamb, recalls a clatter
Of hooves where traffic is flashing in rows;
Then grunts and goes in, with a slam and flick
To beat real iron out, to work the bellows.

The numbered questions in the back of the school anthology are obvious. What is the attitude of the smith to modern civilization? Is it the same as the poet's attitude? And (for advanced students) would you consider the Leavisite views on the organic relationship of work to life relevant? But it should also be obvious that the interest of the poem drops considerably when the human being replaces the object at stage centre. Those hairs in his nose don't do much to establish him, except as a character actor sent down at an hour's notice from Central Casting. If he were more real, his attitudes towards mechanized culture might not fall so pat. Get through that doorway in the dark and you might find him beating out hubcaps or balancing the wire wheels on a DB6—both jobs which can be done with as much love as bending your millionth horseshoe. There is no conflict here: there is just a received opinion expressed in hints and cleverly overblown in unexpected places—that altar, and the unicorn's horn, which ought to be a rhino's only that's too easy. On the page the refined poem has its attractive spareness; it's the implication, the area of suggestion, that worries the reader through the ordinariness of its assumptions about culture. Self-employed artisans are usually tough enough to see reality straight: given the chance, the leather-aproned subject might well remind Mr. Heaney that there ain't no pity in the city.

Things live; animals almost live; humans live scarcely at all. The inverse progression holds disturbingly true in well-known efforts like the poem about the frozen pump, 'Rite of Spring'.

That sent the pump up in flame.
It cooled, we lifted her latch,
Her entrance was wet, and she came.

It's a roundabout way for passion to get into print. The obverse poems to this are 'Mother', in which the lady ends up wanting to be like the pump, and 'The Wife's Tale', a brilliantly tactile poem in which you touch everything—cloth, stubble, grass, bread, seed and china cups—except flesh.

Mr. Heaney's 'A Lough Neagh Sequence' (also available in the *Phoenix* series as a separate pamphlet prefaced by a useful note absent from the present volume) forms an important section of the book and could well be pointed to if one were asked to isolate a thematic area absolutely his.

> They're busy in a high boat
> That stalks towards Antrim, the power cut.
> The line's a filament of smut
>
> Drawn hand over fist
> Where every three yards a hook's missed
> Or taken (and the smut thickens, wrist-
>
> Thick, a flail
> Lashed into the barrel
> With one swing.) Each eel
>
> Comes aboard to this welcome:
> The hook left in gill or gum
> It's slapped into the barrel numb
>
> But knits itself, four-ply
> With the furling, slippy
> Haul, a knot of back and pewter belly
>
> That stays continuously one
> For each catch they fling in
> Is sucked home like lubrication.

Evocation could go no further: the eels ('hatched fears') are practically in your lap. Similarly in poems like 'Bann Clay' and 'Bogland' his grating line, shudderingly switched back and forth like teeth ground in a nightmare, finds endless technical equivalents for the subject described: he really is astonishingly capable. And in 'Bogland' there is an indication that he can do something even more difficult— state the open statement, make the gesture that enlivens life.

> They've taken the skeleton
> Of the Great Irish Elk
> Out of the peat, set it up
> An astounding crate full of air.

The spirits lift to the flash of wit. There ought to be more of it.

Nobody in his right mind would deny that Mr. Heaney's is one of the outstanding talents on the scene, or want that talent to settle in its ways too early.

# (g) ROBERT DUNCAN

## *Selected Poems*

IT HAS LONG BEEN CUSTOMARY to praise a writer for luring his audience into working for him. Following a well-wrought text, readers are prepared to see hints fall and gaps open. If they are, as one says, 'trained' they enjoy completing an author's analogies or connecting his thoughts. But even compliant donkeys want a morsel of carrot to sweeten their task; and even the most difficult poets used to supply some melody or apothegm or delicious sensation to draw one into the activity of perfecting their meaning. Robert Duncan is too high-minded to sully his work with many sweet or nourishing tidbits. As if to set an example, he has said, 'I study out what I write as I study any mystery'. He takes the grandest possible view of a reader's responsibility to live up to an author's expectations. 'You too if you read have written', he says, 'as my poor mind knows not if it has read or written'. Rather than defile our sensibilities with lines of actions or argument, he often presents the verbal materials out of which we may construct the poem of our choice, do-it-yourself kits for the creative audience.

The most tiresome of Mr. Duncan's challenges are old-fashioned experimental work; automatic writing, dada, lists of freely associated phrases beginning with the same words, nursery-rhyme surrealism. Those readers who regard Gertrude Stein as a literary equivalent of the sorcerer's apprentice will wince to find Mr. Duncan producing 'imitations' of her compositions.

Slightly more welcome is another category, namely, poems that seem designed in the mode of *Hamlet* without the prince. For a poet given to afflatus it is a temptation to overlook the simple incident or passion that has started a rapture or fury, and to convey the high mood in terms of a landscape or a moral principle filling his mind during the experience. So long as his poem draws on conventional, public references, the reader is free to enjoy a straightforward pleasure—provided that the poet's expression is adequate to the planned elevation. But if the references become private or eccentric, the reader meets an emotional gap; he is called upon for a response which the verses hardly justify, unless he can build a bridge with his own more or less suitable associations.

In some poems, especially those written more than twenty years ago, Mr. Duncan makes the link between occasion and excitement traceable enough. For example, his creative imagination gives him a sense of divinity; love makes him happy as a god; poetry seems a way both of making love and of receiving Apollo's love; the beloved seems divine; and when the poet loses the beloved, he feels like Apollo mourning for Hyacinthus. This is roughly the plan of 'An Apollonian Elegy', with its intricate parallels between the sun god and the passionate, imaginative poet:

> When I turn, I touch, I, joyous shout;
> face the abyss where the angel of the sun,
> the dreaded, the loved, hovers
> and covers my body with his wings.
> He is gone. And trembling, I face my lover.
> He is more beautiful than the sun. The human
> has in its rest what can be loved
> and yet wrest not from the bone its flesh
> nor from terror its love.

Again, in 'Revival', when Mr. Duncan deals with the ending of a difficult love affair (abruptly closed by a telephone call from the poet's lover), he nicely distinguishes the stages of anxiety; a relation of cause to effect is visible; and we can decide for ourselves how well the verse agrees with the emotion:

> Am I on the brink of happiness?
> Am I on the brink of panic?
> Not even love or not-love
> seems significant
> when I consider
> the panic with which I walk
> toward the house of friends.

But far too often Mr. Duncan places side by side phrases and images that may affect him deeply or hilariously, but that have little connotation for the rest of us:

> Old Mother Anthropos
> refuses to face her hour's mirror.
> You know her. She lives in the shoe
> that fits her.

In the longest and most complex of his works three elements are

L

mingled without differentiation: a theme the poem is presumably
'about'; other themes or images privately associated with this by the
poet; and various perceptions occurring to him while writing the
poem—including observations on the act of composition. Thus one
prose piece opens; 'As we start the sentence we notice that birds are
flying thru it; phrases are disturbd where these wings and calls flock.'
The earlier specimens of this class show more control and have more
power than the later. A long sequence called 'The Venice Poem' is
concerned with jealousy:

> When you lie in bed and know with a start
> that the vows are broken—You face with a grin
> and damn your mind that searches the fact
> that your lover lies panting in a new lover's arms,
> holds on and comes in some secret room
> lifted again to the passionate pitch.
>                              BANG.

Mr. Duncan frames his fairly explicit stanzas, of which these lines are
a part, in a mass of allusions to Shakespeare and Othello, Venice and
Venus, a bust of Louis XIV and a statue of Venus. One can follow
the thematic connexions. But among them he drops a question
apparently directed at the lost lover, and dealing, in a ludicrous
spasm of domesticity, with 'a row of stainless aluminium pots'.
Similarly, a train of remarks on the genitals of Louis XIV and bug-
gery leads into this:

> 'We must understand what is happening';
> watch 'the duration of syllables
>     'the melodic coherence,
>     'the tone leading of vowels'
> 'The function of poetry is to debunk by lucidity.'

Ultimately Mr. Duncan's methods operate best for those who
know him well as a friend. Outsiders cannot hope to appreciate the
subtleties of his technique because they cannot be sure of his tone,
form, or allusions. When the theme of a poem is obvious, as in the
witty 'Re', which is about springtime, we may join the smaller circle.
Otherwise, we must accept our limitations. Not everyone can live in
California.

Together, the two volumes, *The First Decade* and *Derivations*,
comprise a selection of Mr. Duncan's work from 1940 to 1956.
Still waiting for us, therefore, are the achievements of the past
thirteen years.

# 13

# POETS IN CORRESPONDENCE

## (a) EDWARD THOMAS/
## GORDON BOTTOMLEY

AMONG BRITISH POETS, Edward Thomas must surely be unique in that he took up poetry for the first time in his mid-thirties, lived his entire poetic life in less than three years, and died without seeing a single poem published under his name. 'Did anyone ever begin at 36 in the shade?' he asked his friend Eleanor Farjeon. Nobody did, except him, and one wonders at the forces in his nature, in his life, and in society that pressed him to that brief achievement, so personal, so solitary, and so sure.

The story up to the day in 1914 when Thomas became a poet is the dreariest Grub Street history. Married while still an undergraduate, and a father six months later, he came down to London without money or influence or even parental approval, to support his family as a writer. Inevitably he became a hack (and that *is* the right word), editing, compiling, reviewing whatever came along, meeting impossible deadlines, hating his work and himself for doing it. He wrote in all nearly sixty books, of which perhaps seven or eight—mainly the posthumously published poems—could be described as voluntary work. The others were written to order, and at rates that made extraordinary speed necessary (six books appeared in one year, 1911).

At the same time Thomas was reviewing constantly, whatever editors would send him; volumes of mediocre verse, books on books, and more and more, as he established a reputation, books on country life. In 1904 he wrote to Bottomley: "Perhaps the 'man & a landscape" plan has a future for me.' It did: a future of reviewing books called *Peeps into Nature's Ways*, *A Country Diary*, and *Travels round our Village*, and of adding his own titles to that vast Edwardian

---

(a) R. GEORGE THOMAS (Editor): *Letters from Edward Thomas to Gordon Bottomley*. 302 pp. Oxford University Press. £3 3s.

(b) FORREST READ (Editor): *Pound/Joyce*. The Letters of Ezra Pound to James Joyce, with Pound's Essays on Joyce. 314 pp. Faber and Faber. £3 10s.

sub-genre, The English Countryside Book. His first book was *The Woodland Life*, and before his drudgery was done he had also written or edited *Beautiful Wales*, *The Heart of England*, *The Book of the Open Air*, *The South Country*, *The Country*, and *In Pursuit of Spring*, and had written lives of Jefferies and Borrow.

Thomas's nature writing was good of its kind and time—it was accurate of flora and fauna, and made its nightingales sing at the proper season—but it was also decorated, literary, and a bit arch. It was to the great tradition of English natural history what Georgian poetry was to the Romantic tradition—the exhausted fag-end. Thomas himself described his *Heart of England* as 'pseudogenial or purely rustic—Borrow & Jefferies sans testicles & guts', and his harsh judgment will do for more nature-writing of the time than his alone—will do for the *Peeps* and the *Diaries* and the *Travels*, and for most of the country poems in *Georgian Poetry*. The whole lot expresses that Edwardian desire to keep English traditions alive beyond their time that one finds in so many aspects of the prewar period (in the House of Lords, for example). Faith in England and faith in Nature had become conventions, charms to hold the twentieth century at bay.

Thomas's books on Jefferies and Borrow are still worth reading because he cared for his subjects, and to a degree identified with them, but the other literary studies—the books on Maeterlinck, Lafcadio Hearn, Swinburne, and Pater—are less worthy. Like his nature books, they were all done hastily and on commission: none of the subjects appealed to Thomas and some he actively disliked. Because he was a conscientious writer, and because he had a deep love of letters, his criticism was never worthless; but the work is essentially Edwardian literary journalism, and though it is better than most of its kind, it is not good enough to survive. Circumstances compelled him to take whatever work came his way, but he was too serious to write superficially, and too gifted to write badly, and so he made a poor hack. He spent his talents, and most of his life, in the manufacture of literary mediocrity that he could not even do well. Small wonder, one may think, that he was chronically melancholy, that he took opium, that he contemplated suicide.

Thomas's melancholia was more than a consequence of misfortune, though; it was a part of his nature. 'I suppose every man thinks that Hamlet was written for him', he told Eleanor Farjeon, 'but I *know* he was written for me.' He had, as he put it, a habit of introspection and self-contempt, and he brooded self-consciously upon his excessive self-consciousness. What he saw, when he examined his own exist-ence, was a life of labour that was both endless and valueless: 'Think of the pain', he wrote to his friend Bottomley, 'going on living & not being able to do anything but eat & drink & earn a living for 5 people.' Many an industrial worker must have felt that pain before and after, but it was a peculiar accomplishment of late Victorian and Edwardian England that it made the life of letters a dark satanic mill for men as gifted as Thomas and Gissing.

The cure for this state was clear: a decent income and a little leisure. Lacking these, Thomas sought help from nerve specialists and medicines and diets; he gave up butcher's meat and tobacco, and he sought changes of climate and company. Most of all he sought out that stock romantic dose against melancholy, communion with Nature. Alone, or with his wife or a friend, he went on prodigi-ous walks (often note-taking as he went, since there was usually some nature book to be written) until he had a footpath knowledge of most of Southern England and Wales. But all his walking seems only to have proved that Nature *will* betray the heart that loves her, if that heart is troubled enough and poor enough. Thomas remained a tormented man, hating his life and himself, even hating his profile.

Thomas's private letters during those Grub Street years make bitter reading: they are not so much communications as written groans. A change came into his life, and into his letters, in 1914: 'I have given up groaning', he wrote to Bottomley, 'since the war began.' What Nature could not do, War had done. It may seem odd that so catastrophic an event had raised his spirits, but anyone who was young and male in 1939 will recognize the experience; War had taken over, and had liberated individuals from their drab responsibilities. In a nation at war, Thomas's precarious life as a writer was impossible; there was almost no work to be had. The only courses open, it seemed, were emigration to America, or en-listment. For a time Thomas did neither, but simply drifted, 'getting little scraps of work', he wrote, 'that prevent me from quite seriously facing questions'. He wrote one substantial book, a life of the Duke of Marlborough; and having finished it, he wrote to Bottomley in June, 1915: 'Now I am going to cycle & think of man & nature & human life & decide between enlisting or going to America before I enlist.' The next month he enlisted. He served for a time as an in-structor of troops in England, was commissioned in the Artillery, and volunteered for service in France. He was killed there in the Battle of Arras, April 9, 1917.

The sense of relief that one finds in Thomas's letters after August, 1914, is partly his response to the release from responsibility that war, and especially service in a war, brings to men. But in Thomas's case there was an additional factor; shortly before the war he had met Robert Frost, who had told him what perhaps anyone might have said, but Frost had to—that Thomas had been a poet all his life. 'You are a poet', Frost said, 'or you are nothing', and the fact that this was so seems to have affected Thomas as another sort of enlistment; he had joined the armies of poetry.

The effect of Frost on his new friend was instantaneous and striking—the more so if one considers that Thomas had been consorting with poets all his adult life. He had been exchanging letters and visits with Gordon Bottomley for more than ten years, yet Bottomley had not made him into a poet: he knew many of the other Georgians —Abercrombie, Brooke, de la Mare, Freeman, Gibson, Trevelyan —but none had turned him from his prose life. In less than a year of talk and friendship, Frost undammed Thomas's poetic talent, and showed it how to flow.

What Frost did was simply to show Thomas how one might write verse about natural things without sounding like Thomas's own prose—without sounding, that is, like *Georgian Poetry*. Thomas recognized at once what he had been given; his review of *North of Boston*, written in June, 1914, begins, 'This is one of the most revolutionary books of modern times, but one of the quietest and least aggressive'. Farther along in the review he spelt out what he meant:

These poems are revolutionary because they lack the exaggeration of rhetoric, and even at first sight appear to lack the poetic intensity of which rhetoric is an imitation. Their language is free from the poetical words and forms that are the chief material of secondary poets. The metre avoids not only the old-fashioned pomp and sweetness, but the later fashion also of discord and fuss. In fact, the medium is common speech and common decasyllables. . . . Yet almost all these poems are beautiful. They depend not at all on objects commonly admitted to be beautiful: neither have they merely a homely beauty, but are often grand, sometimes magical. Many, if not most, of the separate lines and separate sentences are plain and, in themselves, nothing. But they are bound together and made elements of beauty by a calm eagerness of emotion.

In praising Frost, Thomas was composing his own programme; there is nothing in that paragraph that could not be said of Thomas's own plain and lovely poems.

Though Thomas met Frost in 1913, and saw much of him in the first months of 1914, he did not begin to write poems until the autumn, when Frost had returned to America. Then, with war ahead and his journalistic sources drying up, he could write wryly to Eleanor Farjeon: 'One may as well write poems.' The poems, once he began, came freely, so freely that he worried whether his 'delight in the new freedom' might have led him to write too readily, 'to accept intimations merely'. In a little more than two years' time, of which most was spent on active, wartime service, he wrote the 141 poems that are in his *Collected Poems*.

Thomas's attitude towards his poems shows how different this new life of writing was for him; the poems were written out of private impulses, and he showed no interest in identifying them publicly with the Edward Thomas who wrote prose about nature. The drafts of poems that he sent to Eleanor Farjeon to be typed were often written out without line-divisions, as prose; Thomas explained that when he copied them out he was among his comrades, and he did not want the other soldiers to know him as a poet. Those few that he sent out to editors went under the name of 'Edward Eastaway', and he did not seem troubled when they were rejected. Only a few were published during his lifetime, all pseudonymously.

The pseudonym was necessary, Thomas explained, because people were likely to be prejudiced for or against Edward Thomas—that is, readers would associate the poems with what he had done in prose. By choosing the pseudonym, Thomas accepted the failure of his past, prose-writing self, and buried that self in his name; when he was a poet he was another person. Certainly his friends saw some such transformation take place: the war, Frost observed, 'has made some sort of new man and poet of Edward Thomas'.

The poems that this new man, 'Edward Eastaway', wrote were both new and old. They were new in that they were unlike the fashion of Georgian poetry, and a reaction against it; but they belonged to an old and strong English tradition of nature poetry, and they helped to extend that tradition into the twentieth century. An approximate way of making the distinction clear might be to say that Georgians like Brooke and Abercrombie were poetic 'insiders', and that Thomas belonged to the 'outsider' tradition. The insiders found their relations with Nature comfortable, and their sentiments appropriate and ready, because they wrote from a conventional intimacy with the natural world. The Georgians, one might say, were poetical *rentiers*, spending the capital that their Romantic ancestors had earned.

The outsider is the poet who approaches Nature directly and without assumptions. He will find there emotions that are colder and stronger than an insider would, and he will make cold, strong poems out of them ('a calm eagerness of emotion', Thomas said). Such poetry is solitary, sometimes fearful, never cosy; it is concerned with darkness, and with death, sometimes with violence, and it can be tragic. (The poems of Hardy are full of examples: 'The Fallow Deer at the Lonely House' is a good one that resembles one of Thomas's best, 'Out of the Dark'.) In this poetry, Nature offers no assurances, and only the coldest of comforts: it says, what Georgian poetry never admitted, that man in a landscape is alone.

Thomas's proper poetic company is clear, then: it is that tradition of outsiders which descends in modern poetry from Hardy, through Frost to Thomas, and includes the early, rhyming Lawrence, Edmund Blunden, Robert Graves, Andrew Young, and R. S. Thomas. Together these poets compose a major modern tradition, less noisy than the School of Pound, and without the convenience of a collective name (perhaps that is why this 'quiet tradition' has never been anthologized as a group), but important nevertheless, poets of fine achievement.

'Edward Eastaway' read only one review of his work, that in the *TLS* of March 29, 1917, of an anthology, *An Annual of New Poetry, 1917*, published by Constable, in which six of his poems appeared. The reviewer recognized that Thomas was 'a real poet, with the truth in him', but he also recognized, and was alarmed by, Thomas's 'outsider' quality. Comparing Thomas to Wordsworth, he wrote: 'Mr. Eastaway makes his poem wholly out of the natural fact. Wordsworth passes from it at once to human things.' The point, as he realized, was whether one saw man and landscape as a consoling unity, or as two solitudes. Thomas read the review with approval, and observed, 'I don't mind now being called inhuman'. Reading through the *Collected Poems* one will scarcely think inhuman the right word, but Thomas and his reviewer were justly observing, each in his own terms, a true quality of the poetry—its austere comfortlessness. The natural world is there, in all its beauty, as fact; but in it man lives a mortal and solitary life. The whole attitude is summed up in the last line of one of Thomas's best poems:

There's nothing like the sun till we are dead.

That blunt, monosyllabic line will do as an example of Thomas's formal intentions, too. 'If I am consciously doing anything', he wrote to Eleanor Farjeon, 'I am trying to get rid of the last rags of rhetoric and formality which left my prose so often with a dead rhythm only.' In poetry, honesty has its own sound, and when conventional ideas go the formal conventions must follow. Thomas offended his Georgian friends, with his 'everyday syntax', but it is that rough, blunter-than-conversation style that makes him seem more modern than they (in the same way that Hardy's harshness seems modern); even in his sentimental moods, Thomas's poems have a saving gracelessness.

Because Thomas came late to his poetic life, and left it early, his work has an unusual unity; there are no juvenilia, and no significant variations in matter or tone. The making of the man came first— and the letters record how painful that process was—and then the swift body of poetry that expressed his maturity. 'God bless us all', he wrote to Bottomley.

what a thing it is to be nearing 40 & to know what one likes & know one makes mistakes & yet is right for oneself. How many things I have thought I ought to like & found reasons for liking. But now it is almost like eating apples. I don't pretend to know about pineapples & persimmons, but I know an apple when I smell it, when it makes me swallow my saliva before biting it.

He had come a long way to reach that confidence, where living was like eating apples. And he had brought his troubles, his melancholy nature with him. But he had found somehow the refining process by which melancholy becomes poetry, no longer personal and corroding but creative.

When an edition of Thomas's letters was being considered in the late 1920s, John Freeman wrote:

I doubt if they are of general interest; they are mainly upon purely literary subjects . . . and I don't think they are particularly good or self-expressive. And where they are self-expressive they are inevitably melancholy.

Mr. George Thomas deplores this remark, but the evidence that he offers in *Letters from Edward Thomas to Gordon Bottomley* supports Freeman—these are not particularly good or self-expressive letters. Of the 182 letters Bottomley included, the best—some two dozen—

are quoted in John Moore's *Life and Letters of Edward Thomas*, and
the new ones add little new information. They tell us what a kind and
generous man Bottomley was, and they record Thomas's melancholy
in some detail; but Thomas's friendship with Bottomley was not
really intimate, and one gets a more revealing picture from his
letters to Eleanor Farjeon. On the other hand, the Farjeon memoir
covers only the 'Edward Eastaway' part of Thomas's life, whereas
the Bottomley letters run from 1902 until Thomas's death, and so fill
out the story. For the scholarly student, the Bottomley letters will be
useful, as the Moore and Farjeon books are useful; but the reader of
the poems will not really need any of them—the poems are enough.

## (b) EZRA POUND/JAMES JOYCE

IN DECEMBER, 1913, Ezra Pound and W. B. Yeats were living in
Stone Cottage, Coleman's Hatch, Sussex, 'by the waste moor/(or
whatever)', as Pound recalls that winter in *Canto LXXXIII*. The plan
was that Pound would act as Yeats's secretary. In the event, he also
gave Yeats instruction in the art of fencing, read 'nearly all Wordsworth' and something less than all of Doughty's *The Dawn in Britain*.
Yeats bore with Wordsworth for the good of his conscience, but he
preferred Joseph Ennemosor's book on Magic. Pound was labouring
with Ernest Fenollosa's notes on the Chinese language, writing some
new poems, and preparing *Des Imagistes*. One day he asked Yeats
'whether there were any poets in Ireland fit to contribute to an
anthology of poetry unlike his own'; that is, any Imagists still free
from Celtic twilight. Yeats mentioned a poem beginning, 'I hear an
army charging upon the land', by a young Irishman called James
Joyce. It is clear now that Yeats liked the poem at least partly
because it resembled his own 'I hear the Shadowy Waters'.

Pound wrote off to Joyce, who was in Trieste. At this point he had
not yet read Joyce's poem, but Yeats's word was good enough.
In the first letter Pound introduced himself as a literary man connected with serious magazines like *Poetry* and *The Smart Set*.
Perhaps Joyce might like to send some pieces for publication. 'I
am bonae voluntatis', Pound assured the young man. A few days later
he had read the poem; 'we are both much impressed by it'. 'Despite
the old lavender of his Chamber Music', Pound recalled many years
later, 'this poem, because of the definiteness of the visual image it

presents, had an affinity with the aims of the then nascent Imagist group.' Joyce replied at once, giving Pound permission to use the poem, and sending him a batch of stories from *Dubliners*. Within a few weeks he sent the first chapter of *A Portrait of the Artist as a Young Man*. Pound was delighted, sent the stories to *The Smart Set*, and the chapter to *The Egoist*. A relationship had begun.

Between 1913 and 1920 Pound wrote about eighty letters to Joyce. Sixty-two of these have survived and are now the property of Cornell University Library. Joyce wrote about sixty letters to Pound during the same period, but most of these have been lost. Pound also published several essays on Joyce's work; some of these are readily available, but other pieces have not been reprinted. A few items in fugitive magazines are hard to find. *Pound/Joyce* gathers together, as Mr. Forrest Read says, 'all of Pound's surviving letters to Joyce, most of which are published for the first time, all of his essays and articles on Joyce's work, his radio broadcast, various anecdotes of the time, and a number of miscellaneous pieces and extracts'. The editorial work is excellent, the linking commentary lucid and tactful.

It is a great pity that Joyce's part in the correspondence has been lost. Pound's part was always practical, energetic, selfless. He sent Joyce's stuff to the magazines, lobbied influential men for money, encouraged Joyce in his work, put *Ulysses* into the *Little Review*. He was, in short, magnificent. He offered Joyce advice, but he was not visibly annoyed when the offer was refused: he gave it anyway. When he read the 'Calypso' chapter of *Ulysses* he thought parts of it excessive. 'Leave the stool to Geo. Robey', he advised, 'he has been doing "down where the asparagus grows" for some time.' The *Little Review* had just then been suppressed. If Wyndham Lewis's *Cantleman's Spring Mate* could not get through the law, there was no hope for Leopold Bloom at the jakes. Besides, Pound was not convinced of the artistic necessity. 'The contrast between Bloom's interior poetry and his outward surroundings is excellent, but it will come up without such detailed treatment of the dropping feces.' Lest two inoffensive editresses should go to gaol in a doubtful artistic cause, Pound excised about twenty lines from the description of Bloom on the lavatory. Joyce insisted, of course, that they be restored for the book. When the 'Sirens' chapter arrived, Pound had the same misgivings about asparagus. Joyce had gone down 'as far as the lector most bloody benevolens can be expected to respire'. The subject was 'good enough to hold attention without being so all-bloodily friccaseed'. As a general principle: 'One *can* fahrt with less pomp & circumstance.' Finally, Pound expressed a preference for phallic rather than excremental concerns: 'purely personal—know mittel europa humour runs to other orifice'. Nevertheless, he continued: 'I dont arsk you to erase.'

It was all urbane at this stage. Pound never moved far from his sense of Joyce as a prose Imagist, and he lost interest in the man when he found that sense impossible to maintain in the queer light of *Work in Progress*. The great modern artist in prose was the author of *Dubliners*, the *Portrait*, and *Ulysses*. Pound's position was clear. 'Mr. Joyce writes a clear hard prose', he said in July, 1914, giving in one sentence the gist of his entire critique. He had very little more to say on the subject, but he said the same thing ten times:

It is a joy then to find in Mr. Joyce a hardness and gauntness, like the side of an engine; efficient; clear statement, no shadow of comment, and behind it a sense of beauty that never relapses into ornament.

There was very little English prose worth reading alongside Flaubert: James, Hardy, perhaps Conrad, Joyce and Ford were the new masters. 'Mr. Joyce is the best prose writer of my generation in English.' By these standards, Shaw was trivial, 'the intellectual cheese-mite', Arnold Bennett was cheap, H. G. Wells's style was 'greasy in comparison with the metallic cleanness of Joyce's phrasing', even D. H. Lawrence was inferior with his 'loaded ornate style heavy with sex, fruity with a certain sort of emotion'.

The same standards, and many of the same phrases, are enforced in the *Imaginary Letters* which Pound took over from Wyndham Lewis. In prose, Joyce was the civilized master, the cosmopolitan, 'the stylist', like Ford in *Mauberley*. Indeed, it was probably Joyce's example which prompted Pound to a theory of prose which he outlined in the Henry James number of the *Little Review*; that 'most good prose arises, perhaps, from an instinct of negation; is the detailed, convincing analysis of something detestable: of something which one wants to eliminate'. Poetry, on the other hand, 'is the assertion of a positive, i.e., of desire, and remains, endures for a longer period'. The real function of good prose is to get rid of mush.

Flaubert pointed out that if France had studied his work they might have been saved a good deal in 1870. If more people had read the *Portrait* and certain stories in Mr. Joyce's *Dubliners* there might have been less recent trouble in Ireland. A clear diagnosis is never without its value.

The date is 1917.

So Pound attended to his discovery. In return, Joyce took very little interest in Pound, except as a wonder-working impresario. There is no evidence that he cared, one way or another, for Pound's poetry. He ignored Pound's criticism. It was prudent to keep in with Harriet Weaver, since the customer is always right, but Pound's comments could be disregarded.

I never listened to his objections to Ulysses as it was being sent to him, once I had made up my mind, but dodged them as tactfully as I could. He understood certain aspects of that book very quickly and that was more than enough then. He makes brilliant discoveries and howling blunders.

In any event, Joyce was engrossed in his own case. Pound might be *il miglior fabbro* to Eliot, but he had no such contract with Joyce.

Things began to cool off, as far as the public record shows, in 1926. when Pound received samples of the new work.

I will have another go at it, but up to present I make nothing of it whatever. Nothing so far as I make out, nothing short of divine vision or a new cure for the clapp can possibly be worth all the circumambient peripherization.

*Work in Progress* was an extreme case of Gongorism. Worse, it looked back, and the true direction was forward. Joyce was Lot's wife. Pound never came to terms with the new work, 'that diarrhoea of consciousness', and he resented the fact that Joyce had closed his mind to the twentieth century. At a time when imprudent men were quarrelling over politics, Mussolini, Hitler, economics, American presidents, Major Douglas, Russia, and other contemporary matters, Jim the Penman was otherwise engaged. The rebuke is still couched in Imagist terms, 'Joyce's mind has been deprived of Joyce's eyesight for too long.' And Pound wrote in 1934:

He has sat within the grove of his thought, he has mumbled things to himself, he has heard his voice on the phonograph and thought of sound, sound, mumble, murmur.

In effect, it was the same criticism which Yeats addressed to Pound and Joyce in his essay on Berkeley. Yeats thought both men manifested the new naturalism.

The romantic movement with its turbulent heroism, its self-assertion, is over; superseded by a new naturalism that leaves man helpless before the contents of his own mind.

Wyndham Lewis made a similar report in *Time and Western Man*

and *Men without Art*. Pound thought himself free from this rebuke,
perhaps because of the purity of his intention, his Imagist conviction,
and his concern for the new world of politics. But Joyce, he thought,
was guilty. Pound turned away toward Lewis, Ford, Eliot, Brancusi
and Cummings. 'I prefer *The Apes of God* to anything Mr. Joyce has
written since Molly finished her Molly-logue.' Cummings was good,
*Eimi* was a new thing, looking ahead.

But the cooling off had probably begun long before *Work in
Progress*. When Pound and Joyce met for the first time, in Desenzano
and Sirmione, June, 1920, the occasion went off well. 'Joyce—
pleasing', Pound reported to John Quinn:

After the first shell of cantankerous Irishman, I got the impression that the
real man is the author of *Chamber Music*, the sensitive. The rest is the
genius; the registration of realities on the temperament, the delicate
temperament of the early poems.

But the two men were not really kin. Certainly when Joyce arrived in
Paris in July, he began to move away from his impresario. New ad-
juncts to the Muse's diadem had little or nothing to do with Pound's
interest: Sylvia Beach, Adrienne Monnier, Valery Larbaud, later
Eugene Jolas. Pound himself soon tired of Paris, longed for Italy.
In 1924 he was in Rapallo. In 1926 he refused to help Joyce in an
international protest against Samuel Roth's piracy of *Ulysses*. In
1927 Joyce consulted him on the question of a new collection of
poems, the verses he had written since *Chamber Music*. Pound read
the poems, and told Joyce they belonged with the family album
and the portraits. No, they were not worth reprinting. Joyce was
hurt. But he already felt that he and Pound lived in alien worlds.
Writing to Harriet Weaver in 1928 he said:—

The more I hear of the political, philosophical, ethical zeal and labours
of the brilliant members of Pound's big brass band the more I wonder
why I was ever let into it 'with my magic flute'.

The answer is that he was let into the band because his music reminded Pound of certain indispensable sounds, once heard in Flaubert and Gautier. The proof is in 'James Joyce et Pécuchet', one of
Pound's last and ripest acknowledgements, printed appropriately
in the *Mercure de France*, June, 1922. It was enough for Pound to
discover in Joyce the temper of *Chamber Music* and the style of
*L'Education sentimentale*. What he could not bear, in the later Joyce,
was the egotistical sublime; or the mushy form it took.

He moved away from Joyce, but he never lost his affection for him, or devotion to his genius. *Ulysses* was indelible. The *Portrait* showed how prose should be written. *Dubliners* was the thing itself. Even *Exiles* had its point, though Pound seriously exaggerated its merit when he read it first, thinking that anything by this author must be excellent. Gradually he came to feel that the play was a necessary error, a transition. At the end, he knew that it was not much good. Still, it did not matter. The great work was accomplished, and Pound had helped to bring it out. Perhaps Pound felt that his labour in Joyce's behalf might have been more richly acknowledged. Certainly Joyce's indifference to Pound's own struggles in the *Cantos* was a shabby thing. The only point to be made is that he treated Pound as he treated other writers who befriended him.

It was an interesting relationship, up to a point. But beyond that point its shallowness begins to emerge. Pound's relationship with Eliot is of an entirely different order, much deeper. It is appropriate to reflect upon Pound's critical role in the development of *The Waste Land*; to reflect also upon Eliot's magnanimity, the grace with which he received that favour. To think of Joyce sending chapters of *Ulysses* to Pound is to realize that he treated Pound as his literary agent, his messenger boy, nothing more. There is, indeed, a certain splendour in Joyce's arrogance; it inspires awe. But Pound's selflessness, his care, his generosity; these inspire affection.

But even in the later years the relationship was not completely lost. In December, 1931, Pound wrote to Joyce from Rapallo, taking care to add the words 'Anno X' to the address, the tenth year of the Fascist calendar. He wanted to know something more of Blarney Castle than could be divined from the well-known ballad. Was the custom of kissing the Blarney stone a survival of some fecundity ritual, perhaps?

I mean when did fat ladies from Schenekdety or Donegal first begin to be held by their tootsies with their hoopskirts falling over their privates to in public osculate . . . Whose stone, in short, was it?

Joyce replied:

Dear Pound: There is nothing phallic about the Blarney Stone, so far as I know. The founder of the castle was a cunctator (or perhaps it was the defender of it). He kept on inventing excuses, parlays, etc., during its siege, I think in the time of Essex. The stone is flat and so far as I can remember let into the wall a few feet below a window. I never understood why it could not have been kissed from a ladder. I heard there were double bands of elastic to fasten the women's dresses. I did not kiss the stone myself.

That seemed to dispose of the matter. But many years and many sorrows later Pound recalled the little incident. In *Canto LXXIV*, one of the *Pisan Cantos*, he rehearses old affections:

> Lordly men are to earth o'ergiven
>     these the companions:
> Fordie that wrote of giants
>     and William who dreamed of nobility
> and Jim the comedian singing:
>     'Blarrney castle me darlin'
>     you're nothing now but a StOWne.'

So the affection endured, at least on one side. As Pound wrote in a later Canto,

> nothing matters but the quality
> of the affection—
> in the end.

# 14

# RIOT AND REPRESSION

## (a) MAN BITES YEOMAN

THE 150th anniversary of the massacre at St. Peter's Fields, in Manchester, on August 16, 1819, saw the appearance of three new publications, two of which may be described as occasional. The first is a well-presented folder of plans, prints, and broadsides, prepared by the Manchester Public Libraries. The second is a popular account ('the first book for the general reader', as the blurb has it) by Miss Joyce Marlow. The bias of her book appears to be, like her maternal descent, of 'Radical, Unitarian, small mill-owning stock'; and the general reader may sometimes find that her folksy narrative—'Bamford's wife, Mima, a sterling character, made determined efforts to ascertain what had happened to "our Sam" . . . '—tends to cloy. Miss Marlow offers some general background to explain what led up to Peterloo; this is second-hand and generally over-simplified; but her narrative of the events of the day itself is closely-observed, well-written, and deftly employs a little original material. On this account her book deserves to find some readers; although the *first* book for the general reader must remain, as it has always been, Samuel Bamford's *Passages in the Life of a Radical*.

Bamford's evidence is not, of course, privileged and beyond reach of examination. He was one of the crowd ridden down by Yeomanry and Hussars—a thing likely to induce bias in the victims. And he was later found guilty before a special jury at York Assizes for 'assembling with unlawful banners, at an unlawful meeting, for the purpose of inciting the subjects of our lord the king, to contempt and

---

(a) *Peterloo, 1819.* A Portfolio of Contemporary Documents. Manchester Public Libraries. 20s.

JOYCE MARLOW. *The Peterloo Massacre.* 238 pp. Rapp and Whiting. £2 2s.

ROBERT WALMSLEY: *Peterloo: The Case Reopened.* 585 pp. Manchester University Press. £4 10s.

(b) E. J. HOBSBAWM and GEORGE RUDÉ: *Captain Swing.* 384 pp. Lawrence and Wishart. £3 10s.

hatred of the government', and sentenced to one year's imprisonment. This clear decision in an impartial court of justice suggests him not only as a biased but also as a compromised witness. No matter such as this escapes the watchful eye of Mr. Robert Walmsley.

Mr. Walmsley's *Peterloo: The Case Reopened* is not so much occasioned by the anniversary; it is, in itself, an occasion, and is—the blurb tells us—'the fruit of half a lifetime's research'. The 585 pages of this fruit swing from the impeccable bough of the Manchester University Press. Mr. Walmsley, a Manchester antiquarian bookseller, first had his interest in Peterloo aroused some thirty years ago during the course of research into the family history of the Hultons of Hulton. William Hulton (1787–1864) was chairman of the magistrates who overlooked the field of Peterloo and gave to the Yeomanry the fatal order to advance. In the course of his researches Mr. Walmsley became convinced, not only that William Hulton had been unfairly treated by historians, but that he and his fellow magistrates were the victims of nothing less than a Radical conspiracy to falsify the events of that day—a conspiracy fostered by Hunt, Bamford, and Richard Carlile, furthered by Archibald Prentice (author of *Historical Sketches of Manchester*) and John Edward Taylor (before he sobered down and founded the *Manchester Guardian*), and in which John Tyas (the correspondent of *The Times* who witnessed events from the hustings), the Rev. Edward Stanley, and dozens of others were witting or unwitting accessories—a conspiracy so compelling that even Donald Read, in his sober and by no means radical study of *Peterloo* (1957), failed to detect it.

It is necessary to make clear what Mr. Walmsley's book is not, as well as what it is. It is not a general interpretative account of Peterloo within its political or local background. Nothing is said of radicalism or reaction before January, 1819; very little is said about the government of Manchester in 1819, or to explain the character, role, or reputation of such important actors as Joseph Nadin or Henry Hunt before they emerge on the 1819 stage. This is not a book for the general reader, unless he has taken the precaution of reading (at least) Bamford—or Prentice—and Dr. Read beforehand. Nor is it, altogether, a book for the scholar, although it has competent scholarly apparatus, adequate footnotes and bibliography, and a very good index. It is not based on extensive newly discovered evidence, although Mr. Walmsley introduces interesting new material from the Rev. W. R. Hay (the prominent clerical magistrate) and from William Hulton himself. In particular there has been no new search of Home Office, legal, or military papers in the Public Record Office.

Such new material as there is relates largely to the Hultons of Hulton. We learn not only that there was a Ranulph Hulton who was sub-deacon at Manchester Collegiate Church in 1465 but (more interestingly) that William's mother's horse 'Church and King' won the Kersal Moor races in 1794; and we are given a most revealing view of William himself, addressing the anniversary dinner of the Manchester Pitt Club two years before Peterloo, proposing the toast, 'The Pride of Britain and the Admiration of the World—Our Glorious Constitution', and rolling around the room the unabashed and unalloyed clichés of the British ancien régime:

Under this vast aegis repose our liberties, encircled with wisely-ordained laws, and blessed with the sanction of a pure religion. . . . Shall we then, sell the black-letter volumes of our great charters for any spurious editions printed with type of the National Convention, for Cochrane, Burdett and Company?

If Mr. Walmsley had confined himself to writing a brief biography of William Hulton he would have served historians well. It would have seemed somewhat quaint and provincial, smelling of fine vellum and reverence; and in such a work an exculpatory chapter on Peterloo would have passed without remark. But this chapter has expanded to become some 500 pages of Mr. Walmsley's text, and it cannot pass without remark. Nor has it. One of the book's more ecstatic reviewers (in the *Daily Telegraph*) has declared that Mr. Walmsley's 'massive research challenges the accepted version', his book 'leaves no fact unchallenged and uncorroborated, no document unread *in full*, no source unchecked', and that it 'utterly discredits' the accounts in Prentice and Bamford. Not very many readers, perhaps, will struggle their whole way through the book; and of those who do even fewer will follow, point by point, its exceedingly repetitious, but at the same time involuted apologetics. But all —or nearly all—will come from it with a bemused impression that, in all this turning and wheeling around a few points, something must have been proved, somebody must have been exposed. And as such the book will enter the folklore of history.

Mr. Walmsley is interested, chiefly, in the events of the day of Peterloo, and even more closely in the events of one half-hour of that

day—between 1.15 and 1.45 p.m.—from the time when Henry Hunt
arrived on the hustings to the time when the field was empty of all but
shawls, bonnets, sticks, and cavalry adjusting their saddle-girths.
Obsessively he rides up and down that field and its environs, obsessively he rides up and down the five or ten minutes between the
arrival of the Yeomanry at the edge of the field and the dispersal
of the crowd, summoning witnesses in the newspaper press of the
weeks following, dragging them back by their collars, making them
pace over the yards before and behind the hustings, cross-examining
reminiscences and confronting them with conflicting depositions,
galloping off into the suburbs of the twentieth century to interrogate
suspicious stragglers, like F. A. Bruton, the author of the careful
*The Story of Peterloo* (1919).

At the centre of his obsession is this: what happened on that day
was unintentional, and the crowd (or part of it) was the first aggres-
sor. The magistrates in their house overlooking the hustings were
justly alarmed by the proceedings, both by tumults which had preceded August 16 and by the radical rhetoric and military array of the
crowd on the day. With a nice sense of legalistic propriety they waited
until Hunt and his fellow speakers were on the hustings and then
ordered the constables to arrest them; this Joseph Nadin, the deputy-
constable, refused to do without military aid; the magistrates sent
for Yeomanry and Hussars, and the Yeomanry arrived first, fortuitously; the Yeomanry were ordered to support the constables in the
execution of the warrant, and they advanced in reasonable order and
without aggressive intention or action into the crowd; but the crowd
then closed in upon them in a menacing manner and the Yeomanry
were assailed, at some point close to the hustings, by brickbats and
sticks hurled by a portion of the crowd; most of the Yeomanry
kept their heads until Hunt and his fellows had been arrested, and
then, increasingly assailed by brickbats and hemmed in on all sides
by a threatening crowd, were forced to beat off their attackers (with
the *flats* of their sabres) in self-defence. The magistrates, observing
their predicament in the midst of a threatening multitude, were
forced to order the Hussars to come to their rescue and to clear the
field. All followed on. And the radicals have made party-political
propaganda out of their own aggression ever since.

One needs a book like this, every now and then, to recall that the
patron saint of historians is St. Sisyphus. Before we enquire what
facts he has actually adduced, Mr. Walmsley must be acquitted of

one charge. He is certainly not guilty of wilful suppression or dis-
tortion, although there are many inconvenient facts unmentioned and
others which are bludgeoned into unrecognizable pulp. He could not
have written this book unless he believed in its truth, obsessively. No
one but a true Church-and-King believer, an authentic descendant
and vindicator of the shopkeepers on horseback who made up the
Manchester Yeomanry, could have cantered, brandishing his sword
of polemic, into so many blind alleys of argument as he has. The
printed—and, to historians, long known and readily available—
documents which he quotes, he quotes repetitiously and in full.

Yet the fact is that Mr. Walmsley has *no* new facts to adduce about
this half-hour. His book is a sustained essay in special pleading
about minutiae, in which he is very much disposed to believe that A
did happen and very much disposed to believe that B did not happen.
Such a conviction, sustained over 500 pages, is bound—whatever the
press of defenceless facts against it—to reach the hustings in the end
and to cut down the 'radical' flags. Nevertheless, let us follow Mr.
Walmsley on to his chosen part of the field.

Did the Yeomanry ride quietly up to the hustings to effect the
arrests, or did they (as 'radicals' mythologize) begin to strike out
with their sabres from their first entry into the crowd? Were they
attacked, before they reached the hustings, by sticks and brickbats?
The overwhelming majority of witnesses to these events may be
suspected of 'prejudice', as parties to the event, since the greater part
belonged to the crowd who were ridden into, and the remainder
belonged to the magistracy, special constables, and the Yeomanry
who did the riding. Their evidence is not therefore worthless,
since they were subject to cross-examination in the courts, and betrayed the customary signs of veracity or inconsistency. However,
historians, from 1819 until 1969, have attempted to simplify the extreme difficulties of sifting this evidence (and the reports of partisan
newspapers, on either side) by looking for witnesses who cannot be
accused of belonging, in any obvious sense, to either contesting party.
There *are* a few such observers: uncommitted and merely curious
spectators on the fringes of the crowd: householders whose windows
overlooked the field: and (notably) several press reporters who
were afforded places on the hustings—John Tyas of *The Times*, John
Smith of the *Liverpool Mercury*, Edward Baines of the *Leeds Mercury*
—and the Rev. Edward Stanley, a clergyman who had private business on that day with Mr. Buxton, who owned the house which the

magistrates chose as their headquarters, and who stayed on to observe the whole affair from a window directly above the magistrates.

Mr. Stanley, in a careful account written within a few months of the affair, was unequivocal. On the brickbats, for example: 'I indeed saw no missile weapons used throughout the whole transaction, but . . . the dust at the hustings soon partially obscured everything that took place near that particular spot.' Mr. Walmsley seizes upon this honest statement as merely negative: Stanley could not see the brickbats because of the dust. (He does not notice that, if he accepts Stanley's testimony here, he must for the same reason question Hulton's testimony at the trial of Hunt: 'When the Yeomanry advanced to the hustings I saw bricks and stones flying'—since Hulton's viewpoint was almost identical to that of Stanley, and magistrates must peer through the same dust as clergymen). Uncommitted witnesses, however, can be found on the hustings, beyond the rising dust. Thus Tyas, who was reporting from the hustings, on the Yeomanry's approach to the hustings: 'Not a brickbat was thrown at them . . . during this period.' Mr. Walmsley gets around this by quoting Captain Birley, the scarcely impartial witness who commanded the Yeomanry on the field, to the effect that the first attack was made upon his men at the *rear* of the hustings, which Tyas could not observe. Mr. Walmsley does not report the evidence of Smith (at Hunt's trial) who was over six feet high and had a good viewpoint to the left of the hustings:

I saw no stone or brick-bat thrown at them; in my judgement, if any stones or brick-bats had been thrown I was in a situation likely to have seen it, my eyes and countenance were in a direction towards the military up to the moment of their reaching the hustings.

The question of the manner in which the Yeomanry approached the hustings is much the same. Smith declared in a letter to the Earl of Derby written two days after Peterloo that they 'rushed upon the people, cutting right and left', and repeated the same general testimony in Redford v. Birley three years later. He did not attest to the fact during the intervening trial of Hunt, presumably because, as he was led by counsel through his evidence, he was not asked this question; but Mr. Walmsley finds the omission so significant as to be sinister and to discredit his whole evidence—he 'thought fit to modify' his 'first impressions' when under oath.

The Rev. Edward Stanley receives very much the same treatment.

His testimony (which influenced the accounts of those two 'radical' writers, F. A. Bruton and Dr. Read) was plain:

It has often been asked when and where the cavalry struck the people. I can only say that from the moment they began to force their way through the crowd towards the hustings swords were up and swords were down, but whether they fell with the sharp or flat side, of course I cannot pretend to give an opinion.

Mr. Walmsley demolishes this by showing that, three years later, in the action of Redford v. Birley, 'Stanley's testimony under oath was not the testimony given in his narrative':

Did you watch the advance of the cavalry from their place up to the hustings?
I did.
Did you see either sticks, or stones or anything of the kind used against the cavalry in their advance up to the hustings?
Certainly not.
Did you see any resistance whatever to the cavalry, except the thickness of the meeting?
None.
Do I understand you to say you saw them surround the hustings, or not?
Surround I could not say, for the other side of the hustings, of course, was partially eclipsed by the people upon it.
But you saw them encircle part?
Encircle part.
Did you see what was done when they got there?...
I saw the swords up and down, the orators tumbled or thrown over, and the mob dispersed.

Mr. Walmsley—and it must be insisted that this is a fair example of his method—is seized with the mis-apprehension that the juxta-position of these two passages of Stanley's amount to an astounding discrepancy ('Bruton appeared quite oblivious that these discrepancies existed'), and he canters about the pages with it like a captured Cap of Liberty:

In his printed narrative the 'swords were up and the swords were down' on their way up to the hustings. On oath, Stanley testified he saw 'swords up and down' when they got to the hustings.

But—oh, St. Sisyphus!—there is no discrepancy here at all. Stanley, being led by counsel, had to reply as exactly as he could to the exact question asked, which is, in this case, what he saw done *at the hustings*. And he uses the identical phrase which he had used in his earlier narrative because, being an accurate man (he was later a president of the Manchester Statistical Society), he was describing what he could actually *see* through rising dust at a distance of some hundred yards —the swords rising and falling.

Mr. Walmsley allows that there were one or two other witnesses who shared Stanley's illusions, but he implies that the evidence is slender and unsupported. Such a conclusion is made possible only by the cavalier way in which Mr. Walmsley passes by the evidence adduced in the inquest on John Lees of Oldham, at which at least nine witnesses testified to seeing the Yeomanry cut at the people on their way to the hustings:

Coroner: At what pace did they come?

Jonah Andrew (cotton spinner): I think it was a trot. It was as fast as they could get, and the constables were making way for them.

Q. Did you see them striking any one?

A. Yes: I saw them striking as they came along, and they struck one person when they were about twenty yards from me . . . they squandered to the right and left before they came to me. . . .

Q. Well: What then?

A. Why they began to cut and hack at the people like butchers.

\*

William Norris Buckley (merchant, and nephew to one of the active magistrates): There was a complete convulsion when the soldiers rode their horses among the multitude, and they seemed to be laying about them with their swords, in their way to the hustings; and when they arrived there, they cut down the people that held the flags.

\*

Coroner: Do you know anything of the death of John Lees?

Elizabeth Farren: No. I do not.

Q. Then why do you come here?

A. Because I was cut.

Q. Where were you cut?

A. On the forehead (Here the witness raises her bonnet and cap, as also the bandage over her forehead, and exhibited a large wound not quite healed).

The Coroner: I don't mean that, woman. Where were you at the time you were cut?

A. About thirty yards from the house where the Justices were, amongst the special constables. . . .

Q. Were you cut as the Cavalry went to the hustings, or on their return?

A. I was cut as they were going towards the hustings. I had with me this child (shewing the child she held in her arms). I was frightened for its safety, and to protect it, held it close to my side with the head downward, to avoid the blow. I desired them to spare my child, and I was directly cut on my forehead.

Q. What passed then?

A. I became insensible. . . .

None of this, or similar, evidence at the inquest on John Lees is cited by Mr. Walmsley. The witnesses, and in particular the last one, were clearly highly prejudiced. The counsel for the family of the deceased offered to bring any number of further witnesses to prove the same facts, but were prevented by the coroner; the counsel for the Manchester constables brought forward several witnesses (including Joseph Nadin) who contradicted this evidence (and who saw the controversial brickbats) and could no doubt have brought forward others. All that can be said is that the witnesses for the former appear to be more various in their occupations and commitments and to offer more authentic testimony.

This is relevant to Mr. Walmsley's large claim to have dispersed from the field all previous historians, since his neglect of the evidence presented at this inquest is in striking contrast to the exceptional weight which he places upon the evidence presented for the defence in Redford v. Birley. The Oldham inquest, upon a victim who died, most probably of injuries sustained at Peterloo, was a turbulent and ill-conducted affair, at which the reformers sought to bring forward evidence leading to a verdict of 'wilful murder' against the Yeomanry. But it was held within weeks of the event, when neither the authorized nor the unauthorized versions had congealed; the testimonies have authenticity and freshness, and the very breaches in legal formality lead to scores of revealing polemical encounters. Redford v. Birley, on the other hand, was held *three years* after Peterloo; it was a civil action for damages by one of the injured against the commander and several members of the Yeomanry. In the interval there had been the trial of Hunt, press outcry, parliamentary debates, demands for enquiry; memories had dimmed and the evidence had been many times rehearsed; and the Manchester authorities offered for the first time a unified and well-drilled defence of their actions. Mr. Walmsley has a touching faith in the absolute historical verity of legal decisions (when they confirm his own conclusions), and the fact that the jury found against Redford appears to him to substantiate at every point the tardily mounted official version and, moreover, to brand Prentice and Bamford—who continued to pass on their own version—as wilful deceivers of posterity.

This is central to his argument. The 580 pages of the Oldham inquest are 'interminable proceedings'; which may be largely dis-
counted; but the 632 pages of three-year-chewed cud in Redford v.
Birley are commended as providing a 'cloud of witnesses' to prove
that it was not the Yeomanry at all but the *crowd* which attacked.
But it is characteristic of Mr. Walmsley's polemical method that he
never does settle down, in any systematic way, to examine what
Redford v. Birley did, or did not, 'prove'.

In fact, an analysis of the trial gives these results: on the first of
Mr. Walmsley's disputed points, twenty-nine of Redford's witnesses
swore that they did not see brickbats, stones, or any form of resistance
by the crowd to the Yeomanry before they reached the hustings,
whereas seventeen of Captain Birley's witnesses swore that they did.
Among Redford's twenty-nine witnesses were seven weavers, one
fustian-cutter, one carver and gilder, two cotton manufacturers,
one pattern-drawer, one Church of England clergyman (Stanley),
one dissenting minister, one Quaker surgeon, three gentlemen, one
salesman, four journalists (including Tyas, Baines and Smith),
one chemist, two householders overlooking the field, and one
member of the Manchester Yeomanry. Among Birley's seventeen
were the Deputy-Constable (Nadin), two of the committee of magistrates (Hulton and Hay), one merchant's agent, one calico-printer,
one policeman, two lawyers, one gentleman, one farm steward,
and at least six special constables. The former would appear to be the
more representative group, with the greatest number of independently
placed witnesses.

On Mr. Walmsley's second disputed point—whether the Yeomanry struck out with their sabres on the way to the hustings—the
honours are more even; rather more—and more various—witnesses
said they did than said they did not. The fact that the jury (which
was a special jury) found for Birley does not, in any case, indicate
anything about their judgment on these parts of the evidence, since
they were directed by the judge 'that if the defendants were acting
in the legal discharge of their duty, being called upon by the magistracy to act, the verdict ought to be for the defendants'. Since the
fact that the magistracy ordered the Yeomanry into the crowd is one
of the few facts about Peterloo which was never disputed, the jury
had no alternative; but a verdict reached on such a basis can have
no binding power on the judgment of posterity.

In contrast to his faith in the 'cloud of witnesses' in Redford v.

Birley, Mr. Walmsley evidently found the more authentic evidence given at the Oldham inquest too painful to read with precision. His few, selective references to it are generally inaccurate. Here is an example. He writes that one witness

> testified that he heard one of the Yeomanry say, 'there is that villain Saxton; run him through,' which in the printed report of the proceedings is italicized, apparently to make it clear that it corroborated John Tyas's report in *The Times*. It did. The words were almost identical. Tyas had written: 'There is that villain Saxton: do you run him through the body.' This passage has been cited in modern times [footnote citing E. P. Thompson] as convincing testimony, without adding the information that this witness, 'muttering to himself', was dismissed from the courtroom as an incredible one.

The passage deserves detailed criticism, as exemplifying Mr. Walmsley's pursuit of imaginary molehills and his ignorance of tangible mountains. The suggestion that the words quoted were italicized to indicate that they corroborated Tyas's report is pure attribution; it is very much more probable that they were italicized to distinguish quoted matter from the witnesses' own words. If Mr. Walmsley had been discussing evidence supporting the Yeomanry he would probably have found that two witnesses corroborating each other offered final proof; in this case he suggests that corroboration suggests collusion. The witness, it is true, is reported as withdrawing, muttering, but there is nothing in the report to suggest that he was dismissed as 'incredible'; he was dismissed because the coroner was out of patience, was seeking to abbreviate the proceedings, and was refusing to take evidence which did not bear directly upon the wounding of John Lees by the hustings; and the witness was muttering because he was not permitted to relate all the facts about the Yeomanry which he knew:

> Coroner: Do you mean to state that you saw these two people, Harrison and Shelmerdine, wound any body?
> James Walker: I don't know that I saw Harrison wound any body, but I saw him attempt to wound both me and Mr. Saxton; and if I had not jumped back, I am sure he would have cut me. I saw Shelmerdine inflict a wound upon a person afterwards.
> Q. Near the hustings?
> A. No.
> Q. Then this is the conclusion of your evidence, that you neither saw Shelmerdine or Harrison wound any person at the hustings? Which was it that attempted to strike you?
> A. Harrison.

The Coroner: That is all I ask you.

The Witness: But I have not stated all I know. I saw different men wounded after that.

The Coroner: You are told, that is not evidence. Go about your business.

(The Witness withdrew, muttering.)

The witness was not, in any case, the witness cited by E. P. Thompson unless Mr. Walmsley has access to an edition of *The Making of the English Working Class* which is unknown to us. Mr. Thompson cites Nathan Broadhurst, who appears some 300-odd pages earlier in the inquest, and who also testified (collusively?) to the attack on Saxton, using the words: 'There's Saxton, damn him, run him through.' This witness was not dismissed, nor accused of incredibility, nor did he mutter.

This, then, is Mr. Walmsley's method. He batters away so remorselessly at every piece of evidence accusatory of the Yeomanry that the reader, out of sheer tedium, is inclined to submit. The crowd attacked the peaceable Yeomanry (behind the hustings, where no one but Captain Birley could see it) and all followed on:

All the actors in that tragedy were victims. The radicals on the platform, the militants in the crowd, the peaceable in the crowd, the Yeomanry, the constables, the magistrates in their room, the captives in the New Bayley, were each and severally as much the victims of the tragic chain of circumstances as the dead special constable lying in the Bull's Head, the wounded in the infirmary, and Mrs. Partington, crushed to death, lying at the bottom of the cellar steps.

If a case is constructed largely out of negations, it is logical that at the centre of it there will be, not a fact, but a hole. Mr. Walmsley is well aware of this hole—who *did*, then, attack the Yeomanry?—and he would have been wisest to have left it empty; but he could not resist the urge to fill it, and it is here, at the heart of his thesis, that his special pleading becomes excessive.

There was a row, in *February*, 1819, at Sandy Brow in Stockport, where some cavalry attempted to seize a Cap of Liberty, and where the Radicals beat them off and crowed about it for months afterwards. Therefore it follows, as the night the day, that the hole can be filled by the Stockport contingent. The evidence? They were behind the hustings. That is all: a mountain of speculation labours to produce this poor, moulting mouse of uncertain evidence. No one, at the time or later, noticed what Mr. Walmsley, now that 150 years of dust has settled, can now see; not even Captain Birley.

Moreover the mouse is dressed up as a lion. First Tyas of *The Times* is pressed into service. He mentioned at Hunt's trial that, while the crowd were cheering the Yeomanry on their first arrival at the edge of the field, 'Mr. Hunt desired that some persons on the waggon [hustings] might be removed, as they were neither speakers or writers, and were creating a disturbance.' To Mr. Walmsley, this incident suggests 'a disruptive element in the crowd actively opposing the Huntean mode of proceeding—that of passive resistance'. Well, does it? It seems to suggest an overcrowded stage and people jostling for place. But then, continues Mr. Walmsley, how to account for the sinister evidence of George Swift, himself a radical speaker:

Hunt ordered the people to stand fast. 'If they want me,' said Mr. Hunt, 'let me go—don't resist, don't rush,'—pointing to a place near him, 'If them fellows won't be quiet put them down and keep them down' . . .

More evidence of a 'disruptive element'. And then there is the 're-markable' fact that James Moorhouse, the Stockport leader who ac-companied Hunt to the hustings, was nevertheless not on the hustings during the action. What was he doing? And why did Hunt huff and puff so much about all this at his trial? In fact the reasons for this are ludicrously simple: first—Miss Marlow points out this one—Moor-house had injured his hand in the door of the barouche and retired for medical attention; second, Crown witnesses swore to his presence on the hustings when it was simple to prove that he had been absent, and in all the contentious evidence this was one point at which they could clearly be faulted and even accused of perjury.

But we are allowing ourselves to fall, headlong, into the trap which Mr. Walmsley has spent half a lifetime in baiting. For of course these disputed matters do not affect, centrally, an understand-ing of Peterloo, even if Mr. Walmsley's liberal criticisms of Prentice, Bamford, Bruton and Read, do invite a little of his own kind of correction in reply. Marshalling his thin case in support of the brickbats, Mr. Walmsley avers:

That attack on the Yeomanry, if made, is to be considered as the 'flash-point' from which stemmed the inevitable explosion. Anything could happen after that; and in fact did.

This is the 'heart of the matter', because 'the success or failure of the radical version of Peterloo pivoted on whether this fact of strik-ing the first blow could be pinned on the Yeomanry or not'. But this is not the case. If a meeting of some 60,000 people is surrounded by

cavalry and foot-soldiers and penetrated by hostile special constables,
if Yeomanry are then sent into its midst to arrest its most charismatic
orator, and if a member of the crowd then throws a brick at a yeoman
(which is not proven) are the crowd then guilty of being ridden and
sabred off the field?

*          *          *

Even by the infinitely nice legalisms of Mr. Walmsley's own game,
the military do not resort to instant and massive retaliation at the
moment when one of their members is assaulted. What Mr. Walmsley has almost succeeded in making us do is to distract our attention
from the actual attack on the crowd, and the nature of that attack.
Give or take some emphasis this way or that, the events that preceded this attack are as follows.

A peaceable and fairly good humoured crowd was assembled,
and Hunt began to address it. Immediately the magistrates sent for
the Yeomanry to assist the civil power to arrest the speakers in the
midst of the assembly. The Yeomanry—local shopkeepers, dealers,
dancing-masters and the rest (several of whom were probably
drunk)—rode fast towards the hustings, fanning out in disorder
among the crowd as they came into it. As they reached the thickest
part of the crowd the more disciplined or more humane probably only
brandished their swords to make the crowd give way, but others
struck out, and not only with the flats. The evidence of any brickbats,
&c., being thrown at them until at least several minutes after they
had reached and surrounded the hustings is excessively thin. Hunt—
who until that moment had exerted himself for order and to prevent
panic—was then arrested. Up to that moment the situation had still
not passed beyond control, but simultaneously with that moment
(Hunt disappeared as if he had been shot, said one witness) the cry
went up from the Yeomanry—'Have at their flags!'—and the
Peterloo Massacre really began. Some feeble attempts were made by
the crowd to defend the costly embroidered banners and Caps of
Liberty which the female reformers had worked over so carefully,
and which the reformers had carried so many miles to the meeting.
The Yeomanry struck out right and left and the special constables,
not to be deprived of their share of the trophies of the field, joined in.
The magistrates, seeing the Yeomanry in 'difficulties', ordered the
Hussars to clear the field. On the edge of the field, some of the people,
finding themselves still pursued, made a brief stand.

Mr. Walmsley, who has so much to say about unidentified Stock-

port militants, has almost no comment to offer on this—a moment
of unrestrained aggression which cannot by any special pleading
be offered as self-defence. Nor is there much conflict of evidence
about this, the real 'flashpoint'. Scarlett, who led the prosecution
against Hunt, remained unconvinced about any attack upon the
Yeomanry until this moment, and declared in a subsequent parliamentary debate: 'Had they [the Yeomanry] stopped then no real
damage would have been done, but they then began to attack.'
Tyas reported:

As soon as Hunt and Johnson had jumped from the waggon a cry was
made by the cavalry, 'Have at their flags'. In consequence, they immediately
dashed not only at the flags which were in the waggon, but those which
were posted among the crowd, cutting most indiscriminately to the right
and to the left in order to get at them. This set the people running in all
directions, and it was not until this act had been committed that any brickbats were hurled at the military. From that moment the Manchester
Yeomanry Cavalry lost all command of temper.

Not even Captain Birley disputed the fact of this attack on the flags.
His account (through the medium of Lord Stanley) declared that,
when the magistrates' warrant had been executed,

considerable tumult prevailed, and a struggle ensued between the constables and those persons in the cart, who wished to save the caps of liberty,
banners, &c. Some of those who resisted were taken into custody, and the
soldiers cut with their sabres. In doing this, it was possible that some
persons had been hurt, but not intentionally.

It would perhaps be legalistic to point out that the magistrates'
warrant was for the arrest of Hunt and not of a Cap of Liberty. We
are bereft of independent witnesses to describe the sensation of
being 'hurt, but not intentionally', since neither Tyas (who himself
had been arrested, in error) nor the Rev. Edward Stanley was fleeing
on the field. We must, perforce, supply the hiatus in Mr. Walmsley's
account, by drawing upon the evidence of some of these biased
victims to describe the temper of these moments:

William Harrison (cotton spinner): . . . We were all merry in hopes of
better times.
Coroner: Were you not desired to disperse?
Harrison: Only with the swords—nobody asked us to disperse—only
trying to cut our heads off with their swords.

'The soldiers began cutting and slaying', went on Harrison, 'and
the constables began to seize the colours, and the tune was struck up;

they all knew of the combination.' Amidst such music, few paused to
distinguish between flats and sharps:

Coroner: Did they cut at you near the hustings?
Harrison: No; as I was running away three soldiers came down upon me
one after another; there was whiz this way and whiz that way, backwards
and forwards . . . and I, as they were going to strike, threw myself on my
face, so that, if they cut, it should be on my bottom.
The Coroner: You act as well as speak?
Harrison: Yes; I'm real Lancashire blunt, Sir; I speak the truth; when-
ever any cried out 'mercy', they said 'Damn you, what brought you here'.

Another witness related how a special constable jumped on the
hustings, 'took up the President's chair, and beat it about those who
remained'. Some of the crowd, hemmed in on all sides by Yeomanry,
crawled under the carts which formed the platform for the hustings.
According to one witness, John Lees (who later died) was one of
these:

Jonah Andrew (cotton spinner): I saw several constables round him, and
beating him with truncheons severely. One of them picked up a staff of a
banner that had been cut with a sword, and said, 'Damn your bloody eyes,
I'll break your back'.

This 'self-defence' was pursued by Yeomanry and specials to the
edges, and beyond the edges, of the field. Hunt, as he was taken to the
magistrates' house, ran the gauntlet of special constables' batons.
Even in the side-streets around the field the cavalry pursued the people, cutting at them and saying, 'Damn you, I'll reform you;—
You'll come again, will you?' Outside one house in Windmill Street,
'special constables came up in great triumph, before my door,
calling out *"This is Waterloo for you! This is Waterloo"*.'

\*      \*      \*

Mr. Walmsley is of course wrong to suppose that the sober
accounts of Peterloo by Bruton and Read represent, even if un-
wittingly, a perpetuation of the 'radical' myth. A radical interpretation of the day, derived in part from witnesses such as those just
quoted, would be far more savage than anything published since
Bamford or Prentice. It would see it as a clear moment of class war.
Nor were the warriors only on the side of the magistracy. If Mr.
Walmsley had examined the Home Office papers he would have
found evidence that both before the day (among those drilling on
the moors) and afterwards (among those threatening vengeance)

there were indeed most unpacific 'militants' among the reformers. Bamford was—at least after Peterloo—very probably among them, although he gives himself a more sober character in his reminiscences. If the report of a spy is to be credited, he was still, three months later, venting his feeling in revolutionary rodomontade, and giving in a tavern the toast: 'May the Tree of Liberty be planted in Hell, and may the bloody Butchers of Manchester be the Fruit of it!' As late as April, 1820, there was a fierce tavern brawl in Oldham between soldiers and townsmen, when one of the latter proposed the toast: 'May the skin of every loyal man be taken off his back and made into parchment to beat the Reformers to arms!'

Undoubtedly among the huge crowd which assembled on that day there were some who felt obscurely that something large might come of it, and come suddenly to the raising of the poor and the throwing down of the rich. As one of the contingents marched in that morning they passed Roger Entwisle, an attorney and clerk to the race-course, and later a witness against Hunt: 'Thou hast got a good coat to thy back', one of the marchers shouted, 'but I shall have as good a one as thee before to-night is over.'

* * *

All this was around, before and after Peterloo. But on the day itself the vast crowd was, definitively, under Hunt's control and subjected to his egotistical but emphatically constitutionalist strategy. He had spent the previous week in Manchester, seeing some of the leaders of contingents, and ensuring that his orders for peace and discipline were understood and would be obeyed. They were obeyed, and women and children came with the men upon the field. Hence Peterloo was not only a massacre, but a peculiarly cowardly one. Miss Marlow has discovered letters of Major Dyneley, who commanded the two field-pieces which were held in readiness in the wings on the day: 'The first action of the Battle of Manchester is over', he wrote, 'and I am happy to say has ended in the complete discomfiture of the Enemy.' He had been 'very much assured to see the way in which the Volunteer Cavalry knocked the people about during the whole time we remained on the ground: the instant they saw ten or a dozen Mobbites together, they rode at them and *leathered* them properly'.

A radical interpretation, however, would re-examine with the greatest scrupulousness those parts of the received account which

N

exonerate from blame in these events, not only the government but also the magistracy; or which assume that the magistracy were guilty only of panic or ill-judgment, and that once they had sent the Yeomanry upon the field, all happened fortuitously. Both Prentice and J. E. Taylor offered powerful arguments against this at the time. The official *Papers Relative to the State of the Country*, published by government in November, 1819, and offering a selection of the letters of magistrates to the Home Office, depositions, &c., should be regarded as being just as much a party statement—and should be examined as scrupulously—as any radical account. Historians have not, generally, done this; although the *Papers* were selected and published in order to prevent any parliamentary enquiry; the information (Lord Liverpool admitted privately) 'may be laid safely, and much more advantageously, by Government directly rather than through the medium of any committee'. Many of the questions asked by John Edward Taylor in his brilliant and scathing *Notes and Observations, Critical and Explanatory on the Papers Relative to the Internal State of the Country* (1820) have never found a satisfactory answer.

*     *     *

These questions are of the order most difficult to resolve; questions of intention—did the magistrates intend beforehand that an armed dispersal should take place?—and of complicity—did Sidmouth assent to, or know of, any such intention? Mr. Walmsley himself quotes important passages from a private, justificatory account which the Rev. W. R. Hay drew up for Sidmouth on October 7, 1819, and which was hitherto unpublished. In this he described the actions of the select committee of magistrates which was in almost continuous session in the days leading up to August 16:

The Committee continued to meet, and did so on Saturday, [August] the 14th, Sunday, and Monday. Prior to the Saturday, different points had been discussed as to the propriety of stopping the Meeting and the manner of doing so. They were of opinion that Multitudes coming in columns with Flags and Marching in military array were even in the approach to the Meeting a tumultuous assembly; and it was for a little time under consideration whether each Column should not be stopped at their respective entrances into the Town, but this was given up—it was considered that the Military might then be distracted and it was wished that the Town should see what the Meeting was, when assembled, and also that those who came should be satisfied they were assembled in an unlawful manner.

'Being satisfied', the account continues, 'that in point of Law [the Meeting]if assembled as it was expected, would be an illegal Meeting, we gave notice to Lieut.-Col. L'Estrange . . . of our wish to have the assistance of the Military on the 16th.'

This is a clear enough statement of the magistrates' intention, although it does not amount to proof. It is abundantly evident that magistrates and military had a contingency plan for dispersing the meeting; and, at the very least, it would appear that Sidmouth was informed of this plan, from a letter in the Home Office papers dated August 18, in which Sidmouth conveyed to General Sir John Byng his satisfaction in the judgment of Colonel L'Estrange, the military commander on that day: 'His Judgment has in Lord S.'s mind been evinced by his employing the Yeomanry in the Van agreeably to the Plan on which I know you intended to act.' A contingency plan, it is true, does not amount to a fully-proven intention, even when the first part of it—the assembling of the military forces—is put into effect. But there is altogether too much circumstantial evidence, as well as rumour, circulating on the Sunday and the Monday morning, to allow one to discount the possibility of such a fully-formed intention: the clearing of the field by the authorities, early on Monday morning, of all stones: the industrious preparation by the magistrates of depositions from prominent citizens that they were alarmed by the banners and military array of the crowd: the rumours such as those which reached the ears of J. E. Taylor:

. . . early in the forenoon on August 16th persons supposed to be acquainted with the intentions of the magistrates distinctly asserted that Mr. Hunt would be arrested on the hustings, and the meeting dispersed. I myself was more than once told so, but could not conceive it possible . . .

The intention was expressed, the contingency plan was prepared, the military forces were assembled, the rumours and more-than-rumours were circulating: and yet we are *still* invited to believe that the dispersal of the crowd was fortuitous, and that the magistrates determined to send cavalry into the midst of it to arrest the speakers because one Richard Owen, a pawnbroker, swore an affidavit that Hunt had arrived and that 'an immense mob is collected and he considers the town in danger'. (The affrighted Richard Owen, in his alternating role as a special constable, is supposed to have signally distinguished himself on the field by capturing the black flag of the Saddleworth contingent—'Equal Representation or Death'—the

mere sight of which so many official witnesses at subsequent proceedings testified as having thrown them into consternation and
alarm.)

There is a simpler explanation than Mr. Walmsley's for Peterloo.
There was a plan. It was put into operation. The magistrates knew,
for some hours, and perhaps days, before Hunt arrived on the hustings, what they intended to do; the special constables were expecting
the arrival of the Yeomanry; the Yeomanry did, on the field, very
much what was expected of them, although neither as efficiently
nor as decorously as the authorities might have wished; and the
regulars performed a part in which their officers (like Major Dyneley)
were well versed.

This case has not been established, but it seems, at the least, open
to enquiry. If established, it would not necessarily exclude the
authorities from any larger historical defence. The magistrates
were faced with a new phenomenon of which they had no understanding. The crowd was not attending a Whitsun walk nor even a
miners' gala. Its size, its discipline, its high morale, were ominous
to the old order. Neither in the magistrates' room nor in the crowd
did men look forward complacently to 1832 and all that; it was more
natural, in 1819, when two incompatible social forces confronted
each other, to remember 1789.

Some such historical defence might be offered. Mr. Walmsley,
however, would not wish to offer it. His zealous partisanship is, in a
serious sense, worthy of the Peterloo tradition; and his book, which
has turned over the ground freshly, will certainly join the enduring
literature of the event. But he cannot allow a line of investigation,
nor even of defence, which must also show that Hulton of Hulton
(who denied that the magistrates had any prior intention of dispersing the crowd) was a liar. But Mr. Walmsley, in his zeal, has
provided evidence for this as well. William Hulton had some sort of
stiffening about him which some of his fellow-magistrates lacked—
an absence of humanitarian cant and a contempt for general opinion.
He offered no maudlin apologies for Peterloo; indeed, he later recalled it as the 'proudest day' of his life, and many years afterwards
he kept a Cap of Liberty, captured upon the field, in his study.
A gentleman of Hulton's breed and station does not lie; he merely
has so great a hauteur, so great a distance between himself and the
seditious plebs, that it is a matter of utter indifference to him whether
this or that is true of them or not.

Twelve years after Peterloo, and after fact upon fact had been disputed for as long, Hulton could throw off a public letter containing a manifest farrago of mis-statements about the day—'two people were killed in St. Peter's Field—one, a woman, who having personated the Goddess of Reason, was trampled to death in the crowd. . . . On the succeeding day, an old pensioner was beaten to death with portions of his own loom, because he had expressed a loyal attachment to the King'. He was as inflexibly convinced, in 1831 as he had been in 1817, that the defence of 'this vast aegis' of our liberties required the hunting of Jacobins and the sharpening of swords. The defeat of the Tories in South Lancashire in the Reform election of 1832 led only to an adjustment of tactics. 'A few despondent individuals', Hulton of Hulton later recalled, then met in a common pot-house in Newton-le-Willows: 'It occurred to them that it was their duty to call up every friend to the monarchy and the Church to counteract the machinations of the enemies to both.' As a result of that meeting 'the foundations of the South Lancashire Conservative Association were laid . . . and from that stem at Newton, Conservative associations had branched out all over Her Majesty's dominions.' It is well to remember that British Conservatism has not only been made by the great, the well-endowed, the fluent. It has also had its stubborn provincial grass-roots.

## (b) A VERY ENGLISH RISING

THE TWO NAMES on the cover of *Captain Swing* are a guarantee of sound scholarship, imaginative insight, skilful investigation and intensive, ingenious research. The book itself is a tribute to the wise initiative of their publishers. It promises to be a marvellous tandem; and the promise is maintained. The reader will not be disappointed by this closely-written book, so well constructed that, were it not for the indications provided by the authors, it would appear to have had a single creator. The two authors have shown a remarkable understanding of each other's particular gifts, in the division of the toil; George Rudé is, as always, admirable in the description and the spread of riot, while Eric Hobsbawm displays his usual acuteness of perception, his flair for the striking metaphor and his abundant historical imagination. Such a pooling of skills is of great advantage

to the reader, as well as providing a double stimulus for further
research.

The introduction and the first three chapters (on agricultural England, the rural poor, the village world) are particularly well written,
giving a sensitive and perceptive account of the conditions of the
rural poor in the fifteen or twenty years before the 'Swing' riots of
1830, with special reference to the counties of the South-East, the
South, the Home Counties, and East Anglia. There are brilliant
descriptions of the collective life of the village, of the decline of
paternalism once the farmer has his parlour in which he sits alone
with his family, the changing pattern of work and leisure, the conditions of hirings, the increasing gulf between the in-servants, who
live and eat in the farm and who are employed on an annual basis, and
those who are hired by the day, the importance of the newly established beerhouse as a meeting place for the rural poor, in distinction
to the country public house, where the poor would find themselves
in the presence of their 'betters', the consequent emergence of village
radicals among these beerhouse keepers, as well as among artisans
and itinerants, as the effects of the Poor Law tended to tie the seasonal
labourer or the totally unemployed labourer more and more to the
confines of his parish, depriving him of mobility and of the safety
valve of emigration to London, the importance of Saturday and
Sunday in the genesis of rural riot.

The book opens with a movingly evocative reference to the almost
total isolation of the English agricultural labourer of the southern
counties within a society that either rejected him or totally ignored
him:

If they could write—and in 1830 most could not—they would have little
occasion to, except, perhaps laboriously, to some daughter or sister 'in
service' in a town too remote to be visited, some brother or son in the
army. Except for their gravestones and their children, they left nothing
identifiable behind them, for the marvellous surface of the British landscape, the work of their ploughs, spades and shears and the beasts they
looked after, bears no signature or mark such as the masons left on cathe-
drals.

And, in a very different vein, one can appreciate the pointedness
of Dr. Hobsbawm's sharp comment on the subject of the rural clergy:
'The vicars of Victorian England found medieval documents a less
recalcitrant source than their parishioners.' Others, like Gilbert
White a century earlier, devoted their attentions to the local wild life,

to botany, the early primrose and fifteenth-century reredoses. 'Hodge' (the peasant) scarcely came into their spectrum at all, save in respect of the tithe.

The chapter on the rural poor is one of the best in the book, as good, in fact, as that on Australia. It is an important and compassionate contribution to the still largely unmapped history of poverty at its most dramatic, most shamefaced, least publicized level. There is an abundant literature on the subject of 'dark satanic mills'; but there has been little to recall—perhaps not even a gravestone—the fate of poor men, found dead in ditches, their stomachs full of dandelion leaves, or the bitter humiliation of the upstanding, strong young labourer—a married man and a father—driven to live off the parish, mobilized into road gangs, like a common criminal, and forced to display all the accoutrements of a cruel, derisive, uncharitable charity, with bells and collars, as though he were a performing monkey on an organ-grinder's box. It is an unrelieved picture of utter demoralization, insensitiveness and mental and moral cruelty.

Dr. Hobsbawm, aptly, compares the condition of 'Hodge', in early nineteenth-century England, to that of the inhabitant of the black ghettoes of American cities at the present day. An American visitor to England in the 1840s, ten years or so after 'Swing', was to contrast the broken, 'forelock-pulling', degraded English labourer to the neat, well-organized, independent and self-respecting French peasant of the same period. This was a little more than fifty years after Arthur Young had contrasted the wretched position of the French rural poor, on the eve of the Revolution, with that of the Suffolk farmhand.

The reader is thus well prepared to place in its proper context what represents the core of the book, the closely written, day-by-day, sometimes hour-by-hour, narrative account of the spread of the 'Swing' riots, from East Kent, where they were principally directed against threshing-machines, recently introduced to the Weald, the mysterious Den Country, the Marsh, thence to the Medway Valley, the Tunbridge Wells area, East Sussex, West Sussex, Hampshire, Wiltshire and Dorset, and from Wiltshire and Hampshire to Berkshire, Oxfordshire, Buckinghamshire and Bedfordshire, with a largely independent outbreak in East Anglia (the third of its kind in Suffolk since 1816), in areas that were not contiguous to the rest of the 'Swing' territory, but overlapping into Huntingdon, Northamptonshire and Cambridgeshire.

While the riots thus spread, with great rapidity—less than a week, from Sussex to Hampshire and Wiltshire—acquiring, in the process, particularly alarming proportions in Wiltshire and in Berkshire, disturbances continued endemically in East Kent, in which the movement had originated, and in parts of Sussex to the end of 1830. In most places, it was all over in a matter of a day or two; but in some villages between Canterbury, Ashford and the Marsh, or on the Kent and Sussex border in the Tunbridge Wells area, there were repeated disturbances, taking a variety of forms, from the late summer until the middle of winter. Detailed analysis of this kind, much of it based on county records, brings out all George Rudé's flair for research and dogged persistence; the historian of the 'Flour War' of May, 1775, is once more on the road, and it is fascinating to follow him as the disturbances spread, on an erratic course, westwards, not along the highroads and Roman ways—Watling, Stene—but through semi-secret footpaths or tracks cutting through the greenery, nearly always giving the towns a wide berth, that is, along lines of communication known only to the local man, to the poacher and smuggler, to the ploughman as he plods his weary way back to his airless cottage.

This might account for the peculiar way 'Swing' moved in its western course, disappearing from sight, avoiding a dozen or more villages, to re-emerge in a place twenty or thirty miles away. It might also help to explain the disproportionate fears inspired, among property-owners and parsons, by the activities of very small bands of men—in East Kent twenty or thirty, never more than fifty, and nowhere, even in areas of spectacular sorties, such as Wiltshire, more than 300. The rioters, of course, had other very good reasons for avoiding the highroads, and in East Kent, especially in the Marsh, they were no doubt able to use the green tunnels of the smugglers' routes from the coast inland.

It was not surprising that bodies of cavalry, once they had been sent into the 'Swing' areas, had such difficulty in meeting the bands of labourers on the move, even when they went by day, in their best clothes, and carrying flags and emblems; it was only when they entered towns, called parish meetings, or camped on the rector's lawn, that they were liable to be identified by the authorities. The incendiarists in particular, the men who blackened their faces so effectively, it seems, that hardly any of them were ever identified —and they are indeed the greatest unknown factor in the present book, so that we cannot even conclude whether they were private persons carrying out vengeance against specified individuals, or participants in a mass movement—would have been likely, on the contrary, to have progressed under cover of night through the deep runnels of half-abandoned tracks.

Riot is much more fearful when it moves mysteriously, and it was not surprising that 'Swing', like rural movements in France in 1796, 1812 and 1848, should have been accompanied by the usual outriders of rumour and panic. In East Anglia, much was made of 'gentlemen' —rather seedy gentlemen, it seems, of shabby elegance—'in green gigs', reported in a dozen places at once. There was the usual crop of foreigners and exotics; it was a tribute to the importance of 'Swing', at least in terms of rumour, that it mobilized once again all the Englishman's favourite bogy figures: dark Frenchmen and Flemings, men in black travelling in green, sallow men with blazing eyes, the brutal, violent Irish, the emissaries of the Pope, 'ranters' of strange cults, people who kept mistresses, men who travelled with large sums in Bank of England stock, 'Jew-looking fellows', gypsy pedlars.

On the extent, then, of the 'Swing' riots as well as on their persistence in certain areas, *Captain Swing* would appear to be exhaustive. It is unlikely that any village in which there was any activity at all that could be even vaguely associated with 'Swing' has been omitted. Indeed—and this is a tentative criticism—one sometimes has the feeling that some have been let in on rather slender evidence: one rick burnt, or an assault on an overseer of the poor, or the destruction of a single machine, or a parish meeting to demand an increase in the weekly wage. This is not to suggest that the authors have deliberately inflated their evidence in order to make the 'movement' more impressive in terms of spread and impact; but at times they do appear over-eager to attribute to 'Swing' what may have been habitual forms of rural pressure and protest.

The reader and the future researcher are especially in the debt of the authors for the minute care that they have taken in calculating the extent of the repression—in itself a counter-proof of the extent of the 'movement'—in terms of personal unhappiness, the break-up of families, imprisonment, deportation, and, in nineteen cases, execution. George Rudé is an old hand with prison registers; he has also made admirable use of the Tasmanian penal records, and his account of the subsequent fate of many of these poor ploughmen and village artisans in Tasmania and New South Wales is deeply

moving, as well as illustrative of his devotion both to his subject and
to the human beings that took the leading part in it. Indeed, whatever doubts one might entertain about the total spread of the riots
in terms of localities, one would hesitate to write off as historically
unimportant a 'movement' that resulted in nearly 500 poor country-
men being deported to the Antipodes—and most of them no doubt
were people who had never gone farther from their village than
the nearest market town or the nearest fair (no wonder some of these
rural deportees should have been afflicted, almost physically, with the
nagging anguish of home-sickness), more than 600 condemned to
long terms of imprisonment, and nineteen executed.

Repression, as it generally is, was quite disproportionately severe,
in view of the general mildness—one would be tempted to say deference—of this strangely orderly movement of protest. But this is in
itself important, indicating as it does the extent to which the Government had been frightened by a form of protest which, in extent at
least, appeared to it as quite unprecedented. The Government was
probably wrong—many local authorities thought so, a number of
magistrates played down the whole affair, giving rioters in East
Kent, at the time of the first outbreak, sentences of three or four
days' imprisonment—but the sheer severity of its reaction adds a
further dimension to disturbances that were never consciously
seditious. The Government, on this occasion, over-reacted as it had
done in 1795. It might have turned a deferential and traditionalist
movement into a revolutionary one, but, as it was, repression was
totally effective. Whether one calls 'Swing' a 'movement' or a
'rising', or both, or merely a repetition on an unprecedented scale of
various traditional forms of rural protest, it was the last thing of its
kind.

The authors have taken similar care to calculate the full extent of
the damage caused by 'Swing' activities in the twenty-odd counties
that were affected. It is unlikely that there is a single threshing-
machine missing in their list (their total is 387); the burning ricks
and barns have been counted with similar care, and, with considerable ingenuity, they have drawn on the records of the insurance
companies to assess the financial losses incurred by the victims of
incendiarism. (It is a further compliment to the gravity of 'Swing'
that the Norwich Union and other companies, after August, 1830,
refused policies to farmers in Kent and Surrey!) They have likewise
established definitive statistics on the subject of compensation. The

one thing that has largely eluded them statistically—and not for lack of trying—is the total number of 'Swing' letters actually sent; they have had to make do with those produced by the recipients— certainly a tiny proportion of the total, for people are generally, and understandably, reluctant to admit that they have been in receipt of anonymous threats, as though the fact itself was something shameful.

*Captain Swing* is perhaps even more valuable as an indication of the intense 'localism' both of a 'movement' whose form varied from county to county, even from village to village, and which can only be described at a national level in terms of spread, and of a repression that varied so much as to constitute a sinister sort of lottery. It is apparent from the narrative chapters that the riots could sometimes jump as far as twenty or thirty miles a day, but that the rioters themselves seldom went so far, recruiting as they went their way, and returning to their beds each night, for as long as the disturbances lasted. The mass of rioters were clearly unwilling to go far from their homes, and the actual spread of the movement seems to have taken the form of a sort of relay race rather than of a marathon. In this respect, the authors insist on the importance of localities on the borders of two counties (West Kent and East Sussex: for instance, Frant, Wadhurst, Mayfield, Rotherfield, Goudhurst, Crowborough; West Sussex and Hampshire, in the Selsey area; Hampshire and Wiltshire, Wiltshire and Dorset, Hampshire and Berkshire, South Suffolk and North Essex) for the extension of the riots beyond the county boundary.

Here then are the complete map of 'Swing', its cost, its form and its variety. Here too are the names of many of the leaders, or at least of those who were accused as such and punished accordingly, in Kent and Sussex, lightly; in Wiltshire, Hampshire and Berkshire, very severely. And here the occupations of those deported and sent to prison. First, craftsmen (carpenters, blacksmiths, wheelwrights, tailors, thatchers, sawyers, bricklayers, beerhouse keepers, shoe-makers, cobblers, glovers) amounting variously to a quarter, a sixth or a seventh of those convicted—a very high proportion. Secondly, inevitably, a majority of labourers, with ploughmen, herdsmen, shep-herds in the lead, with not quite so many in-servants. Many of the rioters who were labourers operated, in the disturbances, on the basis of the family unit, or on the extended one of the village (especially in Kent). We have, too, some interesting instances of double or triple employment (labourer, beerhouse keeper and shoemaker, &c.). There are assorted *varia*: an ex-army officer, a pedlar, a horse-dealer (a trade often on the edge of crime and violence), a naval deserter, an ex-policeman—some involved no doubt for motives of private vengeance, for a movement of this kind is bound to draw in a small proportion of misfits and malcontents.

The average age of those deported is between twenty-seven and thirty, most are married (the bachelor would be likely either to become an in-servant, or get out of the village altogether and try his luck, if he came from Kent, in London). From the Tasmanian penal records George Rudé has established the names, professions and places of origin of thirty-eight deportees—not much, no doubt, out of nearly five hundred, but still indicative of the likeliest types of composition. Only one has been identified for East Anglia—a movement which thus remains almost completely anonymous; only four for Kent.

For Hampshire, one is far better informed (nine individuals), there are eight identified for Wiltshire, and five for Berkshire, several from Kintbury. This uneven representation—so thin for some of the most important counties that it is very difficult to make anything more than intelligent guesses about the nature and the composition of 'Swing' there—reflects above all the very unequal weight of re-pression from county to county; the Commissions sitting in Salisbury and Winchester were far more severe than the assizes anywhere else.

So much for the known facts, so carefully enumerated (there is a wealth of research behind each sentence in these apparently straight-forward narrative chapters). One feels, however, that the authors are on more uncertain ground when dealing with general causes, organ-ization, motivation, effects, and when attempting to place 'Swing' in the wider context both of traditional rural protest and of nine-teenth-century social history. Concerned with a 'movement' of infinite variety, unsophisticated, and often quite mysterious in its methods, springing from assumptions unstated because they were probably unstatable—nothing could be more difficult for us than to get into the mind of a Kentish hop-picker or of a Sussex cowman of the early years of the last century—and responding to ancient habits of collective pressure, they try to prove too much, too neatly, on evidence that is often merely tentative and too narrowly statistical. They propose a series of tests, not lacking in ingenuity but somehow too mechanistic. And the answers too, often come out too pat.

In the section on the distribution of riots and in Part Three (on the 'Anatomy of Swing') the authors are rather too ready with their pointers. And when any of their particular 'Swing' theses comes out right, as they so often do, then the lights go on, the letters flash, the buzzers jangle, as when someone has hit the jackpot in a Reno gambling saloon. These two are not hidden persuaders. And something of this is reflected in their style; 'as we shall see', 'it is no accident that'—a revealing remark, for one feels that nothing ever is an accident for them!

Numbers, too, are often not allowed to tell their own story in their own words; both are out with their pointers again, underlining '*no less than*' thirty-five, 300, or whatever, even if the total would appear rather unimpressive. They are reluctant to let the reader make up his own mind; and sometimes they show a tendency to self-evidence, especially when attempting to explain negative factors: the absence of riot, the quiescence of a certain county. They ask, for instance, why, apart from Cornwall, there were so few food riots of the traditional eighteenth-century pattern in 1830. Might the answer not be that there was no food crisis in 1830? They make the point that the people most likely to suffer from incendiarism would be farmers. But ricks do, after all, burn rather better than most things. A similar concern to point the moral, to lead the reader by the hand, and to have an answer to every particularity leads to the repetitive use of the word 'tend'.

If 'Swing' was so multiform—and there is no doubt about that— can it then be described, as the authors insistently do, as a 'General Rising'? One often has the impression that, unconsciously, they are trying to get it both ways and that they have stacked the cards in such a manner that they must win on any count. At one time they are concerned to demonstrate that we are dealing with a 'movement' that responds to certain general forms; and these forms are said to be unique, at least in combination. At another, they insist on the diversity of the 'movement', a diversity which distinguishes it, like its spread, from previous disorders. If it is multiform, this is 'significant'; but if it is confined to a single form of protest (arson, or breaking), this too is 'significant'. Incendiarism, we are told at one stage, is a traditional expression of private vengeance; but, in the 1830 context, it is at times given a political significance, at others it is attributed to the initiative of isolated cranks.

The connexion between arson and the other 'Swing' activities is never clearly established. But, in the period from 1832 to 1835, when the anger of the defeated labourers had changed to desperation, arson once more acquires a political and social significance as the only effective form of protest remaining to the unhappy labourers of the former 'Swing' areas. And since arson is a semi-permanent feature of the English—and indeed of the French or the Irish—countryside throughout the first half of the nineteenth century, one can never make out how much it is characteristic of the specific 'Swing' movement.

The same point could be made for another feature of the 'movement'; the demand by rioters to be paid for machine-breaking and to be given food and drink in the course of their expeditions, the latter a very ancient form of rural protest, at least in France. So much, in fact, of what is said to be characteristic of 'Swing' can be associated with other examples of wide-scale rural disorder in the course of the previous thirty-five years, both sides of the Channel, that one is left wondering what was unique about the 1830 riots; undoubtedly, their spread; secondly, the emergence of the word 'Swing' which personalized a traditional form of collective bargaining; thirdly, the primacy of 'the men out of Kent', whose example was cited in the whole 'Swing' area, including the South-West and East Anglia.

Perhaps the main trouble is this determination to seek a 'pattern' at all, whether one in diversity, like a New England quilt, or whether an all-weave affair. The authors are aiming at 'total history'; but they have not enough evidence, at the village or the human level, to make it 'total'. Facts have first to be established, then accounted for, though quite often they are forced to admit that, 'in the present state of research', there can only be the most tentative answers. What never seems to occur to them is that quite possibly, in the village context, there is no clear answer at all. There is no attempt to 'anatomize' à la Stone or Brinton (on the subject of Revolution) a peasants' revolt, because, as they demonstrate in their brilliant opening chapters, the English labourer of the early years of the last century was unique—he had no European counterpart nor indeed any in Wales or Ireland. (This is perhaps why they do not mention David Williams's book, *The Rebecca Riots*, though it deserved at least a reference, if only as an example of how to exploit personal and family case histories.) Both authors know too much about the European peasantry to make a mistake of this kind.

They never deal with their subjects clinically, because they are compassionate. But often they do try to bully them, to regiment them. Worse, they often seem to be out to bully and regiment events. They are constantly endeavouring to establish rules, albeit county ones. The Kentish game is played this way: arson first, smashing afterwards. In Wiltshire, the game is different. There seems to have been a fairly general, though remarkably vague, appeal back to a Kentish precedent, there are threats about 'men coming out of Kent'; but one hears them, be it noted, in Berkshire, in Buckinghamshire, in Wiltshire, in Oxfordshire, in Dorset, in Gloucestershire, in Suffolk, not in Sussex and Surrey and Hampshire. In the latter counties, people would know that men did *not* come out of Kent; such referances are the empty threats and the characteristic mythology of primitive rural unrest, and perhaps also a folk memory of 1381. The 'men of Kent' are the 'strangers' of the French eighteenth-century provincial disturbance, and 'strangers' become more distinctively 'strange' the farther away they come from.

The authors, too, as we have noticed, make much of the importance of border places, though, in the minute patchwork of England's 'coloured counties', these certainly do not have enormous significance. The Thames and the Severn do not divide a world, a way of life and a mentality. And one is never far from any county border, once rioting has spread east to Goudhurst, Cranbrook and the Tunbridge Wells area, so that news, example and the resultant action are at all times likely to spill over. For the 'Swing' men were not voters, and it is hinted that in the larger villages many of them, especially the artisans, may have been newcomers (one would like to know more about this), and so they were not necessarily given to think either in village or in county terms. Some, no doubt, had been serving in the army, fifteen or twenty years previously.

They make allowance for the elements of accident, of personality, particularly with reference to the exceptional unpopularity of a certain named overseer of the poor and of some great noble landlord (though, on the whole, the great land-owning families get off very lightly; perhaps they were too elevated to come into the spectrum of the poor man's anger and despair). But the local leaders of 'Swing' themselves hardly emerge at all as personalities, and we have only rare examples of their reported speech (there is an eloquent example from Wiltshire: 'We don't want to do any mischief, but we want that poor children when they go to bed should have a belly full of tatoes instead of crying with half a belly full').

London hardly figures at all in this account, because the 'movement' did not even lap its fringes; the authors suggest, as an explanation for this, that much of the population of Middlesex, Surrey and South Essex was employed in market gardening for the provisioning of the capital and that they did not thus belong to the type of seasonal labourer (harvest workers, hop-pickers) that formed the base of 'Swing'. But is not the seasonal labourer the most likely to seek partial winter employment in the metropolis?

Kent above all does not get its due. For here it all began. Why Kent? There are tentative suggestions but some or all could be applied to other southern counties of wheat or hops. And why, in Kent, Lower Hardres? For the business in Orpington, Oxted, Ide Hill and Sevenoaks (what *will* Smith Square make of this?) does not seem very important, apart from the date—it started first—(but, then, does arson ever start, or ever finish?). There must be more to it than just saying that it all started in Kent. The authors do mention contacts with France, the July Revolution, smuggling, law-evasion, desertion, and so on. And soldiers, especially Irish ones, were presumably particularly unloved in a county that, over the centuries, had so often been subjected to their passage out and their passage in —the latter, no doubt, much worse. There were more than milestones on the Dover Road.

Even in the present account, with its insistence on 'the General Rising', 'the Last Labourers' Revolt', and so on, one is constantly amazed at the naturally deferential attitudes of most of the 'Swing' men, when confronted with the authorities: magistrates, landowners, farmers, even the parson. They temporarily abandon their inbred deference only when meting out some conspicuous, but non-violent humiliation on an unpopular overseer of the poor. These are no rural egalitarians, they accept the established order of village society and their expectations are fantastically minimal; a very slightly better wage, the destruction of the machines, the opportunity to work while preserving their dignity. They go about their task of riot politely, dressed according to many eyewitnesses' accounts in their best clothes, seldom using threatening language. Nothing could be more unlike an Irish rising; it is the revolt of the proud, conscious of their own rights and aware that they are not doing anything that their father would not have done. It is a strange sort of rising that goes to the tune of 'May it please you, Sir', and that strictly avoids any form of physical violence against persons (only one person was killed in the whole affair, and he a rioter, by the yeomanry).

This again is not to lessen its importance, at least in the contemporary and local framework. Perhaps this was the English way of rioting; it certainly caused an enormous shock to the higher authorities, no doubt long confident in the ox-like subservience of the dumb, semi-literate 'Hodge'. It was not the tone of the disorders that alarmed, so much as the awareness that the labourers appeared to be able to organize protest far beyond the limits of the parish, on something like a national scale.

The authors tend, in another way too, to give a somewhat inflated view of the impact and, above all, of the diversity and of the multiplicity of the disorders—this applies particularly to the statistical tables with which they so liberally sprinkle both their text and their footnotes—by laying down distinctions that are over-sophisticated between the various forms of 'Swing' action. In this, they have let the lawyers and the police dictate to them their cue. A Kentish labourer, on setting fire to a rick at Oxted, is unlikely to say to himself: 'I am now about to commit a felony, an act of incendiarism, a trespass, an offence against the 1827 Act.' No more will a Suffolk ploughman, when he lights a barn, accompany his gesture with the rigmarole: 'I am now committing a capital offence, am infringing the 1828 Act, am committing a pillage and a breaking-in.' This is the way the forces of repression counted, not the poor rioters who, as they are quoted on a number of occasions, believed that 'we mean no mischief', knew nothing of the infinite variety of legal definitions, and thought in any case that they were acting in their own rights, at least when they held village meetings, or walked out of the church, smoking their pipes in the churchyard, until their wage demands had been met (there was something symbolic, too, about this pipe-smoking, like the emblems, the flags, and the smart appearance).

The immediate cause of the protest—the threshing-machine—seems, at the end, almost irrelevant, for, as far as one can gather from this account, no one wanted the wretched things; the farmers were unenthusiastic about a device whose main effect was to drive a large proportion of the seasonal labourers on to the parish, many justices openly favoured their withdrawal and were not unsympathetic to their destruction. Only the manufacturers—the Ipswich firm of Ransome's above all—cannot have been very happy about a 'movement' which put the threshing-machine out of use for a generation at least. In so far as 'Swing' was about the introduction of the machines—recent in East Kent—then it was indeed a victory, but a victory so many others were quite prepared to concede to the wretched, half-starved, morally humiliated rural labourer, while denying him everything else.

Certainly the most moving and human chapter of *Captain Swing* is that which recounts the subsequent life of the deportees in New South Wales and Tasmania. There is something very touching about the devotion with which George Rudé has followed up every scrap of evidence concerning the fate of these unfortunate country-men.

It is the fault no doubt of the material that one can thus learn much more about their life in exile than about that in England before their brief and tragic incursion into history. Since, like most of the rioters, the deportees were generally young men, there would be much more to know about their new existence, some of them living on to the 1880s and 1890s. This is a serious weakness but it is difficult to see how it could have been remedied.

Perhaps the greatest merit in thus choosing 'Swing' as the subject of a monograph is that it reveals, at least through the distorting lens of repression, a whole layer of English society that had previously been hidden from historical awareness. This is the advantage of defeated protest movements, at least to the historian. But, as is the case with all such movements that go wrong—and most do—our historians must be the police, the magistrates, the parsons, the people in high places. And therefore, knowing so little about the men—even about the leaders—one cannot expect to discover much about the inner motivations of the 'movement'. It is not even sure that those who were deported and who thus acquired an historical identity, *were* the leaders; all we know is that they were singled out from the general mass of several thousand brought to trial, for reasons best known to the repressive authorities.

Is this then *all* that one can go on? Is there no way of discovering what they said to the examining magistrates? And is there no trace of what the magistrates, the rectors, the Government informers, the squires, said about *them*? For if these had been truly, if momentarily, frightened one would expect them—especially the parsons—to put names and faces to their fright. Vengeance, especially class vengeance, is verbose, thick with adjectives and abundant in moral judgments; that such a one was a drunkard, a ne'er-do-well, such another insolent, beat his wife, neglected his children, putting them out naked while he stood in the beerhouse, did not know his place, was a deserter, a criminal, a poacher, a smuggler, a horse thief, was rootless, had come but recently God knows from where, had no ancestral bones in the village graveyard, practised strange, egalitarian, undeferential religions, had his head befuddled with apocalyptic nonsense, used bad words and dreamed, as well as spoke, of blood. For this is the usual stock-in-trade of the repressive vocabulary, when addressed to the lower orders, at any time in the early nineteenth century. The literature of repression, one feels, is far from having been exhausted by the present authors. And one is often driven almost desperate by the blank faces of these desperate men, by their anonymity, by the mystery of their sudden involvement in unprecedented action. There is already a little—but so little —to go on in their strange spelling, in their few, crude slogans.

The answers—some of them at least—are surely to be found in Kent. Let the historian follow Dickens to the Medway Towns, to the Thames Estuary, to the hulks, to the house on the cliff, and to those communities in London, south of the river, where Kentish villages were re-created, all the more self-conscious for having been transplanted. Let him seek, too, the other side of the Estuary, the area where the Essex labourer runs into the Essex porter or artisan, where London and East Anglia overlap. Let him seek in the letters of fashionable people, taking the waters in a developing Tunbridge Wells—Holy Trinity had been built about ten years before 'Swing'—for an event that brought the cavalry to the Pantiles would not easily pass unnoticed in letters and memoirs. Even Jane Austen was aware, a decade or so before, of the dragoon and hussar officers, because they came to hunt balls. And some of the sisters of 'Hodge' must have gone into service in Folkestone, Tunbridge Wells, Ramsgate and Deal (sea-bathing had begun).

What, too, of village memory? Would the men of Deptford have any historical awareness? How did 'Hodge', young 'Hodge', in conversation with his father, or his grandfather, envisage the Kentish past? And if 'Hodge', as it appears in the present study, tended to be an *enfant du siècle*, born about the turn of the century, might not his father or his uncle have served in the army or, in the Chatham area, been pressed into the navy?

There are frequent references throughout *Captain Swing* to the radicalism of rural shoemakers, the authors even suggesting that a village that possessed more than one artisan in that trade would be likely to be that much more radical. Beerhouse keepers—the poor man's publican—are likewise seen as radical forces, a reasonable assumption, for a publican will generally take on the political colouring of the majority of his clientèle, as can be well observed in eighteenth-century France; on occasions, he may also create it. But, while one is ready to accept the radicalism of village shoemakers, one would like to know more about its causes. There are also remarks, almost *en passant*, about certain localities, both towns and large villages, as 'well-known radical centres' (Lewes, Rye, Maidstone, Battle, Horsham, Robertsbridge, as well as Banbury and Ipswich are included in this category). Perhaps they were, as the authors say so; but one would like to know more.

Yet the people who would matter most in rural riot and protest —not so much in its preparation, for here we may accept the importance of the shoemaker and the beerhouse keeper as political educationists of the labourers and as links with the towns — would be the people in the know, above all the blacksmith, so much in the secret of concealed rural wealth and well aware of the size and content of the farmer's establishment: how many hands living in, where they slept, how many dogs, how much cash kept behind the fireplace, how many bushels stored away, how much food and drink in the larder and cellar—information valuable to any form of collective protest and bargaining that would consist in payments, in money and in kind, to the participants.

Dr. Hobsbawm and Professor Rudé have done what they set out to do; to investigate the total spread of 'Swing', to apply to their investigation the techniques and experience of recent work on primitive forms of protest and of rural disorders (both are admirably qualified in this respect), to place 'Swing' in its historical context and to discover why a movement of rural protest, unprecedented at least in its scale and its rapidity, should have occurred in the second half of 1830, and, finally, to examine the composition of the movement and to suggest the motives that sent its participants on the road that, for some, was to end in the prison hulks and Australia. They are more concerned with the various forms that the movement took than with individual commitment to riot and with the exploration of a lost mentality. Their rioters—a few of them—have names, trades, villages, but that is all.

Likewise, in a general study that includes some five hundred place names, it was not possible to explore any single village community in depth—and how to know which to choose before thus mapping out the general picture of the movement?—and they had to make do with such general distinctions as that between large and small villages, and such general indications as corn, hops or pasture, the presence of paper or clothing mills, the proximity of markets, the state of communications, the basic division of England between the higher agricultural wages of the North and the areas of relatively low wages south of Nottingham. Within these terms—precisely stated at the outset—they have produced a work of considerable importance, stimulating and exciting to read.

One may not be entirely convinced by all their claims for 'the General Rising', the 'Last Labourers' Revolt', the 'movement'. How historians, and not only popular ones, and examiners, *love* this word 'movement'! and how unaware of their participation in such a conveniently well-organized, well-defined team are most of those contemporaries thus mobilized at the time. Historians should beware of the word; or they might emulate the anonymous author of a counter-revolutionary pamphlet of 1790. The pamphlet takes the form of an imaginary conversation between an unnamed questioner and a Palais-Royal prostitute given the evocative name of Rose Cutendre. 'Depuis quand', he asks her, 'êtes-vous citoyenne *active*?' To which she replies, from the age of fourteen. The next question is. 'Aimez-vous le *mouvement*?' 'Oui, citoyen, j'aime *beaucoup* le mouvement.' Rose at least, unlike many historians, knew what movement she was talking about. And one remains unconvinced by the way in which so many of the authors' tests, both positive and negative, come out right. These are minor faults of over-exposition; they may have tried to prove too much. What is even more impressive is that, unlike some recent American work on French rural revolt, they have succeeded in completely avoiding the hideous and meaningless jargon of sociology. This is a literate book, about barely literate people, for literate readers.

It is, in fact, a tribute to the stimulus offered by *Captain Swing* and to the fascinating glimpses afforded, through doors pushed ajar, of the dreadful realities of rural life, that, on putting it down, the reader wants to know *more*, his curiosity awakened by its intelligent and imaginative speculations. The greatest compliment that could be paid to the authors is that others should take up where they have left off; and there is every reason to expect that they will, now that the ground has been so carefully surveyed and so minutely mapped out. The facts, the frame, the statistics and many possibles lines of closer approach are to be found in this important pioneering book. And now to the study of Lower Hardres. The many excellent historians of Kent cannot fail to respond to such an inviting challenge.

# 15

# FICTION OF 1969

## (g) PHILIP ROTH

### *Portnoy's Complaint*

WHAT IS 'PORTNOY'S COMPLAINT'? A *cri de cœur* from a Jewish adolescence, a load of specifically Jewish guilt, a casebook of the Jewish blues. It is the most zany, zestful novel Philip Roth has written, and, with all its seeming *non sequiturs*, a classic comic statement of the Jewish condition:

What was it with these Jewish parents—because I am not in this boat alone, oh no, I am on the biggest troop ship afloat . . Only look in through the portholes and see us there, stacked to the bulkheads in our bunks, moaning and groaning with such pity for ourselves, the sad and watery-eyed sons of Jewish parents, sick to the gills from rolling through these heavy seas of guilt . . .

Oh, cameradoes! This is no longer a *Life with some goyische Father*, but inevitably a *Life with Momma*—a life of every nice bright little Jewish boy, publicly pleasing his parents, while privately pulling his 'putz'. Locked in self-love and self-hatred, Alexander Portnoy sits enthroned on the lavatory, masturbating; and the bitter joke is that *all* his fantasies—to his shame—come true. Between a kosher kitchen and these dreams of Onan, what bridge? What salvation?

Yes, shame, shame, on Alex P., the only member of his graduating class who hasn't made grandparents of his Mommy and his Daddy.

While everybody else has been marrying nice Jewish girls, and having children, and buying houses, and (in his father's phrase) *putting down roots*, he has been chasing women, and *shikse* women, to boot!

(*g*) PHILIP ROTH: *Portnoy's Complaint*. 274 pp. Cape. 30s.
(*h*) MARGARET DRABBLE: *The Waterfall*. 255 pp. Weidenfeld and Nicolson. **30s**.
RICHARD WOLLHEIM: *A Family Romance*. 255 pp. Cape. 30s.
(*i*) THOMAS ROGERS: *The Pursuit of Happiness*. 237 pp. Bodley Head. 25s.
(*j*) KINGSLEY AMIS: *The Green Man*. 253 pp. Cape. 30s.
(*k*) HENRY DE MONTHERLANT: *Les Garçons*. 377 pp. Paris: Gallimard. **25 fr.**

Thirty-three years old, *nel mezzo del cammin*, Alexander Portnoy is still roaming the streets with his eyes popping. In Newark and the surrounding suburbs there is apparently only one question on everybody's lips: 'When is Alexander Portnoy going to stop being selfish and give his parents, who are such wonderful people, grandchildren?' If this were just the old masochistic spiral of sexual degradation, these confessions to a psychoanalyst (Spielvogel, O. 'The Puzzled Penis', *Internationale Zeitschrift für Psychoanalyse*, Vol. XXIV p. 909) might verge on pornography. Does not 'Portnoy', the very name, seem some self-inflicted anagram of 'P. Roth' and 'pornoy'? Yet it is the comedy which is triumphant—a peculiarly Jewish comedy on the borderlines of fantasy and despair, exhibitionism and strongly felt ethical impulses, sexual lust and overriding feelings of shame.

It is the same borderline territory where Charlie Chaplin teetered on his tightrope path, or Svevo's Zeno amiably stumbled. Only this, being an American farce, is fiercer, blacker, more outspoken. All are spiritual clowns, wrestling with the swing-doors of a world of matter; all are degraded, only to rise and return as self-appointed saviours. Zeno, too, consulted a psychoanalyst to discover he had an Oedipus Complex. But Portnoy, way ahead of Freud, exclaims:

Dreams? If only they had been! But I don't need dreams, Doctor, that's why I hardly have them—because I have this life instead. With me it all happens in broad daylight!... Doctor, maybe other patients dream—with me, *everything happens.* I have a life *without* latent content. The dream thing *happens*! Doctor: *I couldn't get it up in the State of Israel!* How's *that* for symbolism, *bubi*?

For his tale ends, with blackest irony, in *Eretz Yisroel.* 'Im-po-tent in Is-rael, da da daaah' (to the tune of 'Lullaby in Birdland'), the Jew of the diaspora must return into exile. Thus the irony travels full circle, recalling the pompous rabbi of Portnoy's barmitzvah for whom no word in the English language had less than three syllables, 'not even the word *God*'; and *Israel* sounded as long as 'refrigerator'.

But who is this other rabbi, playbird, Spielvogel? 'Doctor, my doctor, what do you say, LET'S PUT THE ID BACK IN YID! Liberate this nice Jewish boy's libido, will you please? Raise the prices if you have to—I'll pay anything ! Only enough cowering in the face of the deep, dark pleasures!' Portnoy is the victim of a psychological disease and neither his Jewishness nor assimilation (*alias* Alton Christian Peterson, Al Port, Al Parsons), neither Manhattan nor Zionism, can save him. A universal Messiah (Assistant

Commissioner of Human Opportunity for the City of New York)
tormented by lust, he destroys himself by a torturing stream of self-
analysis: 'Spring me from this role I play of the smothered son in the
Jewish joke!' Unsuited to *any* coherent Jewish role, he bungles his life:
reaching for *shikses* he is drowned in *goyim nachus*. Hypochondriac
son of a constipated Life Insurance salesman, he loses his birthright.

Where Bernard Malamud has repeatedly explored fables of the
quest for fatherhood achieved, for adult responsibility won through
suffering, Philip Roth has triumphantly turned the tables. His is
the anguished comedy of Jewish fatherhood evaded and perverted.
Alexander Portnoy is the *schlemiel* quester who fails to win his
freedom. His suffering is for nothing, his life devoid of meaning
since he has not yet learnt that true freedom lies in the willing
acceptance of others. The secret source of his humour, in Mark
Twain's words, 'is not joy but sorrow. There is no humour in heaven.'

# (*h*) MARGARET DRABBLE

## *The Waterfall*

## and RICHARD WOLLHEIM

### *A Family Romance*

MARGARET DRABBLE'S work has been rightly praised, here as elsewhere, for its honesty and elegance. But it has also been disappointing
to see such rational talent so narrowly confined. History as well as
temperament apparently summoned Miss Drabble to the role of a
contemporary George Eliot; to write about work, society, morality
in the widest sense; to indulge an 'unfeminine' intelligence in a
world where women were at last allowed to be as critical as men. Instead, she hugged the domestic shore with a graduate's outboard
motor, and wrote about the 'new woman's' uneasy inheritance of
traditional charts. She spoke for those who secretly feared they had
the worst of both worlds; education without a career, inferiority
without love. Duty loomed large, to fill large gaps.

Her newest heroine takes a new step—though whether forward or
backward is hard to say. She is the first of Miss Drabble's characters
to live mainly, if briefly, in and for love. And it is love of a very old-

fashioned romantic kind: an infatuation, a madness, a disease. It is cloying and deranging, undignified and doomed. The heroine's husband has left her seven months pregnant. Her cousin and her husband come to look after her; but as soon as the baby is born the cousin's husband is lying in her childbed, declaring a (temporarily) unconsummable passion in the steamy heat recommended by the midwife. It is a Keatsian image of sweetness verging on corruption, and promises well. But it also sounds a warning note of similarity with the arbitrary extremism of Iris Murdoch's later novels—an example Miss Drabble might look at with foreboding.

The promise is, in one sense, fulfilled. The waterfall of the title is a metaphor for the female orgasm; it is a method of shuffling cards, where the two halves of the pack interleave by being dropped towards each other. After demonstrating the trick, James finally gives Jane the sexual pleasure she has missed in a lifetime of superior frigidity. ('How I dislike Jane Austen. . . . What can it have been like, in bed with Mr. Knightley?'). But such pleasant triumphs do not make a book. Miss Drabble turns to her heroine's background, and describes her prep-school headmaster father, her weak musician husband, in her familiar sharper style. There is some long-windedness here, a school-mistressish sarcasm clogging a finer irony; a sense of stalling, avoiding the difficult new ground. She can do Jane's solitary obsession very well; her lunatic sufferings when James is away, her eagerness to abandon all scruples about neglecting children or stealing another woman's husband. But she cannot do much with James and Jane together; with the happiness, in fact, which might be the book's theme. 'I did not know how to write about joy', confesses Jane. Nor does Miss Drabble; she borrows from women's magazines:

'All right,' said James, 'all right—' standing there with one hand on the open door, looking for something with the other in his jacket pocket, with such elegance of gesture that her heart stood still, with the vanity of her love.

Such sentimentality should perhaps be punished for aesthetic reasons; but hardly by the conventional mechanism of a car crash, even one so carefully signposted by casual hints that James is a reckless driver. Is it guilt or egoism that makes Jane so sure that she will bring pain on everyone, that her beauty is 'a cruel and disastrous blessing', that her child 'would inherit her disastrous nature as surely as he had inherited the colour of her eyes'? 'Often, in jumping to avoid our fate, we meet it; as Seneca said.' (There is far too much punctuation in this book.) It seems not so much fate as choice. 'I prefer to suffer, I think', the book wanly concludes. Certainly the author prefers her to. The book's moral structure seems a convenience for the teller, not a necessity of the tale; as does the switching between first-person and third-person narrative. This could charitably be read as a conscious device to present a self-absorbed person's struggle for honest self-appraisal. But charity wilts at passages like this:

I began the last paragraph with the word firstly, so I must have been intending to begin this with secondly, but I can't remember what it was or if I can it was too embarrassing and I've repressed it. Anyway, I'm tired of all this. It has a certain kind of truth, but it isn't the truth I care for. (Ah, ambiguity.)

There are too many ahs as well, and too many lovelys; in jumping to meet her talent, Miss Drabble has avoided it.

In case one should think such claustrophobic subjectivity female (and *The Waterfall* is a powerful if not deliberate argument for an old-fashioned view of woman's emotional self-centredness), Professor Wollheim's novel also takes the form of a diary. But here the mould is a far more subtle and more decisive thing. Miss Drabble has never shown much interest in extending the technical limits of nineteenth-century fiction. Many of her best passages are godlike summaries, visions through the wrong end of a telescope. Professor Wollheim's narrator is reading Butor's *L'Emploi du Temps* while keeping his own diary, busily counterpointing epistemological counterpoint with the best of them. But vulgar content creeps up, so that the two novels succumb to instant comparison: London adultery novels, or intellect-at-work on the emotions novels, or novels told by narrator's puppets who would rather suffer or inflict any injury than confess to harbouring second-rate thoughts.

The diarist of *A Family Romance* is impatient of ordinariness. He painfully sets down a dinner-party conversation in order to put down the guests and then wonders why he bothered either to go or to write about it. His wife and mistress occur in his diary as X and Y, and both are subjected to self-justifying tirades. 'Why am I the only one of us all who has a concern for the truth?' Poor Y has another way of describing it:

You talk: I listen. You tell me your problems; I sympathize. You describe to me people I've never heard of; I show interest. You abuse yourself; I try to restrain you. You abuse me; I —join in.—Dave, I'm prepared to help you, a bit at any rate, quite a lot for me in fact. But there just comes a moment when I can't take it any more.

Dave suffers no such moments. Everything about himself fascinates him: his intelligence, his grief at the destruction of London, his tyrannically affectionate father, his unlovably suffering wife, his late-night walks, his conjunctivitis. Interests, but does not involve. 'Perhaps my failing is that I think of everything as somehow extra, or external: talents, body, wishes, wife, love of painting, orgasm.' And, of course, the failing itself. It is the voice of a man who would rather be right than do right.

Perhaps his real aesthetic failing is simply that he talks too much; that his voice, intelligent, articulate, cultured, graceful, finally becomes boring, with the guilt-inducing boredom that very good conversation provokes. Do women suffer more if left for another woman, or simply left? Dave records contradictory but plausible statements on this point, and adds: 'How pathetically convincing any view about human nature is in the abstract.' Dissatisfaction with those abstractions is the starting-point of a novel.

In the absence of passionate concreteness, one turns to ingenuity. Putting his Butor to use, Dave imagines a detective story in reverse, culminating not in discovery but in crime. Spot the moment when the decision is taken, not the identity of the decider. (Patricia Highsmith, as well as Butor, has been here before.) The diary lists poisons and symptoms; it ends with a confession that Dave has poisoned his wife. True, a just indictment of his own indecisive selfishness: or false, a proof of crack-up, a 'family romance' as Freud used the phrase, a fantasy to escape paternal authority? Ah, ambiguity, as Miss Drabble might say, We kill as we have lived; in Dave's case, inconclusively. For all his doubts and self-questionings, he is an oddly complacent fellow; Just as Jane's act of self-forgetfulness, the blissful altruism of love, turns out to be a hothouse of self-absorption. Are intelligent egomaniacs the only people left who care much about love—either way?

## (i) THOMAS ROGERS

### *The Pursuit of Happiness*

THOMAS ROGERS'S FIRST NOVEL has been enthusiastically received in America, praised by writers as unlike each other as Philip Roth and

Elizabeth Hardwick. It deserves to be read and admired here too, though it is just the sort of well-mannered, rather melancholy, humorous novel which crosses the Atlantic surprisingly badly—in both directions. The novel's subject-matter and its pessimism may discourage readers too. Neither should; for Mr. Rogers is an astonishingly skilful writer, able to bring characters to life through dialogue and gesture and to suggest family relationships without resorting to explanatory flashbacks. And he has a deft, sophisticated wit, the kind which has been out of favour recently, replaced by comedy of a really more alien kind; bitter, New York Jewish humour, which English readers seem to respond to without necessarily understanding its sources or nature.

William and Jane are in their fifth year at Chicago University. Their love affair and their political activities have delayed graduation. William comes from a rich and mildly eccentric Chicago family, Jane is Jewish, from the sort of sneering academic background which has undermined her self-confidence while insisting she do something 'worthwhile' with her life. She's refused to marry William until this 'worthwhile' something has been found and by both of them. They're in that slithering mood students sometimes experience in their early twenties. They're disillusioned with student politics, but reluctant to abandon their earlier ardours in favour of the solid life their families would wish for them. Then William accidentally skids his car and kills a middle-aged woman. He is tried and sent to prison for a year. Half-way through his time there he finds himself involved, again quite accidentally, in another killing. This time, a young Negro homosexual, whose love letters William had helped to write, is killed by the brutal protector of the boy the letters were written to. Rather than appear, equivocally, as witness at the trial, William escapes and he and Jane go to live in Mexico. They are left expecting a baby and about to marry, supplied with money by William's family.

The couple are rich, handsome and lucky. They know this and would like to be useful to people who are less privileged, but they doubt their motives and their effectiveness. An accident involves them in that other life they've felt barred from in a way their principles never could. An admiring friend tells William, 'You've accomplished what the rest of us just fool around about. You've outlawed yourself.' This would be a gloomy message if it were a message, but Mr. Rogers is a novelist writing about people who interest him but who he's not prepared to indulge. It is William's family and his largely un-spoken feelings for them which make the novel as rich and enter-taining as it is. His father is a patient, retiring millionaire, who has gracefully allowed his wife to leave him for New York, where she paints gigantic visionary pictures and reads Khalil Gibran. William is the son such a couple would have. Exactly right too are the am-biguities of his relationship with a reactionary grandmother, still living luxuriously in a turreted mansion in what is now an entirely Negro neighbourhood, and with his stuffy, well-meaning Republi-can aunt. He laughs at them, stands up to them, takes their money and will forever be tied to them. The love affair is seen in the same way. William and Jane do love each other, but the affair has its consolatory side, an uneasiness, for it is doomed to turn into an alli-ance in defeat, yet the best either of them is likely to have.

The comedy is always discreet and delicate, and even in a very funny scene with a sponging, lying old tramp who hitches a lift on the way to Mexico, the author is adding something serious and truthful to his portraits. Love and the pursuit of happiness are not made frivolous or simple through the knowledge that half the world is dying of hunger. If the couple are left with a sense of failure, they've at least recognized their own dilemma. How is it possible to make the world a better place, if that better place depends on standards which must be relinquished if it is to be achieved?

## (j) KINGSLEY AMIS

### *The Green Man*

THE NATURAL WORLD has always sorely plagued Kingsley Amis's characters, but in this book, his thirteenth, the supernatural world is drawn on to add to the burden they have to bear. The chief character and victim this time is Maurice Allington, landlord of a Hertfordshire inn. Nature provides him with jactitation (convulsive jerking of the muscles), hypnogogic (onset-of-sleep-accompanying) hallucinations, and the early symptoms of *delirium tremens* (a small bird flying out of the back of his hand)—not to mention a violent hatred of white Burgundies, food and television, women whose personalities infuriate him all the time except when he is actually copulating with them, a father who dies of a stroke over dinner, and a trendy young person who pooh-poohs the notion of immortality at the father's funeral, explaining that Jesus 'can be a bit of a wet liberal when he's not taking off into flights of rather schmaltzy, Semitic metaphor'. The supernatural world provides, on top of all this, a red-haired woman ghost on the staircase of the inn, a seventeenth-century devotee of black magic called Thomas Underhill who returns to earth to show Allington erotic visions, a 'green man' made of foliage who almost kills Allington's daughter (and does kill his cat), and a well-dressed young man who arrests the motion of the world outside while he talks to Allington, and who seems to be some kind of divine agency of which Christ, Satan and death are all 'pieces'.

Every one of these afflictions, and more, are suffered by Allington in the course of the five August days covered by the novel. What he had mainly planned to do over this period was to get his wife and the local doctor's wife into bed as a threesome, and he goes on trying to do this while attempting at the same time to lay the ghosts (in an older sense of the word). In this respect he is quite an heroic figure— never a man to let anything put him off his stroke—though even the little orgy has unexpected consequences.

In composing this whirlwind of events, Mr. Amis is evidently trying, like his hero, to do many things at once. He is offering the reader at least three genres of novel in one. There is a straight, spooky ghost story; there is a moral fable in which Allington is the one who learns the lessons on our behalf; and there is a display of Mr. Amis's distinctive style of comic preaching in which Allington is, on the contrary, the mouthpiece for his creator.

The ghost story is the least successful. One reason is there is no lingering mystery about the status of the ghosts. We are plainly asked to accept their objective existence: at the end Allington's daughter sees the 'green man', and confirms Allington's conviction that he has not been having hallucinations in this respect. However, the objection to this—which boils down to a simple refusal to believe in what we are being told—only manifests itself clearly in the last part of the book. More seriously, from the start there is no atmosphere of spookiness. It was probably a mistake of Mr. Amis's to give Allington all the genuinely hallucinatory experiences as well. It means that the ghosts present themselves to him more as just another problem than as frightening phenomena breaking into an otherwise placid, sane existence. 'Do they exist or not?' is the question that sends Allington looking up old books in Cambridge, digging up a grave at night, and so on. And as it is a problem that will be solved merely at the whim of the author it cannot in itself yield much interest to us. The way Allington drops his inquiries so easily to get on with the sex in his life also makes it harder for us to feel much fear of the ghosts. And yet another reason for the lack of atmosphere in the book is the blunt, explicit way in which Allington's feelings are always described for us. This, as we shall see, is a successful part of the comedy, but it militates against the weird note in the novel.

Finally, the fact that the spirits—especially the young man—are also there to point a moral confuses one's reactions to them. It is not too clear what the lesson is either. Allington's major discovery of his ignorance about other people comes when his wife announces she would be happier with the doctor's wife than with him, and that she is leaving him. This has nothing to do with the ghosts. From Underhill and the 'green man' Allington gets only a heightened vague sense, if one may put it so, of the fact that a man cannot ignore the ever-present threat of destruction and death. As for the pale young man who talks so donnishly to Allington while drinking his Scotch, he mainly affirms a quasi-Miltonic doctrine of God's ways to man (or, as he puts it, 'Some of your chaps have found out quite enough already. Your friend Milton, for instance'); the universe seen as a kind of game, in which both the creator and man are bound by the rules of free will, and there is no 'offending or punishing or any of that father-figure stuff; it is purely and simply the run of the play'. The young man also rams home the reminder of death awaiting: but he adds the thought that if a man behaves too badly he may find his own death presenting itself to him as mere good riddance to bad rubbish (and that perhaps this is the fate of all men, in the end). These are interestingly expressed ideas, if not novel ones, but again they are offered to the reader, as they are offered to Allington, perfectly flatly; there is no slow, subtle dawning here.

The greatest pleasure in the book is the vigour with which Allington expresses his own scorn and contempt for so much of the life about him. The book opens with an extract from the *Good Food Guide* describing Allington's inn, in which those discerning diners have noticed that the wines are good with the exception of the white Burgundies. The first thing we learn about Allington is what lies behind this observation. He hates white Burgundies and loves watching the diners who order them suffer: 'I enjoyed seeing those glasses of Chablis or Pouilly Fuissé, so closely resembling a blend of cold chalk soup and alum cordial with an additive or two to bring it to the colour of children's pee, being peered and sniffed at, rolled round the shrinking tongue and forced down somehow by the parties of young technology dons from Cambridge or junior television producers and their girls.' This inventive irascibility is sustained throughout the novel, and many canting fools get their lot from Allington. A good few innocents who merely annoy Allington also feel his anger, but no great harm is done, it is fiction anyway, and Allington's huffing-puffing exaggerations always have their saving wit.

However, Allington does not quite hold together as a character. Not only is his ability to snap completely out of anxiety about the ghosts into hearty sex-pursuits rather unconvincing (however admirable), but he is also inconsistent in minor ways. He shows a townsman's comic misapprehension of the ways of the countryside one minute, and the next is reeling off the names of the birds and trees in the landscape like an old forester. What is more, he serves a white Burgundy—a Bâtard-Montrachet 1961—at his own dinner party! One scans this passage carefully for signs of some half-hidden significance—or hidden trap—laid there by Mr. Amis. But Allington seems to have no intention, for instance, of punishing himself or his guests at this point (and he is in every other place quite explicit if he has such ideas). In any case, Bâtard-Montrachet 1961 would be a very good white Burgundy by most people's standards—it looks as if Mr. Amis has just forgotten Allington's prejudice. Such slips bode ill for a writer whose great strength has always been his spryness. (He also, to get down to basic carelessness, calls Underhill "Underwood" on page 88.) Altogether, in fact, this rather ramshackle book, though full of good things, cannot be set among Mr. Amis's real successes.

## (k) HENRY DE MONTHERLANT

### Les Garçons

IN THE 1920s AND 1930s Montherlant's literary reputation rested mainly on some distinctive novels—*Les Bestiaires*, *Le Songe*, *Les Célibataires*, *Les Jeunes filles*—and several collections of essays which confirmed his markedly individual qualities of mind and sensibility. From 1942 onwards, with the success of *La Reine morte*, he established and then confirmed a new reputation as a major dramatist. His most recent play, *La Guerre civile*, had a successful run in 1965. During the 1960s, however, Montherlant has also returned to the novel. In 1963 he published the widely praised *Le Chaos et la nuit* and in 1968 the complete version of *La Rose de sable*. He has now written an outstanding new novel, *Les Garçons*—outstanding in its imaginative sweep, its intellectual power, and its quality of sheer writing. Some readers will be irritated by Montherlant's use of footnotes—particularly since some of them are unnecessarily patronizing, as when he explains a reference to *Oedipus Rex* and adds: 'Nous croyons devoir l'éclairer, personne aujourd'hui en France ne sachant qu'il y a un inceste dans *Oedipe roi*'—but these are minor blemishes in the lively dialogue with his readers which he maintains in connexion with all his writings.

Montherlant's concern to enlighten the reader about his ideas and intentions has its useful aspects in the present case. In a careful preface to *Les Garçons* he places the work between *Les Bestiaires* and *Le Songe* so that it forms, with these earlier novels, a trilogy under the general title: *La Jeunesse d'Alban de Bricoule*. The period covered is the end of the *belle époque*, when Alban attends a Catholic school in Paris after his adventures as a sixteen-year-old apprentice matador in Spain (*Les Bestiaires*) and before his experiences on the Western Front in the First World War (*Le Songe*). The period, and the middle-class Catholic milieu, are those to which Mauriac also recently returned in *Un Adolescent d'autrefois*.

In Montherlant's case, much of his novel is concerned with the emotional relationships between the senior and junior boys in a liberal Catholic school, relationships which end in the sudden, hasty expulsion of Alban—and shortly afterwards of a further seventeen boys and one master. The headmaster, Abbé Pradeau de la Halle, had worked to a threefold principle—'Beaucoup aimer. Beaucoup tolérer. Beaucoup prier'—but his experiment is judged a failure and, before the novel ends, he and most of his fellow-masters have also been replaced. It is perhaps worth adding that the school-boy relationships central to the novel are only dimly and often unconsciously homosexual. Purity, selflessness, idealism all play important roles, and Montherlant's treatment of the whole phenomenon has an authenticity and a delicacy (accurate rather than squeamish) which contrast strongly with a novel such as Peyrefitte's *Les Amitiés particulières*.

Those who are already familiar with Montherlant's work will find in the above account echoes of his play, *La Ville dont le prince est un enfant*. The situations and events of both works have many similarities (two scenes from the play are incorporated directly into the novel) and Abbé Pradeau de la Halle and Abbé de Pradts are major figures in both. In fact, Montherlant writes in his preface that *Les Garçons* represents the realization of a long-standing ambition— to treat the same subject-matter in both a play and a novel. A comparison between the different techniques required by the two genres in treating a common theme could be a fascinating exercise.

*Les Garçons* fulfils two further ambitions on Montherlant's part. On and off for the past forty years he had meditated on the possibility of portraying a priest (such as he himself had met) who carries out all his duties, punctiliously, yet is in fact an atheist. In his novel, Abbé de Pradts is the *prêtre-athée*, and he gives Montherlant the opportunity of creating a character of formidable intellectual power and intense psychological complexity. However, quite the most challenging task which Montherlant sets himself is to show the priest's final conversion to the faith at a period (the beginning of the Second World War) much later than that during which the other main events of the novel take place. Montherlant does this with remarkable skill, triumphantly avoids the clichés of a death-bed conversion, and steers clear of all maudlin attitudes. His final comment as the priest dies is typical: 'Dieu rappelait à lui l'abbé de Pradts juste à temps pour qu'il ne fût pas collaborateur.'

The third ambition fulfilled by *Les Garçons* is its analysis of two different kinds of reformist movement and of the way in which each fails. The headmaster displays his liberal, reforming zeal (the date is around 1912) early in the novel with such statements as 'mieux vaut le désordre avec l'amour que l'ordre sans amour' and 'vous en faites plus par un sourire que par des kilos de morale'. Nevertheless, he fails to realize his implied ideals, mainly because his very idealism blinds him to an awareness of reality as imperfect, an awareness that is essential if ideals are to be given effective expression. Within the general system of the school Alban de Bricoule, as one of the seniors, attempts to establish an austere (rather than liberal) reformist movement among the boys themselves. His efforts are largely misunderstood, then widely suspected, and finally rejected with no little hypocrisy and cruelty by his school-fellows. They move in a world of moral assumptions which differ markedly from the Roman austerities and classical stoicism on which Alban's imagination feeds.

One of the lessons which emerges is that genuine selflessness and highmindedness are dismissed as incredible—and therefore become suspect as covers for selfishness and impurity—by the group which, both individually and collectively, fails to believe that certain individuals can genuinely live at such a high ethical altitude. The elitist assumptions implied by Montherlant's analysis of these two failed attempts at reform will no doubt prove anathema to champions of a blind, unquestioning egalitarianism. Within the terms of this particular novel, however, they have both historical and psychological justification.

In the course of giving fictional form to his three ambitions Montherland creates a gallery of wonderfully observed characters. Particularly welcome is the fact that these characters are allowed to behave with spontaneity (to the point of self-contradiction and 'uncharacteristic' behaviour) admirably free from the imposition of prior psychological or sociological conditioning of a systematic, doctrinaire kind. Alban himself has all the intransigence of youth together with a deliberate acceptance of difficulty and danger as means of testing and proving himself. His young friend Serge is the difficult, rebellious schoolboy ('le voyou de l'école') at once loyal and heartless. Apart from the two priests, the remaining major figure is Alban's mother; Madame de Bricoule, a terrible snob and a failed *mondaine*, yet a woman of imagination and warmth in other ways. The relationships between Alban and his mother, compounded of hostility and dependence, is finely analysed, and the account of the increasing estrangement between mother and son—as the former, still in her forties, lies dying of tuberculosis—is among the most moving passages in the novel.

*Les Garçons* is a long novel (more than 370 pages *grand format*), and the farther it progresses the more impressive it becomes. Montherlant writes out of an astonishing abundance of imaginative and intellectual resource; indeed, as he approaches his mid-seventies his creative powers seem to increase. One has throughout this novel the sense of a thoroughly equipped mind working in conjunction with a rich and abundant humanity. The second half of the novel has the general title, 'Les opérations mystérieuses', and the farther we follow the fortunes of the various characters, the stronger is our sense of a mysterious dimension in life (and most obviously in human relationships) which both deepens the experience of living and ultimately puts it beyond the reach of purely rational analysis. This combination of intellectual power and an ability to convey the rich and subtle texture of lived experience makes *Les Garçons* an outstanding novel. To read it is to have one's subsequent attitude to people and events imperceptibly changed for the better.

# 16

# THE EARLY ENGINEERS

THE STUDY of the history of technology is not new. Compilers such as Dennis de Coetlogon and Johann Beckman in the eighteenth century and J. F. L. Williams, Francis S. White and Edward Cresy in the early nineteenth century made some of the first contributions which to a degree are still useful. Throughout the nineteenth and the early part of the twentieth century, important studies were made in England, Germany, France and the United States. The Newcomen Society was founded in England in 1922 and the Society for the History of Technology in the United States in 1960. And it is in the United States especially that this new historical discipline is steadily asserting itself as a valid field of academic study, where careful scholarship will yield results of relevance and interest to a society which, for better or worse, is technological. In Britain, by contrast, the history of technology has been and with some exceptions continues to be predominantly a hobby, although no one would deny that the many amateur experts involved have done work of the first importance.

Britain is responsible also for another step in the right direction. Quite who coined the term 'industrial archaeology' is not a critical question, nor does it matter all that much whether the choice was a good one. The fact is that industrial archaeology is an area of study and research which has experienced an astonishing rate of growth and rise in popularity. There is, however, some dispute over a definition of what industrial archaeology really is, how it differs from the history of technology or whether it is perhaps the same thing or at least a branch of it.

Perhaps the best definition of industrial archaeology is Kenneth Hudson's: 'the field-work aspect of the history of technology'—the word 'industrial', of course, being taken in the widest possible sense

---

SAMUEL SMILES: *Lives of the Engineers, with an account of their Principal Works comprising also A History of Inland Communications in Britain.* New introduction by L. T. C. Rolt. Volume I: 484 pp. Volume II: 502 pp. Volume III: 512 pp. Newton Abbot: David and Charles. £3 3s. each.

to cover not only the manufacturing and processing industries but also transportation, power production and civil engineering works, which in any case are, in the final analysis, closely connected with industrial requirements.

Certainly it is impossible to see the history of technology being adequately studied without 'field-work'. But industrial archaeology is by no means an end in itself. In so far as it is concerned with the discovery, investigation and recording of the surviving physical remains of engineering, industrial archaeology has a vital role to play. But the interpretation of technical history in the broader context of social, economic, political and strategic history, and even religious and legal history, is the end which must be served eventually. Industrial archaeology is without doubt one of the means to this end. It is also the stimulus, in Britain at least, to resurrecting works such as *Lives of the Engineers* whose new publishers have been closely and effectively involved in the growth of industrial archaeology.

The reappearance of the *Lives of the Engineers*, last published in 1904, is welcome and long overdue. For historians of engineering and industrial archaeologists it is probably the most important reprint for some years. Samuel Smiles's writings have had in some ways a curious history.

During his long life, 1812–1904, he was a prolific and dedicated writer, publishing his first book when he was twenty-six and his last when he was eighty-two. His autobiography, edited by Thomas MacKay, appeared posthumously in 1905. During his lifetime and for a decade or so after, his books were immensely popular all over the world and then they sank into oblivion. For nearly half a century they were unread, except by specialists, and cheap to buy second-hand, when they chanced to be available. In the 1930s, L. T. C. Rolt, who has written a short introduction to each volume of the new edition of *Lives of the Engineers*, was able to buy a second-hand copy of the first edition for 7s. 6d. Today the same thing would cost £15 at least. This lapse from popularity of the *Lives* and others of Smiles's writings, only to be followed by a sudden and recent resurgence of interest, in fact has a lot to tell us about the man, his subject and the way he treated it.

Samuel Smiles was born at Haddington, near Edinburgh, one of eleven children of an industrious anti-burgher. He studied medicine at Edinburgh University and took his M.D. when he was twenty.

He practised medicine in his home town for a few years before becoming the editor of the *Leeds Times*, a post which he relinquished in 1842. Subsequently he was the secretary of two railway companies, and, between occupying these positions, made a brief return to medical practice. In 1866 he retired to devote himself entirely to writing. *Lives of the Engineers* was first published in three volumes in 1861–62, but before that the theme which was to dominate almost all of Smiles's writing had become apparent.

In 1838 he published his first book, *Physical Education: or the Nurture and Management of Children*; it was privately printed and was not a success. In it Smiles expounded the theory that physical education was the proper and necessary basis for an intellectual and moral life. In 1859 there appeared *Self Help: with Illustrations of Conduct and Perseverance*. This is the book for which Smiles is most often remembered and it commanded the largest and most international number of readers. Twenty thousand copies were sold in the first year and nearly a quarter-of-a-million by the end of the century. In the introduction to the seventy-second impression in 1958, Professor Asa Briggs has written, 'There are few books in history which have reflected the spirit of their age more faithfully and successfully'; a paperback edition was published by Sphere Books last year.

In *Self Help* Smiles climbed on to the hobby-horse from which he hardly ever again dismounted. He was utterly convinced that success in life could only be achieved by perseverance, self-discipline, thrift, industry, a sense of duty—in short, all those characteristics which are now regarded as typically and ludicrously Victorian were extolled by Smiles as not merely desirable but totally necessary for a man to make his way in the nineteenth-century world. *Self Help* and the gospel it preached gained immediate and widespread popularity. It was translated into every European and many non-European languages. English readers derived immense satisfaction from the knowledge that the Smilesian formula was, so far as they could tell, a guarantee of success in life. In Italy he was especially popular, and he was received by both Garibaldi and Queen Margherita in 1879. Smiles was no doubt much satisfied to learn from the Italians themselves that 'his story of the triumphs and heroisms of English industry was educating the rising generation of Italians in honesty, courage, and perseverance'. From the King of Serbia Smiles received the Cross of Knight Commander of the Order of St. Sava, while the Khedive of Egypt inscribed the walls of one of his palaces with quotations from *Self Help*. The book was also well known in Japan. The theme of *Self Help* was subsequently developed and repeated in books such as *Character* (1871), *Thrift* (1875), *Duty* (1880), and *Life and Labour* (1887).

To Samuel Smiles, the very epitome of the qualities he most admired was to be found in engineers. His first excursion into the study of the life of an engineer began in 1848. In George Stephenson, the key figure among the early railway engineers, Smiles found a man of precisely the right specifications to exemplify his creed. Here was a man of humble but respectable birth who by hard physical work, thrift, study and determination made the railway locomotive a practical proposition and thus brought about the beginnings of a social and economic revolution which appealed immensely to a man such as Smiles.

The life of a railway engineer had yet another attraction. In 1845 Smiles had become secretary of the Leeds and Thirsk Railway, and his close acquaintance with railway matters and well-known ability at the job were factors in Robert Stephenson's giving support to the idea of a biography of his father, even though he doubted that it would be well received. He was wrong. The response to the book when John Murray published it in 1857 was tremendous—five editions in the first year alone and several more at intervals of a few years. Smiles saw what he must do. He would apply himself to the task of studying and recording the lives of those men who had made Britain the first and greatest industrial nation in the world. The *Lives of the Engineers* was the principal result.

In Volume One there are five parts, all devoted to a description and discussion of engineering in Britain in the period up to about 1800. Smiles deals with early engineering works of embanking, drainage, roads and travel, bridges, harbours and ferries, and the lives of Cornelius Vermuyden, Sir Hugh Myddelton, John Perry, John Metcalfe and, most especially, James Brindley. The volume then is a history of civil engineering and particularly of transportation. It is immediately evident that Smiles was as interested in their works as he was in the engineers themselves.

In Volume Two he considers the lives and activities of just three people—John Smeaton, John Rennie and Thomas Telford—three giants of the Industrial Revolution. All were civil engineers and were profoundly involved in opening up Britain's internal and to some extent external communications. Little wonder then that the *Lives* is subtitled 'A History of Inland Communications in Britain'. In Volume Three Smiles presented a revised edition of his 1857 biography of George Stephenson, enlarged to include the life of Robert Stephenson, who had died in 1859. The communications theme is once more paramount.

Thus, quite apart from his admiration for the engineers themselves and his obvious delight in showing how they substantiated his own theories of personal behaviour, Smiles saw clearly that their work was having profound and even revolutionary effects on the nation. He never used the term 'Industrial Revolution' but he sensed what was afoot. His choice of civil engineers as the subject of the *Lives* sprang from his belief that the construction of roads and bridges, canals and tunnels, railways and harbours was vital to the changes being wrought by engineers and the industries they created.

It has been argued that Smiles misjudged the history of engineering by concentrating on transportation and putting forward the hypothesis that this was the key to the Industrial Revolution. True, this is the emphasis which emerges from the *Lives*, but it must be remembered that in other writings—*Industrial Biography*, *Lives of Boulton and Watt*, *James Nasmyth* and *Men of Invention and Industry*—Smiles covered fields such as iron working, tools and machinery and the steam engine. Nor should we lose sight of what Smiles meant by an 'engineer'. The meaning of the name has changed more than once and to Smiles 'engineers' were what is meant today by 'civil engineers'. Smiles referred to mechanical engineers and metallurgical engineers by the terms 'mechanics' and 'iron workers'.

By Smiles's standards, then, the *Lives* are accurately titled, but it is nevertheless valid to ask why he took civil engineers as his first subject and left the mechanical engineers and others until later. Are we to assume that he intended all along to cover everything and merely chanced to take the civil engineers first? This does not seem to be the case. The later biographies seem to be an afterthought—they give the impression that Smiles turned to them after he had exhausted his principal interest. Certainly this is the feeling one gets from the preface to *Industrial Biography*.

In considering Smiles as an historian of technology, then, one starts out with certain suspicions. If he was a historian of technology, then men such as Henry Maudslay, the Darbys, Henry Cort, James Watt and Matthew Boulton, Joseph Whitworth and Henry Bessemer should have been every bit as important to his writings as the 'stars' of the *Lives*. In their various ways, the machine makers, engine builders and iron workers are judged by engineering historians of today as major figures. Their contributions may not have been impressive in terms of cost or the amount of physical work involved or the size of the works they left on the ground, but they were crucial. As examples of technical innovation and of a man's ability to conceive of new ideas and make them work, their efforts are often remarkable. Indeed within the confines of technology pure and simple they were probably much more truly original than the men portrayed in the *Lives*.

There is no doubt then that Smiles did not approach engineering biography as an exercise in engineering history. He was faithful to the notions already mentioned—namely, his conviction that men would improve themselves and become successful if they followed the path of hard work, discipline and dogged perseverance, and that society and whole nations could achieve wealth and prosperity only by allowing engineering to bring about material improvement.

Of the six engineers who make up the bulk of the *Lives*, Brindley, Smeaton, Telford, Rennie and the Stephensons, not all came from equally humble origins. On the one hand, Brindley, Telford and George Stephenson had most inauspicious beginnings. Stephenson's father was a poor fireman at a local colliery and quite unable to support his six children unless they went out to work at an early age and forewent any education. Brindley's father was a layabout, while Telford, after the age of one month, did not have a father at all. Smiles was not slow to tell us how manfully his engineers, with the devoted and selfless help of mothers, relatives and friends, forced their way past this initial hurdle, Brindley less successfully than the other two. Rennie, Smeaton and Robert Stephenson got away to a better start. This was to be expected in the case of Robert Stephenson, as the son of a famous and successful father; while the other two both received a formal education, Rennie to the extent of attending university for three years, the only one of the six to do so.

Yet Smiles is anxious to put even this into his own type of perspective. He writes of Rennie's going to Edinburgh University:

In taking this step he formed the resolution—by no means unusual amongst young men of his country inspired by a laudable desire for self-improvement—of supporting himself at college entirely by his own labour. He was persuaded that by diligence and assiduity he would be enabled to earn enough during the summer months to pay for his winter's instruction and maintenance; and his habits being frugal, and his style of living very plain, he was enabled to prosecute his design without difficulty.

For Smiles's engineers there is no escape. Having picked his men, and he picked them carefully, he does not lose any opportunity to drive home his philosophy and moralize endlessly. Some modern opinion indeed has judged that in trying to praise his heroes Smiles has in fact done them a disservice. Because he was so anxious to exemplify his doctrine of self-help, the engineers are portrayed as paragons of every Victorian virtue, faultless beyond belief. He fails to take into account, even fails to recognize, that his engineers were only human and that in fact their achievements are as much a reflection of their ability to overcome their own failings and those of their environment as an inevitable result of being superhuman beings.

The engineers whom Smiles chose to ignore are as significant in this context as the ones he chose to praise. Certainly he could not have undertaken biographies of all the civil engineers who were laying out the country's communications network, but one omission is outstanding: Isambard Kingdom Brunel. Smiles cannot be excused on the grounds that there was insufficient material or that Brunel's career was incomplete. In fact Brunel and Robert Stephenson both died in 1859, Brunel being the younger by three years, and their careers had followed similar lines and were equally interesting and important. Indeed, judged purely as an engineer, Brunel is probably the more fascinating—highly original and diversified in his work, enigmatic in character. But Smiles would have none of him. He received brief mention in Volume Three, but then only as a foil for praising Robert Stephenson and his work. Smiles is hard on Brunel at virtually every point; he sees Robert Stephenson as a man who was essentially 'inventive, practical, and sagacious'. Brunel by contrast he describes as 'ingenious, imaginative and daring'. The former qualities suited Smiles down to the ground but of the latter he was suspicious and disapproving.

On purely technical grounds he exposes himself totally. He writes:

But Mr. Brunel had always an aversion to follow any man's lead; and that another engineer had fixed the gauge of a railway, or built a bridge, or designed an engine in one way, was of itself often a sufficient reason with him for adopting an altogether different course.

Brunel was by no means so technically perverse. He was a good engineer with vision and imagination. True he had his failures, the

Atmospheric Railway and the Great Eastern, but his successes, such as the Great Western Railway (the 7 ft. gauge was used on purely technical grounds and was much the best scheme), the Great Britain and Great Western steamships, and the bridges across the Avon and Tamar, were engineering achievements of the first magnitude and Smiles should never have ignored Brunel in writing a history of engineering.

In comparing the Stephensons and Brunels, Smiles lets fall another interesting thought: 'The former were as thoroughly English in their characteristics as the latter perhaps were as thoroughly French'. In fairness though, Smiles does not totally ignore the work of foreign engineers.

Vermuyden, a Dutch engineer, gets two chapters in Volume One, and in the 1874 edition of the *Lives*, an expanded version of the first edition, the work of Pierre-Paul Riquet on the Canal de Languedoc is covered in an appendix. But it need hardly be added that Riquet had to overcome many difficulties in his enterprise, and evidently Smiles was more impressed by Riquet's perseverance and courage than by the technical content of the greatest engineering feat of the seventeenth century.

*Lives of the Engineers* went through a number of editions up to the last five-volume 'popular edition' of 1904. By then, however, the Smilesian philosophy had worn thin; people had ceased to be impressed by his catalogue of Victorian virtues. They began to view his emphasis on work and duty as a manifestation of guilt and an escape from freedom. As Thomas Parke Hughes has written recently:

After the burst of energy and material achievement ending about the last quarter of the nineteenth century, the sophisticated, sensitive, and affluent began to lament what had been lost on the way up—Smiles had been preoccupied by the way up.

The gospel according to Smiles had been exposed.

So for half a century Smiles's writing receded into the background. But now in the past three years there have been four reprints: *Selections from Lives of the Engineers* (1966), *Industrial Biography* (1967), *Self Help* (1968), and the present complete first edition of the *Lives*. Does this mean that the Smilesian view of life is once more in vogue? The answer, of course, is no; the reason is to be found in the upsurge of interest in the history of technology and the phenomenon of industrial archaeology.

It is worth wondering, however, to what extent Smiles is a useful

source book one hundred years after its first publication. We have
seen from what angle Smiles was looking and the sort of theme he
wanted to develop. Is it possible that the *Lives* can now adopt a new
role and become a study in the history of technology? Smiles
was not after all an engineer, nor was he an historian. On purely
technical grounds he was occasionally liable to serious errors, sometimes quite extraordinary ones. When discussing Roman roads
(Volume One, page 158) he claims that they were built absolutely
straight because the Romans had no knowledge of pivoted leading
axles in four-wheeled vehicles and hence they were obliged not to
attempt the turning of corners! But by and large errors of this type
are not numerous and where modern scholarship has had cause to
correct Smiles it is a healthy sign that this research is being done.

The most welcome aspects of the *Lives* for modern readers are its
interest in human beings and the scale on which it is conceived. Technology is today sadly lacking the personal element. Engineers are
obscured behind the complex they have created, and to a large extent
this is inevitable. Smiles's engineers were by contrast clearly seen;
they were public figures who were well known as the sole masters of
the projects they controlled. Smiles saw them through rose-coloured
spectacles but at the same time there was nothing wrong with his
vision. He did after all live close to their own time and has left us
information and details which could not now be uncovered. He has
given us an impression of what these individualists among engineers
were like at a period when British engineering reigned supreme and
was the product not of anonymous assemblies of 'back-room boys'
but of confident and dedicated pioneers who were obliged to stand
in the full glare of publicity and criticism if they were to achieve
anything at all. Few historians of Victorian engineering have not
depended on his accounts, and in the case of John Smeaton, Smiles's
life is still the only one we have. (On this point it is fortunate that
both the 1862 and 1874 editions are identical on the life of Smeaton.
Moreover the later version in five volumes actually contains much
extra material on other engineers, including the whole volume,
first published separately in 1865, on Boulton and Watt. Except on
the grounds of price, it is a great pity that the 1874 edition of the
*Lives* was not chosen for reprinting.)

By no standards was Smiles a technical antiquarian. Merely
to list details and data or compile facts and figures was not his
purpose, and it is a pity that in the case of some historians of tech-

nology and industrial archaeologists the degeneration has occurred. The history of technology is intimately linked not just with technical progress but also with social and economic causes and consequences. Smiles saw it this way. His view was biased, perhaps, but there is no denying his appreciation that technology stimulated economic development and brought about social change. He believed that nothing but good would result, a view that was already transparent by the beginning of the twentieth century and is rightly regarded with alarm and suspicion today. No one writing on the history of technology today would adopt Smiles's point of view. But his broad view of the subject is in principle one to be applauded and, if the reprinted *Lives* serve as a reminder that the history of engineers and engineering can be much more than a chronicle of inventions and patents, technical developments and new techniques, then the reprinting has been worthwhile.

Smiles lived at a time when British engineering was altering the course of the world's history. In his own way he sensed that this was so, even though he overstates the case for the benefits to be derived from engineering and glorifies his engineers and their characters unnecessarily. They were able, even brilliant men without being 'deified', and were at the heart of a momentous and uniquely British achievement. In the arts, science, philosophy, and other fields, Britain's contributions to the world are probably comparable to those of other countries but not markedly superior. But technology was our contribution alone: the industrial revolution occurred in Britain. There were many unhappy and inhuman sides to it but at the same time it set in motion a new era, one in which we are still living and which is not going to end. The technological clock cannot be set back. Britain and her engineers founded the means to improve the lot of mankind by whole orders of magnitude. Smiles knew this and we too should recognize it.

But in fact we, as a nation, are extraordinarily unaware of and unconcerned about our finest historical achievement. We cannot bring the engineers back to life in order to honour them, but a lot more thought and attention should be given to preserving something of their efforts for the interest of posterity and the sheer satisfaction of looking after our national heritage. Britain's future, so we are told, is technological. In which case there is all the more reason for reminding ourselves that in the past we led the way.

A great deal of preservation has already been carried out. A number of museums exist which have fine technical collections, and various trusts look after things like the Newcomen engine at Dartmouth, the Conway bridge, the Avon suspension bridge. Much however remains to be done. In *Industrial Biography* Smiles described the work of Abraham Darby the third in erecting the Iron Bridge across the Severn at Coalbrookdale. This was not only the first iron bridge in the world but the first really big iron structure of any sort. Whereas an earlier French attempt at an iron bridge had been a failure, Abraham Darby succeeded brilliantly, and this most impressive and important of engineering achievements still stands.

It must be said, though, that despite the efforts and concern of many people who are acutely aware of the significance of this unique monument, it is now in a disgraceful condition and any further deterioration may make it impossible to save the bridge. It will be a tragedy, not to say a national scandal, if the Iron Bridge is not preserved with as much pride and care as is lavished on old houses, stone circles, and other ancient monuments.

The Iron Bridge is an extreme case, it is true, but there are other examples of bridges and buildings, machines and engines, many of which are the work of the men described by Smiles in the *Lives* or somewhere else, and which in spite of their age have survived to the present day. Smiles was perceptive enough to recognize their importance and so too should we be.

Fortunately moves are afoot to do something about improving the processes of preserving something of our engineering history and extending the scope of preservation. Numerous museums or new museum departments are projected in various places, even to the extent of huge open air complexes where large items will appear in their original settings or something very like them. Such schemes, however, are expensive and future progress will undoubtedly experience severe financial problems.

Efforts are being made to assess what there is to be preserved and which items are most deserving. The Industrial Monuments Survey has been busy for some years collecting information on a particular group of relics, while the more recently begun Victorian Technology Survey is concerned with all branches of technology in a given period, 1815 to 1914, and thus covers more or less the period when Smiles was writing and being read. The extent to which these surveys can help the cause remains to be seen, and in any case neither is concerned directly with the difficult practical and financial problems of preservation itself. For these to be overcome, there needs to be conviction throughout the country that engineering is historically Britain's finest achievement and worthy of the interest and admiration not just of historians of technology and industrial archaeologists but of the nation as a whole. Samuel Smiles's *Lives of the Engineers* should help this process of education, and its reprint deserves to be widely read.

# INDEX

This index, in addition to referring to articles and reviews in the present volume, also shows other major reviews of the year which have appeared in the *T.L.S.*
Date references and page numbers *in italic* are to articles and reviews in the *T.L.S.* not reprinted in this volume. Page numbers in parentheses are given only where the reference is not immediately obvious from the article.

235

238            *Index*